"The sin of believing in a false document,
is not much greater than disbelieving the truth."

M. W. Shapira, 28 August 1883

The Moses Scroll

ROSS K. NICHOLS

HOREB PRESS
Saint Francisville, Louisiana

Horeb Press
P.O. Box 695
Saint Francisville, Louisiana 70775

Printed in the United States of America

Cover design, map, and illustrations by Daniel M. Wright.

ISBN – 978-1-7366134-0-5 (paperback)
ISBN – 978-1-7366134-1-2 (eBook)
ASIN – B0967DYGC4 (Kindle)

www.themosesscroll.com

For Moses, Rosette, Augusta, and Maria.

נבחר שם מעשר רב מכסף ומזהב חן טוב
Proverbs 22:1

May the Shapira name henceforth be for a blessing.

Contents

Index of Illustrations

Foreword

I first heard of Moses Shapira in the summer of 1976. At the time, I was in graduate school at the University of Chicago. I remember the specific time because I was preparing for my Ph.D. exams, which included reading selections of the Dead Sea Scrolls in manuscript form. Fortunately, David Wilmot—who was a brilliant up-and-coming Scrolls scholar—had agreed to guide me through some of these original texts so I could get used to reading the ancient scripts. Wilmot was a legend; his specialty was the mysteriously cryptic *Copper Scroll.*

I recall that Wilmot and I discussed the fact that two major copies of the so-called *Damascus Document,* dating to medieval times, had been discovered in Egypt in 1896 in the old Cairo synagogue *genizah*—a storeroom for discarded manuscripts. Solomon Schechter published them in 1910 under the title *Fragments of a Zadokite Work,* though he had no idea what they were. It was only with the sensational discovery of the Dead Sea Scrolls fifty years later, in caves around the ancient site of Qumran, that scholars found other fragments of this work and realized the *Damascus Document* dated to the first century BC.

I asked Wilmot if any other Dead Sea Scrolls had ever turned up anywhere before their discovery in 1947–1952. He told me there were accounts of such manuscripts being discovered in caves around Jericho in the third century AD and later again in the ninth century AD, but no copies had survived. He then paused and added, *"Of course, there was also the notorious case of Shapira, a Jerusalem antiquities dealer back in the 1880s. He claimed that he had purchased a scroll from bedouin who said they found it in a cave on the east side of the Dead Sea. Shapira tried to sell it to get rich, but it turned out to be a forgery, and Shapira, thoroughly exposed and shamed, put a bullet in his head."*

Shapira the Forger. The label and Wilmot's brief description stuck.

Over the following decades, whenever the name Shapira came up in academic circles this basic storyline was repeated and assumed. I never gave it a second thought, nor was I curious enough to find out about the purported contents of the infamous Shapira forgery. I remember that many years later *Biblical Archaeology Review* ran an article by Fred Reiner that laid out the details of the Shapira story under the heading "A Bible Scandal Revisited." Frankly, I did not pay much attention to it, and just now in writing this foreword had to look it up. It was 1997—and by that time I had been teaching for twenty years—including regular courses on the Dead Sea Scrolls. In fact, in the 1990s I was even involved in the release of the unpublished scrolls and had participated in three separate excavations at Qumran. In 2002 Hershel Shanks rehearsed the story again in *Archaeology Odyssey* under the provocatively simple title "Fakes!" End of story.

All that changed dramatically for me in November 2019. Shimon Gibson and I were flying back from the annual "Bethsaida" conference at the University of Nebraska at Omaha, where we had presented papers. We are colleagues at the University of North Carolina at Charlotte and have been excavating together on Mt Zion in Jerusalem since 2004. Shimon is a seasoned archaeologist with extensive experience in digs in the Holy Land over a range of ancient periods, but he just happens to have another area of expertise. He has studied and published extensively on the *history* of the exploration of the Holy Land in the nineteenth century (see the bibliography at the end of this book). We sat together on the flight home so we could debrief one another about the conference we had just attended and discuss future excavation plans. Somehow, the name Moses Shapira came up as we talked about the possibility that further Dead Sea Scrolls might still be found. I was completely surprised to learn that Shimon had become quite a "Shapiraologist," as he put it, in the course of his work on the archives of the Palestine Exploration Fund offices in London. He had collected thick files of materials on Shapira and commented that many of the story's reported facts were inaccurate.

He then shocked me. He said he thought the Shapira forgery case needed to be reexamined in light of the discovery of the Dead Sea Scrolls since Shapira's manuscript might well turn out to be authentic. Of course, the problem is that it disappeared not long after Shapira's suicide, so we have not been able to examine it. We moved on to other subjects on that flight, but a seed had been planted in my thinking. I wanted to know more about the whole Moses Shapira story.

As fate would have it, about a month later I had my third "Shapira" encounter. I was doing some Google searching, totally unrelated to the subject, and saw a notice about a book titled *The Lost Book of Moses: The Hunt for the World's Oldest Bible,* published in 2016 by journalist Chanan Tigay. I was immediately intrigued. Reading the review, I realized it was about the case of Moses Shapira and Tigay's own search for this lost scroll! I ordered the book that day, received it a few days later and read it straight through, hardly putting it down. I also alerted my friend Ross Nichols, author of this book, as I knew he would likewise be intrigued. For the past two years, Ross had been working on his own critical study of the book of Deuteronomy. He was influenced, as it turns out, by Chanan Tigay's father, Jeffrey Tigay, professor at the University of Pennsylvania who authored the *Jewish Publication Society Torah Commentary on Deuteronomy,* which we both owned! Small world.

Ross and I were both hooked—passionately so—by Chanan's quest for the scroll, what we began to learn of the scroll itself, and the figure of Moses Shapira. Beginning that week of 15 December, we both dove deeply into anything and everything we could find about Shapira and his "Deuteronomy" strips, as Shapira called them. Ross was particularly intrigued with the possibility that we might "recover" much of the scroll, written in paleo-Hebrew, from the notes and transcriptions that had appeared in 1883—along with Shapira's extensive comments in his personal correspondence. By February 2020 Ross had decided to write a "small book" on the subject, not just on the scroll itself to the extent it could be recovered and compared with our own version of Deuteronomy, but the entire Shapira saga. Little could he have imagined in those early weeks how much would unfold. We traveled to Israel together in late February 2020—just before Covid-19 shut down the world—to excavate at biblical Tamar (En Hatzeva) in the Negev for a week. We also met with Yoram Sabo, one of the world's greatest experts on Shapira. And who did we meet at the airport? None other than James Charlesworth, just arriving in Israel on the same flight. As we greeted one another and told Charlesworth what we were up to, mentioning Shapira, he said, out of the blue, "Well, you know his scroll was authentic, don't you? It needs to be reexamined!"

I was completing my own latest book, a historical study of Mary the mother of Jesus, so as intrigued as I was with the topic, I cheered Ross on heartily from the sidelines and followed the research every step of the way, contributing as I could with a steady stream of texts, emails, and extended phone calls. It has been an amazing journey of discovery and new insights.

I just finished reading Ross's finished manuscript and stand amazed at what he has produced. I have read every book and major article or study on Shapira over the past many months, and clearly *The Moses Scroll* represents a sea change in Shapira studies. Not only does it reveal much that was previously unknown about the Shapira saga itself, but for the first time we have a critical edition, with translation and notes, so much as it can be recovered, of the "Deuteronomy" fragments themselves. The book is a thrill to read—part detective saga and mystery—but solid historical documentation based on newly assembled sources that offer an entirely new look at both Shapira and his scrolls. I think Gibson and Charlesworth—and pioneers such as Menahem Mansoor, John Allegro, Helen Jefferson, Shlomo Guil, Yoram Sabo, and Matthew Hamilton—are correct. In light of the discovery of the Dead Sea Scrolls, Moses Shapira and his "leather strips" deserve a new hearing in the academic world and among the countless thousands who follow new discoveries related to biblical studies with such passion.

James D. Tabor
Department of Religious Studies
University of North Carolina at Charlotte
February 21, 2021

Preface

On the afternoon of 27 April 2019, I presented a paper at the 76th Annual Conference of United Israel World Union titled *Finding the Hand of Moses—THE Torah within OUR Torah*.[1] In that lecture I presented my proposed solution to the long-debated question about what, within the Pentateuch, could be reasonably attributed to Moses based on (a) the words of the Hebrew Bible and (b) the findings of generations of text-critical scholars. I intended to present my conclusions in a book that I began writing on 10 May 2019.

The book was progressing nicely when, on 15 December 2019, I received an email from Dr. James D. Tabor that put the project on an entirely new trajectory. His note contained a link to an online article in the *Harvard Gazette* with the tantalizing title "The Hunt for a Lost Book of Moses."[2] As I scrolled down, I read in bold type, "Radcliff scholar tried to track down what could be a forgery, or the oldest bible in the world."[3] James and I were both intrigued and promptly ordered the book, but never could I have imagined that after reading it I would spend the next year investigating the most controversial cold case mystery in the history of biblical scholarship. During that time, other close associates joined our investigation. Together, we collected, studied, and catalogued hundreds of documents, including newspaper reports of the day, debates contained within the pages of academic journals, and published reports from the Palestine Exploration Fund. The more we researched, the more we found. We shared our findings almost daily, and rarely a week passed in which someone didn't come across an interesting piece of the puzzle that we had not seen before. We traveled to Israel to meet with one of the world's top Shapira experts, corresponded with another in Australia, and members of our small team translated, or had translated, into English dozens of documents that were originally published in Hebrew, German, French, or Dutch.

The basic story was that in 1878, Moses Shapira, a Jerusalem antiquities dealer and agent of the British Museum, came to possess sixteen leather strips. Written on those strips, in Paleo-Hebrew script, was a version of the words of Moses that purportedly had been discovered in the mid-1860s by bedouin in a

---

[1] United Israel World Union, Inc. is a religious educational research organization founded in 1944 by David Horowitz (1903–2002), who devoted his life to its goals and purposes. Its primary focus is to function as an association of any and all who are drawn to the One God of Abraham and the revelation of the Holy Scriptures (the *Tanakh* or Hebrew Bible). To learn more about David Horowitz and the organization he founded, see Ralph Buntyn, *The Book of David, David Horowitz: Dean of United Nations Press Corps and Founder: United Israel World Union* (Asheville: Chiron Publications, 2018).

[2] https://news.harvard.edu/gazette/story/2019/12/radcliffe-scholar-seeks-the-oldest-bible-in-the-world/.

[3] The Radcliff scholar was Chanan Tigay, an award-winning journalist and professor of creative writing at San Francisco State University. See Chanan Tigay, *The Lost Book of Moses: The Hunt for the World's Oldest Bible* (New York: Echo, an imprint of HarperCollins, 2016).

cave east of the Dead Sea. Shapira believed that the manuscript was both ancient and authentic. In the summer of 1883, he presented the strips to leading experts in Europe who debated the manuscript's authenticity in the leading papers of the day. Two scholars in Germany and one in England also independently produced and published transcriptions of the document. In the end, the manuscript was declared a forgery. The entire drama—from the time the manuscript was shown to Europe's top scholars until Moses Shapira was found dead in a hotel room in the Netherlands—played out in a single year. The case might have remained closed had there not been another great discovery eight decades after the reported discovery of Shapira's scroll. That discovery was also made by bedouin, but in a cave west of the Dead Sea. Those scrolls proved to be unquestionably authentic and were more than 2,000 years old. The world now knows them as the Dead Sea Scrolls. We must now ask, Could the nineteenth-century scholars have been wrong about Shapira's scroll?

The Moses Scroll reopens the case, chronologically documenting the dramatic story from available accounts, and then reexamines the evidence for authenticity in light of what we know today. While the book chronicles some of what others have covered, it also contains much new information.

At present, the whereabouts of Shapira's leather strips remain an unsolved part of the mystery. Nevertheless, we can study and debate the internal merits of the manuscript thanks to the meticulous transcriptions of able nineteenth-century orientalists.[4] To facilitate this debate, we have included a new and accurate transcription that for the first time combines into a single document the two independent transcriptions of the Hebrew text as seen through the eyes of the three Semitic scholars who scrutinized it. The book also includes an English translation of the Moses Scroll based on this new Hebrew transcription, complete with notes.

Admittedly, the research behind the writing of this book was a collaborative effort, but I take responsibility for any shortcomings in the finished product. Other members of the team may have told the story better or even come to different conclusions, but they allowed me to take the lead and generously provided assistance in many forms. Since receiving the email from James Tabor on 15 December 2019, I have devoted more than a year to this project. Exactly one year later to the day, the first draft was completed. Following Tabor's advice, on 14 January 2021 I made the official announcement about the book. The date seemed appropriate to us since the corresponding date on the Jewish calendar was the first day of the eleventh month—the day on which Moses delivered the words of his scroll to the children of Israel (Deut 1:3). The book's release date of 8 March 2021 was also purposely chosen. Moses Shapira died on 8 March 1884, and as far as we know, the last public sighting of his scroll was 8 March 1889. It seemed apropos to share the scroll anew with the world on that same fateful day.

---

[4] It should be noted that when one reads "orientalist" today it generally denotes the Far East. In the nineteenth century it was a reference to the Middle East. It is used in this sense throughout this book.

The story I relate on the following pages is engaging, compelling, and accessible to interested laypeople. I hope it is also academic enough that scholars will read it. I want to believe that this book achieves a happy medium between the two. At the outset I must tell you that many "experts," both then and now, have declared Shapira's manuscript a forgery. At the conclusion, after seeing the evidence, you will decide whether I have made a successful case or come up short. I ask the reader to consider the advice of Christian David Ginsburg, who said, "May I suggest that those scholars who may wish to take part in the discussion on the nature and character of these fragments should first inspect them before they commit themselves to any strong opinion? An examination of the slips themselves is alike due to the fair criticism and to Mr. Shapira."[5]

I would ask that you not approach this task with a preconceived conclusion, but rather that you carefully consider the evidence put forward in the following pages. Remember the following words as you embark on your investigation into the genuineness of Shapira's manuscript. They are the wise counsel from one scholar to his young protégé regarding his investigation into the authenticity of the strips. "It is no art," he said, "to declare suspicious things false, but it takes courage and certain knowledge to publicly declare that which is tainted with the smell of the fake, is still genuine. Good luck!"[6] You now are the jury in this celebrated case. Will you be impartial?

Those who contributed in the realization of this work are recognized in the acknowledgments at the end of the book. At this point I wish to thank you, my readers, for choosing to consider the case of *The Moses Scroll*. I close my preface with the words of Moses Shapira, who said, "I will also ask pardon for all of my daring suggestions and for you to give me your candid opinion about it, should you or your friends find it so interesting as I flatter myself it to be."[7]

The Moses Scroll has been the most stimulating study of my life. I am pleased to share it with you.

Ross K. Nichols
Saint Francisville, Louisiana
United Israel Center South

---

[5] "The Shapira MS. of Deuteronomy," *The Athenæum,* no. 2911, 11 August 1883, 178.
[6] Letter from George Ebers to Eduard Meyer, 10 July 1883, "Der Briefwechsel zwischen Georg Ebers und Eduard Meyer (1874–1898)," Vorbemerkung von G. Audring. https://www.geschichte.hu-berlin.de /de/bereiche-und-lehrstuehle/alte-geschichte/forschung/briefe-meyer/ebers.
[7] Moses Shapira, letter to Hermann Strack, Jerusalem, 9 May 1883, "Papers Relative to M.W. Shapira's Forged MS. of Deuteronomy (A.D. 1883–1884)." *Add. MS. 41294* (London: British Library).

Note to the Reader: The Hebrew language has twenty-two letters and this book is arranged in twenty-two chapters, each with a corresponding Hebrew letter. The graphics at the beginning of each chapter are based on the Paleo-Hebrew script of Shapira's scroll. The English transliteration of the letter names appears alongside the chapter designations in the upper left. There are several acceptable methods of representing these names in English. We have used the following:

א   Aleph

ב   Bet (pronounced bait)

ג   Gimel

ד   Dalet

ה   He (pronounced hay)

ו   Vav

ז   Zayin

ח   Khet (the initial letter has a soft ch, pronounced chait)

ט   Tet (pronounced tait)

י   Yod

כ   Kaph

ל   Lamed

מ   Mem (pronounced maim)

נ   Nun (pronounced noon)

ס   Samek

ע   Ayin

פ   Pe (pronounced pay)

צ   Tsade

ק   Qoph (rhymes with loaf, pronounced Kofe)

ר   Resh (pronounced raysh)

ש   Shin (pronounced sheen)

ת   Tav

The Moses Scroll

Sixteen Leather Strips

In July of 1878, a well-known sheik, accompanied by an entourage of Arabs from various tribes, walked past the Turkish guards stationed at Jerusalem's Jaffa Gate and made their way to Christian Street. Throngs of locals wearing kaftans, turbans, and tarbooshes crowded the narrow street, along with beasts of burden carrying wares from near and far. A growing number of tourists were traveling to Jerusalem to visit the places mentioned in the Bible, and many hoped to take a piece of the Holy Land home with them.[8] Carts filled with oranges from the Jaffa coast lined the street and the aroma of oriental spices permeated the hot, stifling air. An occasional cry of *Yallah* rang out above the din of the crowd.[9]

The men's destination that day was the best tourist shop in Jerusalem's Old City, so described in Baedeker's travel guide of 1876.[10] The shop was situated on one of the main thoroughfares of the Christian Quarter.[11] It offered a plethora of items for sale—all the expected charms and trinkets, along with books in many languages, from novels to travel and guidebooks. There were also prayer books, Bibles, postcards, photographs, clothing items, and countless Holy Land souvenirs. Particularly popular were fans, which, when opened, revealed all the principal sacred sites of Jerusalem. Patrons could also purchase dried flowers

---

[8] The nineteenth century saw a growing number of tourists and visitors in Jerusalem, mainly drawn by an interest in the Bible; among the more famous were Herman Melville and Mark Twain. Thankfully, we do not have to imagine the atmosphere in the streets of the Holy City. Through written and photographic records, we can see Jerusalem through their eyes. Of special note in this regard are the works of Dr. Shimon Gibson, renowned archaeologist and leading authority on nineteenth-century Jerusalem. See his excellent volume *Jerusalem in Original Photographs, 1850–1920* (London: Stacey International, 2003), and Shimon Gibson, Yoni Shapira, and Rupert L. Chapman, *Tourists, Travellers and Hotels in Nineteenth-Century Jerusalem* (Leeds, UK: Maney Publishers, 2013).

[9] Arabic for "Hurry up," Come on," or "Let's go."

[10] Karl Baedeker, ed., *Palestine and Syria: Handbook for Travelers* (Leipzig: Karl Baedeker, 1876). On page 145, in a section on Jerusalem, under the heading "Books, Photographs," the entry reads, "Shapira, Christian Street, is the best shop."

[11] The description of Moses Shapira's shop in this chapter is based largely on the recollections of his younger daughter, Maria Rosette, who wrote under the pseudonym Myriam Harry. I relied on the English translation of the French original in Myriam Harry, *The Little Daughter of Jerusalem,* trans. Phoebe Allen (New York: E. P. Dutton & Company, 1919). See also Shlomo Guil, "In Search of the Shop of Moses Wilhelm Shapira, the Leading Figure of the 19th Century Archaeological Enigma." Academia.edu (2012): 1–20. https://www.academia.edu/2127379/In_Search_of_the_Shop_of_Moses_Wilhelm_Shapira_the_Leading_Figure_of_the_19TH_Century_Archaeological_Enigma. Following clues primarily provided by Myriam Harry, Guil determined that "the shop of Shapira is the present day shop at number 76 Christian Street but the original shop, covering the full façade of the house, included also the present day adjacent shops at its right and left sides." Guil, "In Search of the Shop of Moses Wilhelm Shapira," 19.

from various holy places and items of olivewood, including made-to-order Bible covers with Hebrew engraving.[12]

The shop faced the cosmopolitan Christian Street, while the back of the store overlooked Hezekiah's Pool. The two views perfectly represented Jerusalem, one a picture of modern life and the other a reflection of glory days long past.

By the end of 1871, the owner, Moses Shapira, had also become a dealer in antiquities, eventually specializing in manuscripts.[13] Thanks to successful ventures into Yemen and elsewhere, Shapira acquired a valuable collection of Hebrew and Arabic manuscripts.[14] The Royal Museum at Berlin purchased some of them, and the famed British Museum purchased many others.[15] Suspended outside the shop, a white sign bearing gold letters read *Moses W. Shapira, Bookseller and Antiquarian*. The five-fold Jerusalem Cross occupied the center of the sign and beneath it was the designation *Correspondent to the British Museum*.[16]

Figure 1–Author's conception of the sign outside Shapira's shop.

The Arab visitors entered the cluttered shop and made their way past piles of coats and leather boots. They passed through a wider corridor lined with shelves full of books for sale and found Shapira in his usual place. He sat at a table in a little nook, the dim light from outside penetrating the otherwise poorly-lit shop, surrounded by a precious collection of copies of the Koran, Talmud tractates, gospels, and Torah scrolls.

However, Shapira's visitors had come to speak of other matters. In the course of their conversation, one of his guests leaned forward on the deep-cushioned divan and mentioned a chance discovery of some blackened leather strips with

---

[12] These Bible covers were popular at the time. Mark Twain purchased one for his mother during his 1867 Holy Land trip, though not from Moses Shapira. Twain wrote to the book binder, a Mr. Esais, detailing his order. He had the Bible inscribed, "Mrs. Jane Clements – from her son – Mount Calvary, Sept 24, 1867," further instructing Mr. Esais, "put 'Jerusalem' around on it loose, somewhere in Hebrew, just for a flyer." See the account in Gibson, Shapira, and Chapman, *Tourists, Travellers, and Hotels,* 173–202, which includes, among others, this story with photos of the Bible and the letter.

[13] In a letter to Christian Ginsburg dated 6 August 1883, Shapira wrote, "My business with antiquities begins from the end of 1871." The letter is preserved in an 82-page dossier in the British Library, catalogued as *Add. MS. 41294*, "Papers Relative to M. W. Shapira's Forged Manuscript of Deuteronomy (A.D. 1883–1884)."

[14] For details on the extensive manuscript acquisitions of Moses Shapira, see Paul B. Fenton, "Moses Shapira's Journey to the Yemen," in Ayelet Oettinger and Danny Bar-Maoz, eds., *Mittuv Yosef, Yosef Tobi Jubilee Volume, Volume Two, The Jews of Yemen: History and Culture* (The Center for the Study of Jewish Culture in Spain and Islamic Countries, University of Haifa, 2011). Fenton also reports of a visit to Shapira's shop by a group of Mormon pilgrims in 1872. The relevant quote relates that they "visited Shapira's collection of antique parchments, some of which are very ancient, rescued beneath the ruins of synagogues in Palestine as well as in Arabia." Fenton, "Moses Shapira's Journey to the Yemen," lxx.

[15] A sales catalogue, "dated 1881, contains 47 leaves and the description of 126 manuscripts. This is the only one to contain the account of his journey [to Yemen], and it is to be found in Ms. Or. 1343 in the Staatsbibliothek in Berlin, which had purchased 13 of Shapira's manuscripts. A second, which appears to cover the same material as the previous item except for the travel account, is housed in the British Library. A third catalogue, or rather several catalogues, was donated in 1887 to the Berlin library by Shapira's widow." Fenton, "Moses Shapira's Journey to the Yemen," lxxi.

[16] The description of the sign is based on an account in Harry, *The Little Daughter of Jerusalem,* 59.

barely discernible writing on them. Shapira's interest was piqued. The sheik invited him to his home the following day to discuss the matter further.

The next day, Moses Shapira set out on his white mare heading east toward neighboring Abu Dis, a village of moderate size situated on a bare flat ridge and surrounded by deep valleys.[17] Abu Dis was home to a few hundred residents who lived in some fifty houses, the largest of which belonged to his friend Sheik Mahmoud Erekat.[18] Sheik Erekat's intimate acquaintance with the land and competing Arab tribes eastward toward Jericho and the Jordan Valley was an invaluable resource for tourists, pilgrims, and explorers who sought safe passage through those troubled and dangerous territories.[19] For a mere sixteen shillings one could hire an escort from Sheik Erekat, often his son, dressed in glorious apparel and armed with a revolver and sword to protect against ambush, robbery, or even death.[20] Shapira had made the journey east on several occasions, but this visit to see the sheik was not to secure safe passage—it was to learn more about the blackened leather strips he had heard about the previous day.

The sheik welcomed Shapira into his home, which was already full of guests seated on the floor savoring the ample selection of food. Soon after his arrival, the conversation turned to antiquities.[21] One of the bedouin, taking a deep drag on a *nargileh*[22] and exhaling the smoke into the crowded room, noted that antiquities bring blessing to the place where they are discovered. The sheik added that this belief among the bedouin makes it especially difficult to acquire such items. Undeterred, and himself quite familiar with the ways of these desert tribes, Shapira pressed for more details. Where precisely were the leather strips discovered? As smoke from the pipes wafted through the air, one of the bedouin began to describe the circumstances surrounding the discovery that had brought Shapira to Abu Dis.

---

[17] Claude R. Conder and Horatio H. Kitchener, *The Survey of Western Palestine: Memoirs of the Topography, Orography, Hydrography, and Archaeology* (London: Committee of the Palestine Exploration Fund, 1883).

[18] V. Guérin, *Description Géographique Historique et Archéologique de la Palestine* (Paris: L'Imprimerie Nationale, 1874), 160–163. Guérin notes that the largest house belonged to the sheik.

[19] See Reverend James Smith, *A Pilgrimage to Palestine—An Account of a Visit to Lower Palestine 1893–1894* (Aberdeen: Lawrence and Bullen, 1895), where he records, "The Sheikh of Abu Dis, Rasheed Erekat, promised to guarantee the safety of European tourists and pilgrims on the journey down to Jericho and the River Jordan."

[20] James Kean, *Among the Holy Places: A Pilgrimage Through Palestine Between 1895 and 1907* (London: T. Fisher Unwin, 1908), 129–130.

[21] The details of the meeting in Sheik Erekat's home, the discovery of the scroll fragments, and how Moses Shapira came to possess them is based primarily on three accounts: (1) a letter to Hermann Strack dated 9 May 1883, contained in *Add. MS. 41294*; (2) a written account given to Walter Besant and Claude Conder in July of 1883; and (3) an account reported in Hermann Guthe, *Fragmente einer Lederhandschrift enthaltend Mose's letzte Rede an die Kinder Israel* (Leipzig: Druck und Verlag von Breitkopf & Härtel, 1883). In this book I have made use of an English translation funded by David and Patty Tyler. Hermann Guthe, *Fragments of a Leather Manuscript Containing Moses' Last Words to the Children of Israel* (unpublished, 2020). Translated by Mitchell Golde, with preface, introduction, and Hebrew text by Ross K. Nichols.

[22] An oriental pipe in which tobacco is placed in a bowl and heated with burning charcoal, producing smoke that is drawn through an urn of water that cools it and then into a long tube with an attached mouthpiece. Also called a *hookah*.

About ten years earlier, the bedouin recounted, the wali of Damascus implemented reforms in the tribal territories east of the Jordan, exerting Ottoman power and forcing recognition of Turkish sovereignty over the bedouin tribes.[23] Refusing to submit to these Tanzimat reforms, as they were known, and the accompanying persecution by the aging Ottoman Empire, a group of bedouin fled south. They found refuge in a cave east of the Dead Sea, high above the Wadi Mujib. The wadi, known from biblical times as the Arnon River, was located in the ancient territory of Moab. Inside the cave they discovered a bundle wrapped in cloth. Hoping to find gold or other treasure, they quickly unwrapped the outer layers of moldered material, but to their disappointment found only blackened strips of leather. Assuming the strips to be worthless, they cast them aside. One of the bedouin, however, thinking the blackened leather strips smelling of asphalt might prove to be some type of talisman, took them back to his tent. Over the next ten or so years he acquired many sheep and became quite wealthy. He attributed his improved station in life to the strips of leather. Further, the pieces were said to contain ancient writing, although no one thus far had deciphered their message.

The story gripped Shapira. He knew the area well, having been there on previous expeditions; one in particular with Dr. Almkvist from Uppsala, Sweden, in 1875, came to mind.[24] He recalled several caves high among the cliffs facing

---

[23] *Wali* is an administrative title used in the Ottoman Empire and elsewhere to designate governors of administrative divisions. In Ottoman Turkey, the division governed by a wali was called a *vilayet*.

[24] The 1875 trip to Moab with Dr. Almkvist is mentioned in a letter dated 1 November 1877 from the German consul in Jerusalem, Freiherr von Münchhausen, to "My dear Mr. Shapira," published with the title "The Moabite Pottery" in the *Palestine Exploration Fund Quarterly Statement* 1878: 41–44. Shapira also

the Wadi Mujib. A cave could protect its contents from the seasonal winds and rain. Shapira and his Arab friends discussed the possibility that such an environment might indeed allow for the preservation of an ancient manuscript, possibly as old as some that had been discovered in Egypt. Shapira felt confident that if he could inspect the blackened strips he might be able to establish their approximate age and determine whether the Moabite discovery was treasure or trash.

Shapira asked Sheik Erekat if he might be able to arrange an examination of the fragments. Once again, the sheik mentioned the difficulty of convincing the bedouin to part with their treasures. Still, upon a promise of a reward for his success in this endeavor, Sheik Erekat informed Shapira that he knew a man who would be willing to do anything, including selling his wife or even his mother, for a small price.[25] The sheik wasted no time.

The day following the meeting in Abu Dis, an Arab named Selim appeared at Shapira's shop on Christian Street. Shapira was not at his shop at the time but returned to find that, for a modest sum, his shopkeeper had purchased a black strip of leather consisting of five connected columns of a scroll. The five-columned strip was in poor condition, but Shapira could discern the faint presence of lettering. He asked for more details about the seller and learned that Selim was a member of the Hajaja tribe who dwelt east of the Aravah and south of the Wadi Mujib and Kerak. The Hajaja had a reputation as robbers, conducting raids on both the eastern and western sides of the Wadi Aravah.[26] Unfortunately, Shapira was told, Selim's return to the shop was unlikely since there was a matter of bloodguilt on him or his tribe and that reentering the city might lead to trouble if he were recognized and detained. Shapira knew that if he wanted to see more of the mysterious blackened scroll, he would need to work through Sheik Erekat to meet with this wanted man. He immediately enlisted the sheik's help in arranging another meeting with Selim.

The meeting was to take place on a Sunday, less than two weeks after Selim delivered the first leather strip. For the price of a *baksheesh*,[27] the bedouin from the Hajaja tribe handed over another piece of the leather scroll, this one consisting of four columns on which only a few words were discernible. Shapira and Selim agreed to meet again the following Sunday. This time Selim delivered fourteen or fifteen columns of text, these being more legible than the previous ones. The two arranged to meet one more time, ten days later, at which time Selim brought Shapira three or four more blackened fragments. Shortly after the last meeting between Selim and Shapira, Sheik Erekat died unexpectedly. Shapira would never see Selim again. Without the sheik's help, Shapira had no way to contact him.

---

mentioned the trip in some detail in a letter he wrote to Hermann Strack. The letter, dated 9 May 1883, is housed in the British Library *Add. MS. 41294*.

[25] Shapira used the phrase "for a few medjedes," referring to a small Turkish coin of little value.

[26] See Eveline van der Steen, *Near Eastern Tribal Societies during the Nineteenth Century: Economy, Society, and Politics between Tent and Town* (New York: Routledge, 2013), 49.

[27] A tip or bribe paid to expedite services.

According to Selim, in their final meeting he had delivered to Shapira everything that had been discovered in the Moabite cave more than a decade earlier. In all, there were sixteen leather strips. The height of the strips ranged from 7.6 to 9.7 centimeters, or approximately three to four inches. The length of the strips varied. Those that were single panels consisting of only one column of text measured fifteen to sixteen centimeters (about six inches). Other strips contained two, three, four, and even five panels of text.[28]

Shapira's newly acquired strips consisted of five individual columns of text, two strips of two columns of text, five strips of three columns of text, two strips of four columns of text, and two strips of five columns of text.

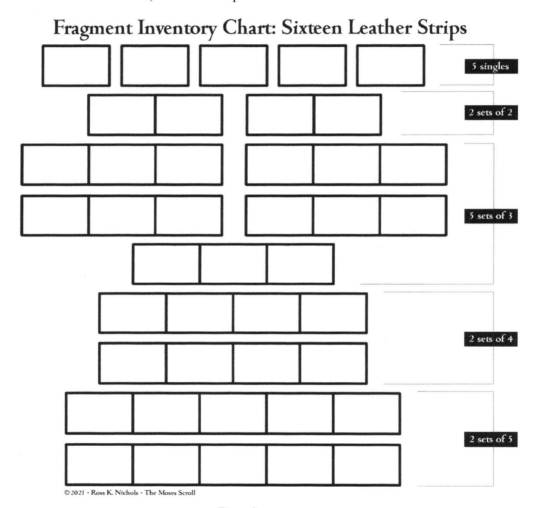

Fragment Inventory Chart: Sixteen Leather Strips

5 singles

2 sets of 2

5 sets of 3

2 sets of 4

2 sets of 5

© 2021 - Ross K. Nichols - The Moses Scroll

Figure 3

---

[28] The description of the physical characteristics of the fragments is based largely on the details provided by Hermann Guthe, *Fragments of a Leather Manuscript,* 3–4.

The longer strips, consisting of multiple columns, were creased along the narrow side of the panel. There were holes here and there in the fragments, and the worst deterioration was along the edges. Some of the leather crumbled easily, even with careful handling. The backside of the strips was coated with an asphalt resin of varying thickness. In places, the coating could be scraped off with a fingernail. Shapira noticed within this coating the imprint of woven fabric. In multiple areas, embedded in the black substance were small pieces of brownish, weathered, fragile cloth, some of which measured nearly one square centimeter. He assumed these pieces of material were the remains of the outer cloth with which the leather strips had been wrapped before being deposited in the Moabite cave.

The face of the strips varied from light brown to dark brown to almost entirely black. The strips were folded so that the surface containing the text always touched another surface containing text; in no case did the lettering contact the asphalted backside of the strip. To picture this, one only has to imagine a series of postcards connected on the narrow side, which, when folded, are text side to text side and backside to backside, accordion style.

For several weeks, in a workspace above the best tourist shop in Jerusalem's Old City, the sixteen leather strips with their forty-two columns of text began to yield their long-held secrets. The message on the Moabite manuscript amazed Shapira. He soon came to believe that he might have before him the most significant archaeological discovery of all time. Yes, Shapira thought, this Moabite scroll would undoubtedly earn him a place of distinction, forever saving his name from the stain of a previous unfortunate episode associated with discoveries from the sands of Moab. Moab had nearly ruined Shapira then. Perhaps Moab would save him now.

ב

The Land of Moab

The bluish-purple hills beyond the Sea of Salt lured Moses Shapira. The untamed wilderness regions east of the Jordan served as an escape from the modern world and his mundane life as a shop owner. Shapira frequently journeyed into these enchanted lands ruled by roaming bedouin tribes. He felt at home among the desert dwellers and made many associations with the Transjordanian tribesmen, even befriending the chieftains of various clans. These relationships allowed Shapira to conduct research and lead expeditions into lands inaccessible to most outsiders. They also placed him front and center in several of the most significant archaeological discoveries of all time from the land that once belonged to the Bible's ancient Moabites.[29]

The Hebrew Bible frequently mentions Moab and the Moabites. Their progenitor was born through an incestuous union between Abraham's nephew Lot and Lot's elder daughter. According to the biblical account, both of Lot's daughters became pregnant by their father and named the sons who were born of these illicit unions Moab ("From father") and Ben Ammi ("Son of my people"). So begins the story of two prominent peoples dwelling beyond the Jordan, east of the Dead Sea. According to the Bible and using anachronistic language, Moab "is the father of the Moabites of today" (Gen 19:37 JPS).[30]

The Moabites and the Israelites were adversaries for the duration of the biblical period. We meet the Moabites during the final stage of the wilderness wandering, when King Balak of Moab hired Balaam (of talking donkey fame), a soothsayer from the east, to curse the children of Israel (Num 22–24). God intervened to annul the intended curse, and the soothsayer pronounced a blessing instead. Even so, this favorable act by the God of the Hebrews did not prevent Israel from committing harlotry with the daughters of Moab or from participating in the worship of Moab's gods (Num 25).

It was also in the land of Moab that Moses delivered his final words to the children of Israel, words that are preserved in the book of Deuteronomy. Moab was the closest Moses would ever get to the promised land. The Bible says that

---

[29] The nineteenth-century discoveries made in the ancient territory of Moab, "across the Jordan," and the personalities behind these discoveries play into our story and therefore form a necessary backdrop to everything that follows.

[30] Unless otherwise noted, Scripture quotations throughout this work are from the Jewish Publication Society translation. Adele Berlin, Marc Zvi Brettler, and Michael Fishbane, eds. *The Jewish Study Bible* (New York: Oxford University Press, 2004).

Moses "died there, in the land of Moab, at the command of the LORD. He buried him in the valley in the land of Moab, near Beth-peor; and no one knows his burial place to this day" (Deut 34:5–6).

The book of Judges records only strife and wars between Israel and Moab. The biblical authors, in fact, rarely have anything good to say about Moab. The Moabites are at the top of a list of King Saul's enemies; this hostility continued throughout the monarchical period. Ruth seems to be the sole exception to an otherwise exclusionary rule regarding the Moabites (Deut 23:3).[31] She was the great-grandmother of King David, and so in a strange twist of irony the Moabites made their way into the bloodline of the celebrated Davidic dynasty.[32] This familial link with Moab likely earned David's parents a haven in 1 Samuel 22. But later, even David made war with his distant maternal relatives (2 Sam 8:2).

The seeds of the end of Israel's united monarchy were sown in the days of David's son Solomon. The eventual division of the kingdom was the direct result of his love for foreign women. King Solomon's women, numbering in the hundreds, included Moabites and Ammonites, but his passion for foreign women seems only surpassed by his affinity for their gods. Among his many apostasies, he "built a shrine for Chemosh the abomination of Moab on the hill near Jerusalem." "And he did the same," continues the scribe, "for all his foreign wives" (1 Kgs 11:7–8).

The Second Book of Kings begins with the notice that Moab rebelled against Israel after the death of King Ahab, husband of the infamous Jezebel (2 Kgs 1:1; 2 Kgs 3).[33] Moab's King Mesha apparently decided that the turmoil in Israel provided an opportunity to cease paying the exorbitant demands of the Israelite monarchs. Ahab was replaced by his son Ahaziah. Two years later, Ahaziah too died, and his brother Jehoram succeeded him on the throne.

Mesha underestimated the attention that Jehoram paid to such international affairs. Jehoram mustered his troops and allied himself with Jehoshaphat, king of Judah, and the king of Edom in preparation for an invasion of Moab. The battle plan involved a southerly attack through Edomite territory, but a shortage of water made them wonder if the mission would end in defeat. Jehoshaphat desired to consult a prophet, and at the king's bidding the famed Elisha arrived to give counsel. Elisha was no fan of Jehoram. If Jehoshaphat had not been a member of the party, Elisha would have refused to seek the LORD on their behalf (2 Kgs 3:14). Elisha called for a musician, and as the musician played, "the hand of the LORD came upon him," and he began to utter a message. Lack of water was not going to be a problem. The wadi would be filled with pools for the soldiers and their animals, which would occur without wind or rain. Equally welcomed was the

---

[31] See 1 Samuel 14:47: "After Saul had secured his kingship over Israel, he waged war on every side against all his enemies: against the Moabites, Ammonites, Edomites, the Philistines, and the kings of Zobah; and wherever he turned he worsted [them]."

[32] On Ruth's Moabite origins, see Ruth 1:4, 22; 2:2, 6, 21; 4:5, 10.

[33] Ahab was a king over the northern kingdom of Israel in the ninth century before the Common Era (BCE).

word that the LORD guaranteed success against the Moabites. Every fortified tower and every splendid town would fall, and the land of Moab would be ruined.

The next morning the Moabites advanced toward their enemies, but the sunlight reflecting off the newly formed pools of water gave the appearance of blood. They supposed that this was the blood of their attackers, who must have fought among themselves, killing each other. However, their hopes were soon dashed when the Israelites, Judahites, and Edomites rose from hiding and launched their attack. The Bible's account of the battle seems at first to correspond point for point with the prophetic utterance of Elisha. All that Elisha said would happen the Bible is careful to say did happen. That is, until King Mesha, seeing that he was losing the battle, took hundreds of warriors and attempted to penetrate the battle line of the Edomites. He failed, and in desperation offered his firstborn son as a burnt offering upon a fortress wall. Mesha may have thought this would appease his god Chemosh, garnering the deity's favor and enlisting him in Moab's defense.

Then, to our surprise, the story ends. After all the buildup, in a few short words the biblical record simply adds, "... great wrath came upon Israel, so they withdrew from him and went back to [their own] land" (2 Kgs 3:27b). We are left wondering how and why great wrath came upon Israel. Does this indicate that Moab was finally victorious? Did the king's depraved act inspire the Moabites to fight more ferociously, seeing that their leader had invested so high a price in the battle? We may never know why the story breaks off so abruptly. For more than 2,500 years the Hebrew Scriptures contained the only known record of this battle fought by four kings. That would change in August of 1868 when a missionary took a pleasure trip into Transjordan.[34]

---

[34] The details of the discovery of the Moabite Stone, also known as the Mesha Stela, and of the attempts to acquire possession of it are extensively covered in several sources from the period. I relied on many of these, taking careful notes for the retelling contained in this chapter. Particularly helpful were the following:

Frederick Augustus Klein's personal account of the discovery. This was originally addressed in a letter to Mr. Grove and appeared in the 19 April 1870 edition of the *Pall Mall Gazette*. The letter was republished as Rev. F. A. Kline, "The Original Discovery of the Moabite Stone," *Palestine Exploration Fund Quarterly Statement* (March 31–June 30, 1870): 281–283.

Christian D. Ginsburg, LL.D., *The Moabite Stone; A Fac-simile of the Original Inscription, with an English Translation, and a Historical and Critical Commentary*, 2nd ed. (London: Reeves and Turner, 1871).

Rev. James King, M.A., *Moab's Patriarchal Stone: Being an Account of the Moabite Stone, Its Story and Teaching* (London: Bickers and Son, 1878).

Taylor & Francis Online (tandfonline.com) was the source for the following:

Online reports on the Moabite Stone by Captain Warren, Mr. Grove, Mr. E. Deutsch, and Monsieur Clermont-Ganneau appear in (1869) "The Moabite Stone," *Palestine Exploration Fund Quarterly Statement*, 2:5, 169–183, DOI: 10.1179/peq.1869.036.

Online report by Herr H. Petermann, Prussian consul in Jerusalem, appears in H. Petermann (1871) "The Moabite Stone," *Palestine Exploration Fund Quarterly Statement*, 3:3, 135–139, DOI: 10.1179/peq.1871.014.

Online report by Rev. F. A. Klein on his initial discovery of the Moabite Stone appears in F. A. Klein (1869) "The Original Discovery of the Moabite Stone," *Palestine Exploration Fund Quarterly Statement*, 2:6, 281–283, DOI: 10.1179/peq.1869.048.

Online report on the shape of the Moabite Stone appears in (1876) "The Shape of the Moabite Stone," *Palestine Exploration Fund Quarterly Statement*, 8:4, 181–182, DOI: 10.1179/peq.1876.8.4.181.

In August of 1868 Frederick Augustus Klein, a Prussian-born Anglican minister and member of the Church Missionary Society in Jerusalem, took a trip east of the Jordan Rift, a rare experience for a European due to the inherent danger in that untamed region. Few Westerners had made the hazardous hike into these lands that played such a notable role in biblical history. Klein traversed the land of Gilead, visited the Jabbok River where the patriarch Jacob wrestled all night with the One who changed his name (Gen 32) and then made his way southward toward the ancient territory of the Moabites. Due to the potential of meeting an untimely end at the hands of unwelcoming tribes, Klein was guided and protected by Sheik Zattam, the son of Fendi-l-Fäiz, the notorious sheik of the Beni Sakhr tribe.

On the afternoon of 19 August, about a ten-minute walk from the ruins of ancient Dibân, the reverend and his guide reached the encampment of the Beni Hamîdé. Klein and his Beni Sakhr guide were greeted with typical oriental hospitality extended to those to whom such cordiality was deemed due. With its plenteous shade, carpets, and soft cushions, the sheik's tent provided a welcome respite from the scorching summer sun. Reclining on a sofa and smoking his *nargileh,* Zattam took the opportunity to surprise his missionary friend, hoping that what he wanted to share with him would be the highlight of the trip. From the outset, Zattam had made every effort to impress Klein with interesting sites. "I want to show you something that no Frank has ever seen," he told Klein as he exhaled the smoke from his pipe. "There is, only a few minutes' walk from this very place, a stone upon which is written an ancient inscription that no man has read. Since you are my honored friend, I want to show it to you." Zattam and the Beni Hamîdé sheik expressed in various ways how fortunate Klein was to have them both as guides. Knowing that this flattery was likely a ruse to encourage a worthy *baksheesh,* Klein was nonetheless anxious to see this hitherto unknown regional wonder.

The first sight of the relic dismissed any doubts Klein may have had. Lying fully exposed on the ground among the ruins of ancient Dibân was a beautiful basalt stone in a perfect state of preservation. The stone was nearly four feet long, half as wide, and slightly more than a foot thick. Both its upper and lower corners were rounded. The inscription covered the entire surface, but Klein had no idea what it said, nor did he fully understand the importance of what lay before him. Klein had four of those present with him lift the stone to see if the other side contained writing. It did not; the backside was perfectly smooth.

With the stone lying at his feet, Klein sketched out the shape and noted that the inscription consisted of thirty-four lines of text, each about an inch and a quarter below the preceding one. The upper and lower lines of text were slightly shorter in length to accommodate the narrowing of the stone at its top and bottom. With sundown approaching and realizing that he lacked the skill to make a complete transcription, he drew in his sketchbook one of each of the unique characters on the stone. Klein also recorded some of the groupings of letters, which he presumed to be words, choosing them from random lines of the stone. As he put his sketchbook in his pack, Klein hoped that upon his return to Jerusalem more learned men might ascertain the language of the basalt relic from his drawings. That evening, while resting near the ruins of Dibân, he wondered about the message engraved in stone. The next morning, Klein and his guide bid farewell to their hosts and began the trek back to Jerusalem.

The day after he arrived in Jerusalem, Rev. Klein went to see Dr. Petermann, the Prussian consul in Jerusalem. Klein hoped that Petermann might confirm his suspicion that the Moabite relic was of great value since the latter was interested in archaeology and experienced in paleography. Klein related his story to Petermann and three others, presenting his sketch of the basalt stone and his crude reproductions of the mysterious characters. Dr. Petermann immediately recognized the letters as Phoenician and realized the potential importance of acquiring the stone. He wasted no time. On 29 August 1868, Petermann dispatched a letter to the directors of the Berlin Museum informing them of the discovery and asking whether they were willing to pay one hundred napoleons to secure the stone on behalf of the Prussian government.[35] He stressed the urgency of the matter, knowing that the Jerusalem stones might cry out and expose the news of the discovery, thus alerting other eager buyers to move in and steal the prize. On 15 September, Petermann received a telegram authorizing the requested expenditure. He then cautioned his colleagues to keep the matter private but soon learned that one of them had already informed Dr. Barclay of the matter. Barclay was the chief of the English Jewish Mission, and so it was almost certain that he had already passed the information to Captain Charles Warren, or would very soon.[36] The race was on!

With approval to proceed on behalf of his government, Petermann consulted with Klein about the best method of acquiring the stone. Klein was the most knowledgeable; he knew Arabic and had contacts with those who lived in the region where the stone lay in the sand.

The two determined that a letter to Sheik Fendi-l-Fäiz was the best approach given the acknowledgment of his authority by the bedouin of Dibân. The letter requested the sheik's assistance in obtaining the basalt object, expressing honestly that they wanted to purchase it as cheaply as possible. Klein sent the letter by his assistant Behnam, a bright young Arab known to the sheik. Planning for the possibility of success, Behnam took a supply of felt to pack the stone for its safe journey to Jerusalem, but the response was not what the Prussians had hoped. At the end of September 1868, when word finally arrived from the sheik, it became apparent that the matter was more complicated than initially thought. Since the stone was in a region belonging to the Beni Hamîdé, transport had to be arranged with yet another tribal sheik named Ahmed Ibn Tarif. Rather than work the deal,

---

[35] The napoleon was a French 20-franc gold coin.

[36] Charles Warren (1840–1927) was an officer in the British Royal Engineers. He was one of the earliest European archaeologists of the biblical Holy Land, and particularly of the Temple Mount.

Fendi-l-Fäiz traveled to Damascus. Upon his return he notified Petermann and Klein that there was nothing he could do. What had appeared to be their best method of acquiring the stone proved unsuccessful.

Petermann knew from the start that if they were unable to negotiate a deal with the modern-day dwellers of Moab quickly, others would grow weary of waiting and begin to compete for the treasured antiquity. When he heard that Dr. Barclay knew about the stone, he worried that Captain Warren would also learn of its existence. Warren indeed heard, but not from Barclay. Captain Warren would later report that toward the end of September an Arab from Kerak told him about the inscribed stone and offered to show it to him. However, since he knew that the Prussians were working to secure it, he refrained from moving forward with any effort to undermine the negotiations already underway.

More than six months had passed since Klein had seen the stone, and with the first failed attempt to purchase it, Dr. Petermann and Rev. Klein devised another plan. This time they engaged an Arab teacher from Jerusalem named Saba Cawâr to serve as an intermediary between them and the bedouin. Petermann sent him off with fifty-three napoleons, three for travel expenses and the remaining fifty to use for the purchase. If he could safely bring the stone back, no questions would be asked as to what he paid for it. Any leftover funds would be his keep. In addition, Petermann guaranteed him a fifty-napoleon bonus upon delivery of the stone.

Cawâr returned without the stone but with some news, both good and bad. The Arabs had allowed him to "peep at" the stone but had moved it to a concealed location and raised the asking price ten times. What was once a hundred napoleons was now a thousand! The owners were finally gaining a sense of its worth. The Arabs insisted that the increased price was to compensate for the loss of blessing from the ancient stone, which, if removed from its place of origin, would likely bring calamities to their land.

This turn of events prompted Petermann to write to authorities in Berlin on 19 March 1869 requesting help from the Turkish government in securing the stone from the bedouin. They reached an agreement and the Turkish grand vizier wrote to the pasha of Jerusalem, but by the time the letter arrived the pasha had gone to Beirut.[37] The correspondence was then forwarded to the North German Consulate in Beirut so it could be delivered personally, but the pasha returned to Jerusalem while the letter was en route to Beirut. Again, the connection was missed. Finally, on 23 June 1869, the message reached its intended recipient. As it turned out, the matter of the stone was outside the jurisdiction of the pasha of Jerusalem. To complicate matters, the pasha of Nablus, despite having jurisdiction over the area beyond the Jordan, could do nothing without the blessing of the governor-general of Syria. The pasha of Jerusalem then sent a request to the wali of Damascus

---

[37] A provincial governor or other high official of the Ottoman Empire.

asking him to get involved and provide direction. This move would soon change matters, but not for the better.

Dr. Barclay had patiently waited for the Prussians to complete the transaction with the bedouin. He had learned of the stone from one of the four who were present at the initial meeting when Kline first returned from his trip, but out of respect had not gotten involved in the matter. Now, in the spring of 1869, seven months into the affair, Barclay invited Captain Warren and a young French dragoman[38] named Charles Clermont-Ganneau to meet and discuss what was known about the ancient relic. After the meeting, Warren and Barclay requested an update from Klein and learned that the Prussians were still actively pursuing the purchase of the stone. Warren informed the secretary of the Palestine Exploration Fund and Emanuel Deutsch from the British Museum of the latest developments. The Prussian efforts finally seemed to take a step forward when, in June of 1869, a *firman* was granted the Prussian consul.[39] Warren would wait for word from Berlin before he felt free to get involved. Klein and Cawâr also learned that the bedouin had buried the stone. Now, nearly a year after Klein first laid eyes on the artifact, no one was any closer to acquiring it.

Seven months after his initial attempt to secure the Moabite Stone, Saba Cawâr met with Herr Von Alten, Petermann's successor as the new Prussian consul. Cawâr informed him that an arrangement was in the works to purchase the stone from the sheik of the Beni Hamîdé for the reasonable price of 120 napoleons. Funds were dispatched immediately. The new consul even contributed twenty napoleons of his own to make up the difference between the amount granted by the Berlin Museum and the sheik's latest asking price. Cawâr had until the end of November to complete the transfer, after which, if unsuccessful, he would need to return the funds. He agreed and immediately set out to finalize the agreement with the sheik.

At last, it seemed that the bedouin would transfer ownership of Moab's much sought-after treasure, but once again tribal conflicts in Transjordan prevented the deal. Kaplan, sheik of the Adwân tribe (situated north of Dibân), refused to allow the stone to pass through his territory. Cawâr sent word to the Prussians that unless the wali of Damascus involved himself in the affair, the difficulties would not be resolved. Despite Von Alten's repeated pleas, referencing the firman and providing proof of the agreement, he received only excuses about why no help would be forthcoming. Von Alten and the wali of Damascus met on 13 November 1869. The consul was advised to deliver the contract and demand assistance from the Syrian

---

[38] An interpreter, translator, and official guide between Turkish, Arabic, and Persian-speaking countries and political entities of the Middle East and European embassies, consulates, vice consulates and trading posts. A dragoman had to have a knowledge of Arabic, Persian, Turkish, and European languages. Charles Clermont-Ganneau was born in 1846 and was only 22 years old when he was assigned to the role of dragoman at the consulate in Jerusalem. His involvement with the Moabite Stone would launch his career, and subsequent events from the land of Moab would place him at the center of our unfolding story of Moses Shapira.

[39] A *firman* was a written decree or permission granted by the appropriate Islamic official at any level of government.

governor-general in securing the stone's passage to its legal owners in Jerusalem. Saba Cawâr waited.

While everyone else was waiting for a solution from Damascus, Charles Clermont-Ganneau made his move. Having closely followed the unfolding debacle since he learned of it from Dr. Barclay, and with the aid of an Arab named Selim al-Qari, the Frenchman obtained a rough copy of just enough lines from the stone to realize its significance.[40] Clermont-Ganneau employed an Arab by the name of Yâqoub Caravacca and sent him, along with two others, to make a squeeze of the inscription.[41] With some difficulty, Caravacca and his two companions received permission to make the squeeze. But before the paper was fully dry, a commotion broke out between competing tribal members and violence erupted. Caravacca was stabbed in the leg, and in the confusion one of the other two with him (named Djemîl) ripped the not-yet-dried paper from the stone, tearing it into seven pieces. The three men miraculously escaped with their lives— and with a less-than-perfect impression of the stone.

Meanwhile, Clermont-Ganneau was working every possible angle. He entered into negotiations with a Beni Sakhr sheik named 'Id el Faëz. They agreed on a sum of 400 *medjidies,* and with half of the sale price in his hand, the sheik went to purchase the stone. Simultaneously, the wali of Damascus sent a letter to the pasha of Nablus, who had jurisdiction over Transjordan. The note authorized him to demand that the stone of Dibân be handed over to the Prussians. The involvement of the wali of Damascus was the final straw for the Beni Hamîdé.

---

[40] It should be noted that this Selim is not the same Selim who acquired the leather strips for Moses Shapira. But Shapira knew him, as we will soon see. This Selim was known for his abilities in ancient scripts. See A. S. Yahuda, "The Story of a Forgery and the Mesa Inscription," *Jewish Quarterly Review,* Vol. 35, No. 2, (Oct. 1944), 145. Here Yahuda, claiming to have met Selim, says, "On this occasion he revealed to me that his surname al-Qari, which means 'the reader,' was given to him by the Bedouins, because he could read all sorts of inscriptions 'in every language in the world.'" Clermont-Ganneau and Selim al-Qari worked together to acquire the Moabite monolith. It is interesting to note that when Klein was shown the now-famous stela, "the stone was lying among the ruins of Dibân, perfectly free and exposed to view, the inscription uppermost," See Klein, "The Original Discovery of the Moabite Stone," 282. One has to wonder how it became exposed. Who unearthed it? According to the recollections of his daughter, it seems that she suggested that it was Moses Shapira! She said, "He [Clermont-Ganneau] was keenly interested in making antiquarian researches, and had taken Selim [al-Qari] ... into his service. The latter ... had guided the French consul into the Bedouin's country and had actually helped him secure a certain monolith which [Mr. Shapira] himself had unearthed. This was naturally more than enough to create the worst feelings between the rival Europeans." See Harry, *The Little Daughter of Jerusalem,* 102. This rivalry between Clermont-Ganneau and Moses Shapira forms a dramatic backdrop to our story. [Clarifications within brackets throughout this work are supplied by the author (RKN).]

[41] A squeeze is a copy of an inscription produced by placing damp paper over it and pressing it into the engraved surface. Once the paper is dry, it is carefully removed, and the result is a reversed impression of the inscription.

7

Moabite Treasures

Sir Walter Besant recalled in his autobiography that the two most conse-
quential discoveries during his time at the helm of the Palestine Exploration Fund
came from the land of Moab.[42] Both of these involve the same *dramatis personae*.
One of these, often overlooked, was the wali of Damascus. In the mid-1860s the
wali of Damascus launched campaigns of aggression against the Transjordanian
bedouin tribes. These aggressive actions resulted in the discovery of Moses
Shapira's scroll and the near loss of the Moabite Stone.[43]

Mehmed Rashid Pasha was the wali of Damascus at that time. He was born
in Egypt in 1824, where his father was an aide in the Egyptian government. Rashid
went to France to study in 1844, completing his education five years later. He
began a life of government service in 1851 in the Ottoman capital of Istanbul
under the mentorship of the grand vizier Mehmed Ali Pasha, a major figure in the
Tanzimat reforms. Rashid's career in government was exemplary. In 1866 he was
named Wali of Syria Vilayet, a role that placed him as governor from Tripoli (in
modern-day Lebanon) in the north to Palestine and Transjordan in the south.

Rashid saw himself as a revivalist of the Ottoman Empire and set out to
implement reforms aimed at achieving greatness for the governing Turks. He is
known for his work in infrastructure—public works, roadways for improved
trade, and telegraph for enhanced communications. He also advanced the cause
of literacy, prompting a sort of renaissance in his time. Newspapers, journals, and
the arts and sciences improved under his leadership. As wali, he saw a strong
military presence as the necessary means to enforce his reforms, and he was not
afraid to use force when he felt it was required.

Military manpower was supplied by conscription, which, like all other
programs, was financed through taxation. Despite the Ottoman gains, a problem
existed in the empire—the bedouin.[44] Rogue elements of these desert dwellers
refused to consent to modernization. They avoided conscription and paid no taxes.
Competing tribes roamed without constraint, instilling fear, particularly in the

---

[42] Walter. Besant, and Samuel Squire Sprigge, *Autobiography of Sir Walter Besant, with a Prefatory Note*,
(New York: Dodd, Mead and Company, 1902), 161.

[43] Moses Shapira related that the sixteen leather strips were discovered by bedouin "about 1865," during a
time of "persecution … in the mid-1860s, when the Wali of Damascus forced the East Jordanian tribes … to
recognize Turkish sovereignty."

[44] For information on the social environment of the Transjordanian region in the nineteenth century I relied
on Eveline van der Steen, *Near Eastern Tribal Societies During the Nineteenth Century*.

Transjordanian Belqa region, an area between the Zarqa River in the north and the Wadi Mujib in the south. Bedouin tribes demanded payment from peasant farmers in exchange for peace. Those who refused to pay suffered raids and robberies. Consequently, there were few settlements in the area. Rashid realized that these extreme elements within the Ottoman Empire must be forced to submit, so he personally led aggressive campaigns into the rebellious region.

Beginning in the summer of 1867, Rashid initiated several campaigns to subjugate the bedouin. As early as 1863 the previous wali had made an effort to enforce reforms over the tribes, but Rashid was more determined. He even demanded payment of past-due taxes. Throughout August of 1867, led by Rashid himself, Ottoman military forces engaged the bedouin of the Belqa region, driving them southward and ultimately forcing long-time rival tribes together in a desperate attempt to survive. By the summer of 1869 the Adwan and Beni Sakhr tribes had formed a precarious confederation to resist the destruction of their way of life by the unrelenting wali. Hatred for Rashid had finally surpassed the hostility between the desert tribes.

Now, as if unaware of what was happening right next door, the Prussians requested assistance from the much-hated wali of Damascus in acquiring the stone that Rev. Klein had seen in August of 1868. This would prove to be the final straw.

The wali passed the oversight of transporting the Moabite Stone to the pasha of Nablus, who, in turn, instructed the modir of Salt to pressure the tribes to relinquish the relic.[45] When word reached the Beni Hamîdé that Rashid had ordered them to hand over their treasure to the Prussians, they resolved to show their nemesis, through one great act of defiance, that they would not submit. The Moabite Stone, bearing a message from antiquity, would be sacrificed on the altar of rebellion.

Tribesmen built a massive fire and heated the basalt monument until it turned from its original black appearance to a glowing hue. To achieve maximum heating they piled coals on the face of the stone; finally, they doused it with cold water and cast large rocks against it. The abrupt temperature change, coupled with the impact of the rocks, shattered the coveted relic.[46]

The destroyers shared the fragments and reportedly placed the chunks of basalt in their granaries, thinking they would bring blessings. Never again would the stone be seen intact. Now, the only hope of learning its message depended on

---

[45] The modir was a regional official, or governor, but subordinate to the Ottoman pasha. The name es-Salt refers to the biblical location of Ramoth-Gilead. The literature at times refers to this official as the modir of Salt and at other times the modir of es-Salt.

[46] Myriam Harry put it this way: "To make matters worse, the Turkish government intervened and laid claim to the ground where the excavations had been undertaken, taking advantage of this pretext to levy a heavy tax on the rebellious tribe. A sharp skirmish ensued between the soldiers and the sons of the desert … In the end, the Turks were driven back beyond the Jordan, but the Bedouins, convinced now that their misfortunes were due to the excavations which had taken place amongst their ruins, blew up all that remained of the latter with gunpowder, destroying thereby several valuable specimens which had already been exhumed." Although Harry's work may not be historically reliable on some points, there seems to be a recollection of things that she must have heard at the time. It is interesting to note that in the context of the destruction she has Clermont-Ganneau and Selim al-Qari working together and even being "attacked and robbed by brigands" on an expedition to Moab funded by Shapira. See Harry, *The Little Daughter of Jerusalem,* 106–107.

the squeeze of Charles Clermont-Ganneau and the few lines he had received from Selim al-Qari.

As Captain Warren was returning from a trip to Lebanon in November of 1869, a bedouin from the Adwân tribe met him as he approached Jerusalem. The bedouin, named Goblan, informed him that the stone of Moab had been broken into pieces; as proof he presented a sample containing a few letters. Captain Warren made a squeeze of the fragment and forwarded it to the office of the Palestine Exploration Fund on 22 December 1869. He then gave Goblan some squeeze paper and sent him to try to obtain a copy of all the fragments he could find. Warren retained the piece that Goblan had given him, but he feared that the world might never know the whole message engraved on the monument from Moab.

Clermont-Ganneau informed Warren that he had obtained an imperfect squeeze of the entire stone and showed it to him. Warren, in turn, let Clermont-Ganneau see the fragment in his possession and informed him of Goblan's mission. The two determined that by working together they would improve the chances of recovering the full text of the ancient stone.

On 13 January 1870, Goblan returned with two excellent squeeze impressions taken from as many fragments. Those pieces appeared to make up about half of the original stone. Together, the impressions contained 508 characters of the ancient Phoenician script. Additionally, Goblan gave Warren a dozen more pieces of the stone, each containing one or two letters.[47] The same day, Djemil, the Arab who had miraculously escaped with the imperfect squeeze of the entire stone, and whom Clermont-Ganneau had dispatched again to Transjordan, also retrieved a few small pieces of the stone. Clermont-Ganneau set to work immediately with these paper impressions and fragments to create a copy of the inscription. Just four days later, on 16 January 1870, he completed his work of producing a transcription of the Moabite Stone in Hebrew as well as a French translation.

Monsieur Clermont-Ganneau's work served as the basis for much scholarly discussion. The stone told a story that was familiar to Bible students, but it offered a different perspective. The Moabite Stone was a stela erected by King Mesha, mentioned in the Hebrew Bible. Specifically, it seemed to contain a Moabite version of the battle mentioned in 2 Kings 3. All estimates dated the Mesha Stela to the ninth century BCE. One scholar, Christian David Ginsburg, published a thorough work on the subject in 1871.[48] His 57-page book, titled *The Moabite Stone*, contained the following sections: preface; dedication; an inscription of the original; an English translation; a history of the discovery; the restoration and present condition of the text; contents, division, and date of the Moabite Stone;

---

[47] Sir Walter Besant reported that he assisted in the work of photographing the squeezes, adding further, "When we had our photographs, the squeezes became less valuable. We sent copies round to the best-known Hebrew scholars, and all began to write books and monographs. We found a great quantity of things in the course of our excavations and our surveys, but never again did we make so splendid a 'find' as that of the Moabite Stone." Besant, *Autobiography,* 161–162.

[48] Christian D. Ginsburg, LL.D., *The Moabite Stone*.

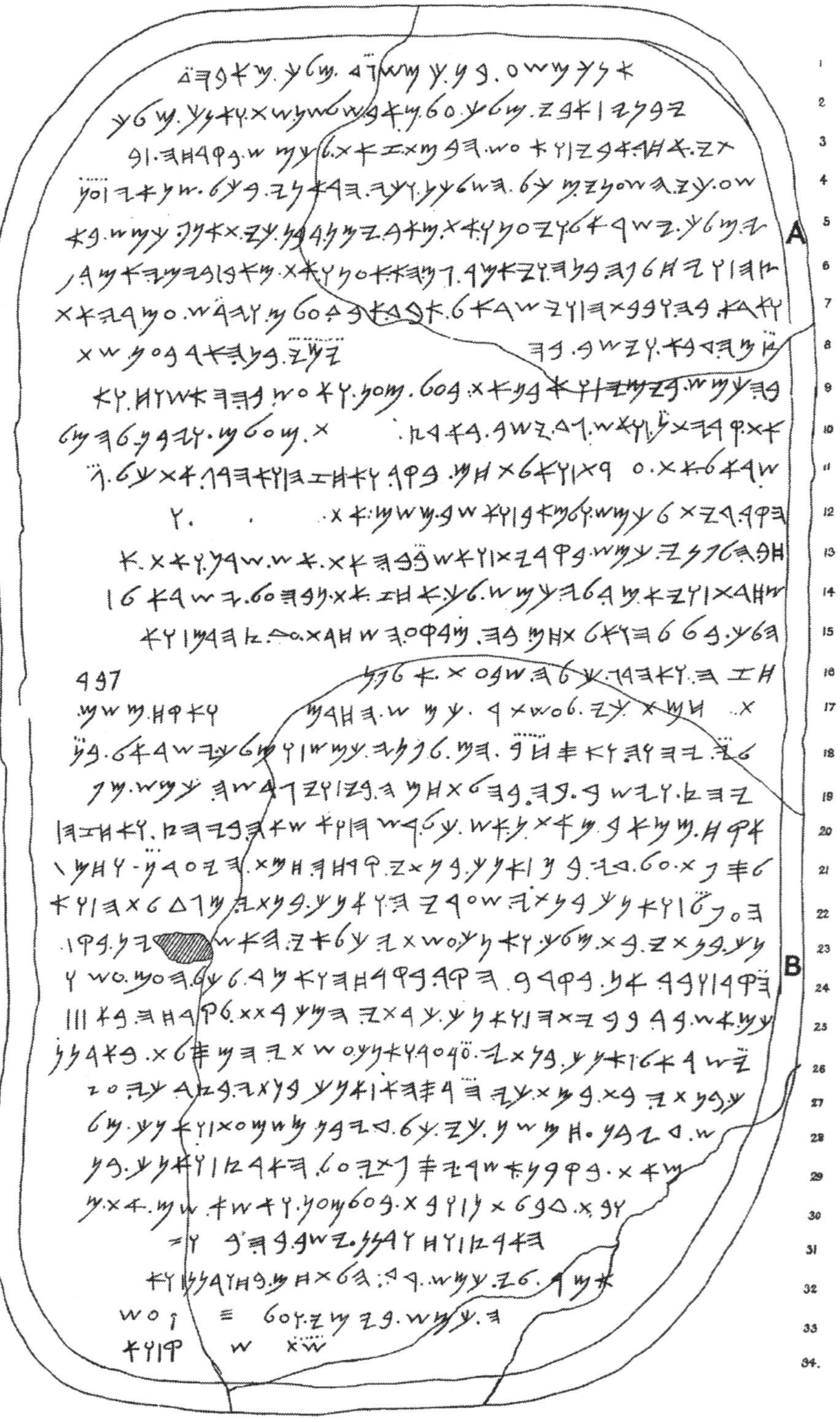

THE MOABITE STONE.
REDUCED TO ONE-THIRD OF THE ORIGINAL.

Figure 4

the relation of the inscription to the biblical narrative; the importance of the Moabite Stone historically, theologically, linguistically, and paleographically; literature about the Moabite Stone; a commentary; various translations in parallel columns; and a vocabulary guide. Ginsburg's work also included an artistic reproduction of the stone and a map of Moab produced by the Palestine Exploration Fund.

In the process of researching and writing his book, Ginsburg expressed both compliments and criticism of the parties involved. In his assessment, blame for the destruction of the stone lay squarely at the feet of Monsieur Clermont-Ganneau, whom he referred to as a "young French savant ... with more enthusiasm than discretion."[49] He further noted that Clermont-Ganneau's initial publications made no mention of Rev. Klein as the stone's discoverer or that the Prussians were actively engaged in its acquisition. He stated that by such omissions Clermont-Ganneau showed that "he was more jealous to appear as the original discoverer of the monument than to give credit where credit is due."[50] Ginsburg even went so far as to say that the "very oldest Semitic lapidary record of importance yet discovered, which had defied the corroding powers of more than 2,500 years, was at last broken up, through the unwise measures adopted by a young French savant, who, despite knowing that others were first in the field bidding for it, was determined to outbid them, in order to secure it for his own nation."[51]

In August of 1868, Rev. Klein provided his own account of the discovery in a letter to a certain Mr. Grove, who published it in London's *Pall Mall Gazette* on 19 April 1870. Given all the attention the matter was being afforded by the academic world, Klein wanted to set the record straight. In addition to providing details that only he could give, he wanted to clarify the inaccuracies of Clermont-Ganneau's work, principal of which was the shape of the stone before being shattered. Describing its shape, he said, "The stone is, as appears from the accompanying sketch, rounded on both sides, not only at the upper end as mentioned by Monsieur Ganneau." He went on to suggest that Clermont-Ganneau was "wrongly informed" about this matter and therefore made the stone square at the bottom in his reproduction.[52] Near the end of his account, Klein added that a "scientific expedition to Moab is a great desideratum and could but greatly enrich our knowledge of Hebrew archaeology."[53]

---

[49] Ginsburg, *Moabite Stone*, 10. Walter Besant held a different view altogether. He stated, "Most unfortunately, Mr. Klein withheld his discovery from his countryman M. Clermont-Ganneau, who, had he been left alone, would certainly have obtained an exact copy, and probably have secured it." See Walter Besant, *Twenty-One Years' Work In The Holy Land, a Record and a Summary, June 22, 1865–June 22, 1886* (London: Richard Bentley & Son, 1886), 161.

[50] Ginsburg, *Moabite Stone*, 10. Indeed in some of the first accounts of the discovery of the Moabite Stone it was Clermont-Ganneau who was credited rather than Rev. Klein.

[51] Ibid. Christian David Ginsburg will play a major part in our unfolding narrative. At this point it is important to note his assessment of the French dragoman Clermont-Ganneau.

[52] In Ginsburg's publication, he presented the shape of the stone according to Klein's description and not that of Clermont-Ganneau.

[53] A *desideratum* is something considered necessary or highly desirable.

Outmaneuvered by the crafty Frenchman, the Prussians lost the race to obtain the precious relic. They quietly accepted defeat as the world debated the treasure that had slipped from their hands. The well-intentioned Klein simply was not equipped to compete with the likes of Clermont-Ganneau, who proved himself willing to stop at nothing to achieve fame and recognition. Aside from an enormous ego, the young Frenchman possessed great skill and a healthy supply of luck. The Prussians needed someone who might enter the scene and earn them a place at the table of academic discussion. Besides being one of their own, the candidate would need the strength to engage with men such as Monsieur Clermont-Ganneau. The man who destiny chose for the job had joined their ranks a decade before the discovery of the Moabite Stone. His name was Moses Shapira.

Shapira was Jewish by birth, born in Kamenetz-Podolsk in 1830.[54] At the age of twenty-five he left his country and his kindred and joined his grandfather on a journey to Palestine—his ancestors' homeland. The trip included an extended layover in Romania. Several months in Bucharest with Christian missionaries led to the young man's conversion to Christianity. However, while he adopted a new religion on the journey, he was compelled to forfeit his passport as well as Russian protection.[55] He arrived in Jerusalem in 1856 and joined the Anglican Community at Christ Church near the Jaffa Gate, where he occupied several positions. But providence had bigger plans for the new immigrant.

Frequent illness ultimately put the young Shapira in the hospital, where a German nurse named Rosette Jöckel cared for him. After recovering, his involvement with the German woman led him to appeal to the Prussian government for protection and a passport on 7 April 1860.[56] His appeal was granted, and adding Wilhelm to his birth name he became known as Moses Wilhelm Shapira. Moses married Rosette on 23 April 1861 and opened his shop on Christian Street a short time later.[57] Shapira's reputation and business grew steadily over the next decade. He sold everything from souvenirs to valuable manuscripts, but it was the discovery of the Mesha Stela that would launch Moses Shapira into the headlines.

One of Shapira's employees was an Arab whose job it was to seek out Christian tourists in the Old City and bring them into the shop. However, over time his familiarity with the territory east of the Jordan proved more valuable to the business. He had close connections with tribal members, having earned their trust, or at least having bought their affection, with supplies of tobacco, sugar, and coffee.[58] He also possessed artistic skills, and he was a linguist or at least pretended to be, claiming that the name al-Qari celebrated his prowess for

---

[54] Located in modern-day western Ukraine.

[55] Personal information about Moses Shapira comes from a letter written by him on 7 April 1860. I used the English translation in Yoram Sabo, "Between Apostate and Forger: Moses Wilhelm Shapira and the Moabite Pottery Affair," 5. Academia (n.d.). https://www.academia.edu/24911481/Between_Apostate_and_Forger_Moses_Wilhelm_Shapira_and_the_Moabite_Pottery_Affair.

[56] Ibid.

[57] Ibid.

[58] Ibid., 9.

languages.[59] This was the same Selim who was dispatched by Charles Clermont-Ganneau.

Working through an intermediary named Bergheim, toward the end of 1869 Selim had given Clermont-Ganneau a sketch of what would soon be known throughout the world as the Mesha Stela. The initial sketch contained enough information to prompt the Frenchman's involvement in the pursuit of the relic. Later, Selim's transcription of lines 13 through 20 of the stone's text only heightened his interest. Selim's sketch proved helpful to Clermont-Ganneau in his later publication, and as the Frenchman wrote, even "served to correct many of my readings."[60]

Selim's primary Bedouin contact in Transjordan was a sheik of the Adwan tribe named Ali Diab. In the wake of the scholarly world's excitement over the discovery of the Moabite Stone, Selim, and in turn Shapira, realized there was an enthusiastic market for antiquities from the land of Mesha. The Adwan sheik could help supply the growing demand. The promise of treasures from Moab and a ready and willing supplier led to Shapira's entry into the antiquities market in 1871. Expeditions proved fruitful. Selim sometimes ventured into bedouin territory unaccompanied, returning with Moabite figurines packed safely in sacks of grain for the journey back to the shop.[61] At other times, when arrangements were coordinated with Sheik Diab, Shapira would mount his white mare and join in the adventures. Shapira especially loved these expeditions into bedouin country, where he could be more than a shopkeeper. There, he was the "king of the desert."[62] On other occasions, Sheik Diab came to Jerusalem to meet with his friends. There seemed to be no end to the treasures, and the Prussians wanted in on the latest finds. This time they were determined to let no one beat them.

Soon the little shop on Christian Street was bursting with hundreds of Moabite treasures. Earthenware jars and figurines flowed into Shapira's shop and quickly became the talk of the scholarly world. Members of the newly-formed Palestine Exploration Fund visited Shapira, mainly to see what the antiquities dealer had most recently added to his growing collection. Captain Claude Conder and Charles Tyrwhitt-Drake took the time to make numerous sketches of the Moabite pottery and forwarded their drawings and enthusiastic reports to headquarters.[63] Some of the Moabite figurines were erotic and grotesque in nature.

---

[59] Yahuda, "The Story of a Forgery and the Mesa Inscription," 145.

[60] Clermont-Ganneau, "The Shapira Collection" (and letters from other authors), in *Palestine Exploration Fund Quarterly Statement* (1874), 204.

[61] The details related to the nineteenth-century Moabitica affair are covered extensively in many publications of the Palestine Exploration Fund, but especially helpful was the work of Martin Heide, whose excellent paper is filled with many relevant footnotes and a well-documented bibliography. See Martin Heide, "The Moabitica and Their Aftermath: How to Handle a Forgery Affair With an International Impact," in *New Inscriptions and Seals Relating to the Biblical World*, ed. Meir Lubetski (Atlanta: Society of Biblical Literature, 2012), 193–241.

[62] Harry, *The Little Daughter of Jerusalem*, 8.

[63] Claude R. Conder, Charles Tyrwhitt-Drake, and Charles Frederick, "Notes on the Drawings and Copies of Inscriptions from the 'Shapira Collection' Sent Home by Lieut. Conder and Mr. Drake," in *Palestine Exploration Fund Quarterly Statement* (1873), 79–80.

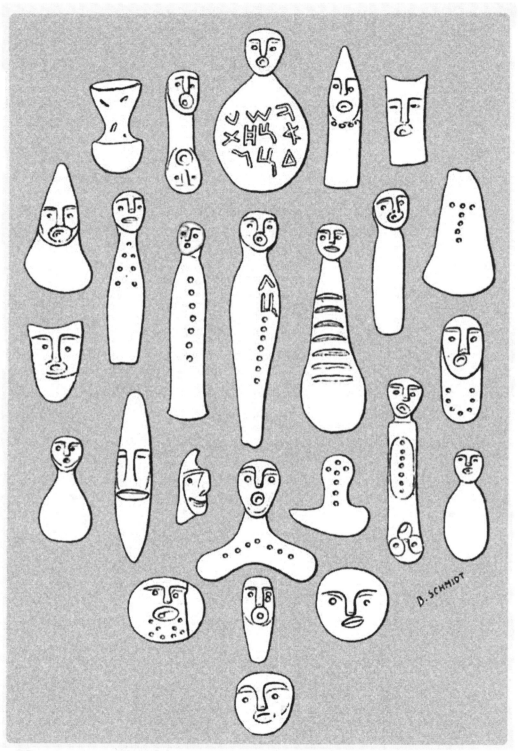

Nº 17. — SPÉCIMENS DE FAUSSES POTERIES MOABITES.

Figure 5–Samples of the fraudulent artifacts from the land of Moab.

Though this was shocking to some, it was no surprise given the biblical picture of the people with whom ancient Israelites had participated in sexual sin centuries earlier.

By the time Conder sent his sketches to Europe, he had reported that the Prussian government, through an agent, had purchased the first series in the Shapira Collection, consisting of 911 pieces. In the end, the Prussians, determined to win this race, bought 1,700 pieces of the Moabite treasure from Moses Shapira for a price of 22,000 *thalers*, 2,000 of which came from the emperor's personal funds.[64] With a portion of his newfound wealth, Shapira moved his family into a lovely new home. His daughter later recalled that her father "could not live any longer in the ugly house on the Russian Hill, and that they must move elsewhere."[65] The new residence was known as the Villa Rachid. It had been built only a few years prior by a wealthy Arab named Aga Rachid Nashashibi, "partly in European and partly in Mussulman style."[66]

Shapira's name was becoming known worldwide and was associated with great discoveries, some ranking his Moabite potteries alongside the Mesha Stela in terms of their archaeological importance. For nearly three years experts openly debated the authenticity of Shapira's Moabitica collection. *The Athenæum,* the Palestine Exploration Fund, and various academic journals, including *Zeitschrift der Deutschen Morgenländischen Gessellschaft* [the *Journal of German Oriental Society,*] published articles written by proponents and opponents.

Many leading scholars of the day believed that the Moabite finds were authentic relics and testaments to that ancient culture. Among these was Professor Konstantine Schlottmann of Halle University.[67] He and other believers provided their interpretations of the finds for everyone to see. Professor Schlottmann's enthusiasm for the Moabitica played a crucial role in boosting the Prussians' confidence, leading them to purchase the collection.

Despite the positive views of many, and the ongoing discussion of Moabite culture prompted by the clay discoveries, not everyone believed in the authenticity of the latest finds. Some suggested that a forger was behind the Moabitica Collection. To counter the accusations of forgery, some participated in sponsored expeditions into the land of Moab. Reports of these expeditions, some with and some without Shapira and Selim, made their way into print. Professor Schlottmann continued to declare the Moabitica authentic and went so far as to claim that the expeditions proved their authenticity beyond question. He also

---

[64] Thalers—any of numerous silver coins that served as a unit of currency in certain Germanic countries between the fifteenth and nineteenth centuries. Also called *talers.* According to some currency conversion models, 22,000 thalers is estimated to be equivalent to nearly $400,000 in 2021 dollars.

[65] Harry, *The Little Daughter of Jerusalem,* 173.

[66] See the description of the house and property in Harry, *The Little Daughter of Jerusalem,* 175–177. The house was purchased in 1924 by ophthalmologist Dr. Abraham Albert Ticho and his artist wife Anna. The property now belongs to the Israel Museum and features the art of Anna Ticho. The Ticho House is located at HaRav Agan 10, Jerusalem.

[67] Schlottmann learned of the inscribed artifacts of Moab from his former student Hermann Weser, a pastor of the German Protestant church in Jerusalem. "Weser had seen them in Shapira's antiquities shop." See Martin Heide, "The Moabitica and Their Aftermath," 194.

complimented Shapira's merits, expertise, diligence, and trust among the desert tribes as further proof. At the same time, two German professors, Socin and Kautzsch, published a 191-page book arguing that the entire collection was a fraud.[68] One other skeptic of the Moabite treasures tipped public opinion toward forgery more than any other—Charles Clermont-Ganneau.

The French savant entered the fray expressing his opinions as to the falsity of the Moabitica by stating that he "did not see, in the whole collection, one single object which could be regarded as genuine."[69] Clermont-Ganneau, acting as a detective hot on the trail for clues, conducted an investigation in Jerusalem that resulted in confessions from everyone involved in what he termed "this colossal deception."[70] Later, some of those who had confessed claimed that they made their admissions under threats and coercion. Nevertheless, public opinion was settled— the entire collection of Moabitica was deemed to be fake.

Shapira was given a pass but was considered the first dupe of the now-infamous forger Selim, who reportedly fled to Alexandria, Egypt, in the aftermath of the affair. Professor Schlottmann endured the shame of having championed the authenticity and having convinced his country to purchase the forgeries. Monsieur Clermont-Ganneau was the hero, earning his place as the one who uncovered the colossal deception. For his part, Shapira went about his life as a shop owner, focusing his energies on valuable old manuscripts and hoping that the whole matter would soon be covered over like ancient treasures buried in the desert sands.

---

[68] Emil Kautzsch and Albert Socin, *Die Aechtheit der Moabitischen Altertümer Geprüft* (Strasburg: Trübner, 1876). The English translation of the title is "The Authenticity of the Moabite Antiquities Investigated." As noted by Heide, Emil Kautzsch "is still known for his revised edition of Gesenius's Hebrew Grammar." See Heide, "The Moabitica and Their Aftermath," 204.

[69] Clermont-Ganneau, "The Shapira Collection," 116.

[70] Ibid., 115.

The Words of the Scroll

By the end of August 1878, Moses Wilhelm Shapira had in his possession the sixteen strips of a blackened leather scroll discovered in a cave in the land of Moab. As soon as Shapira acquired the strips, he began to decipher their content. Now, with the entire manuscript in his possession, he set to work in earnest on the texts before him.

He slowly began to read, transcribe, and finally grasp the message of the leather strips. The work was tedious due to the condition of the strips. Where the surface was light brown, the characters were easier to read, but on the darker brown and black pieces the process was more difficult and sometimes nearly impossible. At times, when exposed to proper lighting, the dull letters became barely visible. At other times, soaking the strips in a special mixture of spirits seemed to be the only way to cause the letters to appear, but only for a short time between the wetting and drying processes. Then, and with considerable effort, Shapira was able to make out some of the letters. He was thrilled to find that the ancient text was written in letters similar to those on the Mesha Stela. Would the scroll prove to be as old as the Moabite Stone?

Letter by letter, word by word, the forty-two panels of text grudgingly divulged their ancient message. The scroll began: "These are the words that Moses spoke, according to the mouth of Jehovah, to all the children of Israel in the wilderness, across the Jordan in the Aravah." Shapira recognized the narrative as a version of the Bible's book of Deuteronomy, but with notable differences. Like Deuteronomy, Shapira's scroll contained a version of the famous Ten Commandments, but with noteworthy variants.

Additionally, Shapira's scroll only contained the four-letter name of Israel's God in its opening and closing lines, using the more generic *Elohim* in all other references to the Deity.[71] He noted alternate word usages and divergent spellings throughout. Shapira's "Deuteronomy" also included details that in the standard biblical text occur in Exodus, Leviticus, and Numbers. One particularly intriguing feature of the document was that it consisted of *two* copies of the same shortened unorthodox Deuteronomy.

---

[71] In the Hebrew Bible, the name of Israel's God is represented by four Hebrew letters—יהוה. They are referred to as the Tetragrammaton (four letters). The name is generally represented in English as *Yahweh* or *Jehovah*, though most English translations use LORD whenever the Hebrew name occurs. The name יהוה occurs approximately 7,000 in the Hebrew Bible. *Elohim* is typically translated as God.

Shapira was anxious to share the remarkable discovery, but with the Moabitica scandal only two years behind him, he needed to proceed with utmost caution. The Halle professor Konstantine Schlottmann had been one of Shapira's few supporters during the Moabitica affair. So on 24 September 1878, after nearly a month of work, Shapira sent professor Schlottmann his transcription of the newly-discovered—and in his mind, potentially the oldest—version of the sacred text along with a commentary detailing the variants between his manuscript and the traditional text of the Bible. The Halle professor shared Shapira's transcription and commentary with Franz Delitzsch who was visiting to work on a revision of the Luther Bible.[72] The two German scholars agreed that in their estimation, the manuscript was a "sophisticated, but at the same time crude, forgery."[73] Schlottmann and Delitzsch thought the text of the manuscript was "striving to give … the appearance of antiquity," and worse in their minds, that it supported the findings of higher biblical criticism. Together, the two deemed it appropriate to give Shapira a stern rebuke, so on 7 October 1878 Schlottmann penned a letter to Shapira declaring the Deuteronomy scroll a fraud.

Shapira later recalled the exchange. He said, "I have sent a transcription of the most of it, to Prof. Schlottmann in 24 Sept 1878 asking him his opinion—to which I got only a rebuke saying, 'How I dare to call this forgery the Old Testament? Could I suppose for one minute that it is older than our unquestionable genuine ten commandments?'[74] That it is not genuine, he went on, he can prove, 1st that it contradicts the Bible (it has Elohim instead of Jehovah)." Shapira continued to relate a few examples supplied by Schlottmann, intended to show that "the writer [of the manuscript] was so ignorant not to know," after which the professor remarked on several variations between Shapira's manuscript and the authorized text. Schlottmann concluded his objections saying, "This is also the opinion of Prof. Delitzsch."[75] Franz Delitzsch also reported this collaboration on the rebuke of Shapira saying, "It seemed appropriate, however, to give him a serious warning, and I authorized my esteemed colleague and friend [Schlottmann] to write to Jerusalem that I, like him, consider this Deuteronomy to be the work of a hideous fraud."[76]

---

[72] See Franz Delitzsch, "Schapira's Pseudo-Deuteronium," *Allegemeine Evangelisch-Lutherisch Kirchenzeitung,* no. 36 (Sept 7, 1883), 844–846. Delitzsch would publish a six-part series on Shapira's 'Fake Deuteronomy.' Franz Delizsch, "Schapira's Pseudo-Deuteronomium," *Allegemeine Evangelisch-Lutherisch Kirchenzeitung,* no. 36 (Sept 7, 1883): 844–846; no. 37 (Sept 14, 1883): 869–871; no. 38 (Sept 21, 1883): 893–894; no. 39 (Sept 28, 1883): 914–916; no. 6 (Feb 8, 1884): 129–130; and a final piece titled "Die Handschriftlichen Funde Shapira's," *Allegemeine Evangelisch-Lutherisch Kirchenzeitung,* no. 15 (Apr 11, 1884): 343–344.

[73] Delitzsch, "Schapira's Pseudo-Deuteronomium," no. 36.

[74] Eduard Meyer reported to Georg Ebers, that when "Schlottmann, whom he informed of this, simply declared it forged, old Delitzsch made the indignant remark: 'Don't touch our Decalogue!'" Letter from Eduard Meyer to Georg Ebers, 8 July 1883, "Der Briefwechsel zwischen Georg Ebers und Eduard Meyer (1874–1898)," Vorbemerkung von G. Audring. https://www.geschichte.hu-berlin.de/de/bereiche-und-lehrstuehle/alte-geschichte/forschung/briefe-meyer/ebers.

[75] Letter from Shapira to Professor Hermann Strack, written 9 May 1883, contained in the British Library *Add. MS. 41294.*

[76] Delitzsch, "Schapira's Pseudo-Deuteronomium," no. 36.

The main reason for Schlottmann's and Delitzsch's rebukes seemed to be that Shapira's scroll deviated from the traditional text of the Bible.[77] Adding insult to injury, Schlottmann made the Prussian imperial consul to Jerusalem aware of the matter hoping to prevent Shapira from making any further moves to publicize the find.[78]

Shapira reviewed and carefully considered Schlottmann's objections. He realized that some of them were the result of his own errors in the transcription that he had sent to Schlottmann, but having narrowly survived the previous charge of forgery he decided to store the manuscript in a secure location and go about his regular endeavors. It was not the time to debate the soundness of Schlottmann's rejection. That would have to wait. Shapira reluctantly put the scroll fragments in a vault designed for securing gold and other valuables at the Bergheim and Company Bank. Located on David Street, the bank was opened in 1851 by Melville Peter Bergheim. The senior Bergheim was assisted in the banking business by his sons Peter and Samuel.[79] With the manuscript safely secured in the Bergheim bank, Shapira continued to operate his popular tourist shop on Christian Street, but his real passion was antiquities, and particularly manuscripts of great age and value. He preferred trips into untamed and uncharted areas over days in the shop selling souvenirs to tourists.

Over time, thanks to several successful ventures into Yemen and elsewhere, Shapira acquired numerous valuable manuscripts.[80] These he sold to wealthy private collectors and to the British Museum in his role as an agent for that esteemed institution. It seemed that Shapira had found his niche and a way to escape the mundane role of a shopkeeper. He had an uncanny ability to find remarkable works, and the desire to see his latest treasures brought some of the greatest minds of the day to his famed shop.

Jerusalem was teeming with discoverers. Archaeologists and explorers made their way to the Holy Land, regularly arriving with "Bible in one hand and spade in the other," hoping to achieve fame and glory. Institutions were formed to explore sites associated with the biblical stories, and lovers of Scripture the world over eagerly anticipated the next great discovery.

In 1880 a young man named Jacob Eliyahu was wading through the Siloam Tunnel in Jerusalem when he chanced upon a hitherto unknown inscription. The passageway, also known as Hezekiah's Tunnel, was discovered by Edward Robinson in 1838. It had been determined to be the tunnel that the Judean king

---

[77] The response of Schlottmann and Delitzsch was clearly influenced by theology rather than by scholarship. This is not to suggest that the two men were not accomplished and capable scholars. Heide refers to Schlottmann as "an open-minded and serious scholar," and then goes on to list several reasons for this assessment. See Heide, "The Moabitica and Their Aftermath," 213. Delitzsch, a well-known Hebraist and prolific writer, was also known for his involvement in evangelism, particularly among Jews. In 1880, Delitzsch founded the Leipzig chapter of the Institutum Judaicum, an organization whose object it was to train and equip Christian missionaries for evangelistic work among the Jewish people.

[78] At the time, the Prussian consul of Jerusalem was Freiherr von Münchhausen.

[79] See Gibson, Shapira, and Chapman, *Tourists, Travellers, and Hotels,* 111 n. 95, 199.

[80] For details on the extensive manuscript acquisitions of Moses Shapira, see Fenton, "Moses Shapira's Journey to the Yemen."

dug to bring water from the Gihon Spring into the city of Jerusalem (2 Kgs 20:20; cf. 2 Chr 32:3–4). The newfound inscription told the story of the construction of the ancient waterway. Upon hearing of the discovery, Shapira hurriedly made his way to Siloam, "a village notorious for the fanaticism of its inhabitants," to obtain a copy of the newly found inscription.[81] Shapira began work immediately to translate and interpret the meaning of the Siloam Inscription. At the time of the discovery Shapira made the acquaintance of a young German scholar by the name of Hermann Guthe who was excavating in Jerusalem near the place of Jacob Eliyahu's discovery. The shared interests of the two Hebraists resulted in many discussions about the Siloam Inscription as well as frequent visits by Guthe to Shapira's shop. Guthe said that his repeated visits to the shop were "primarily to regard various Hebrew and Arabic manuscripts, particularly ones pertaining to the

Figure 6–The Siloam Inscription.

[81] Harry, *The Little Daughter of Jerusalem,* 126.

Bible, which Shapira had acquired in Yemen and meanwhile sold, some to the Royal Library in Berlin, some to the British Museum in London."[82]

Guthe published a work on the Siloam Inscription.[83] Others, too, entered the academic discussions surrounding the latest find—among them Moses Shapira. In an article published in the July 1881 *Palestine Exploration Fund Quarterly* by Claude Conder we read about Shapira's contribution to understanding the Siloam Inscription. Conder wrote: "Mr. Shapira gives a different interpretation to the text, explaining it as referring to the cutting of the tunnel from two opposite ends. This we know was really how the excavation was effected, and Mr. Shapira's intimate acquaintance with the Hebrew idiom (as a Talmudist of 20 years' education) seems to render his opinion worthy of consideration." Shapira's interpretation was ultimately recognized as the correct one. The reputation of Moses Wilhelm Shapira was on the rise. He was soon accepted into the small circle of intellectual elites who had turned on him in the wake of the Moabitica affair only a few years earlier.

About this same time, Shapira came upon a book by a German scholar named Friedrich Bleek, published in 1860 under the title *Introduction to the Old Testament*.[84] This work changed everything. Based on Bleek's book, Schlottmann's arguments were no longer proof that his manuscript was a forgery. Professor Schlottmann had rebuked him, saying that a chief evidence against the manuscript's authenticity was that it contradicted the Bible, specifically highlighting the point that Shapira's scroll used Elohim instead of the divine name Jehovah. According to the German Bible critic, the earliest strand of the Pentateuch was an Elohist document that was later edited in the evolution of the texts to include the divine name. If Bleek was correct, thought Shapira, then perhaps his manuscript represented an older version of the text, written before this editing process. Stated plainly, Shapira learned that the German scholars had concluded that the Pentateuch in its present form was not written by Moses or even during his time. Critical scholars supported this hypothesis by evidence found within the texts of the Bible. As he considered the arguments of the textual critics, he observed that the passages identified as later interpolations were not present in his manuscript.

It had been nearly five years since Shapira had secured the sixteen strips of his Moabite scroll in the Bergheim and Company Bank of Jerusalem. Fittingly, around Eastertime of 1883 he decided to resurrect them. As he made his way to retrieve his manuscript, he could never have imagined what the next year would hold for him. This decision would alter the course of Shapira's life and put him at center stage in one of the most significant religious debates of modern times.

---

[82] Guthe, *Fragments of a Leather Manuscript*, 2.
[83] See Hermann Guthe, "Die Siloahinschrift," in *Zeitschrift der Deutschen Morgenländischen Gesellschaft*, 36 (1882), 725–750.
[84] Friedrich Bleek, *Einleitung in das Alte Testament* (Berlin: G Reiner, 1860).

Shapira had gained considerable knowledge and experience since he last examined the leather strips. His newly acquired knowledge of biblical criticism gave him a reason to examine the scroll again. This time he was better prepared to make an informed assessment of the scroll and counter the arguments of the Schlottmanns and Delitzschs of the world. Now, with the ancient fragments spread out on the table before him, and reconsidering the October 1878 rebuke, Shapira began to realize that Delitzsch and Schlottmann were more than likely wrong in their negative appraisal of the manuscript. Perhaps his scroll was considerably older than what Schlottmann called the "unquestionable genuine." Errors in his previous transcription were now apparent to Shapira. He began to correct them in a new and more accurate transcription. He carefully noted variations between his manuscript and the canonical texts and noted pros and cons for the possible authenticity of the scroll fragments.

The scroll had every appearance of antiquity, and his experience with manuscripts convinced him that nothing like it had ever been found. The leather was considerably thicker than what was typically used for scrolls, of which he had collected many examples. The ancient script was similar to that found on the Mesha Stela and the Siloam Inscription, yet it exhibited differences from both. Having studied the two famed inscriptions closely, Shapira was quite familiar with both scripts. He couldn't help but wonder if these external pieces of evidence didn't evince a very early date. Just how early was impossible to tell, but Shapira was not ruling out the possibility that he possessed the oldest copy of a sacred text ever discovered. He soon found himself consumed with his work on the fragments.

Shapira labored tirelessly for days on end. Letter by letter, word by word, he became ever more convinced of the scroll's authenticity. He even began to entertain the possibility that what lay on the table before him was the original book of Deuteronomy! And to think that he had acquired these leather strips for "a mere song in Arabia."[85] "If," he confided to his daughter, "we can establish their authenticity, which I am pretty sure we can, they will turn out to be the very oldest manuscript in the whole world, actually the original, Mosaic Deuteronomy!"[86]

Shapira was so engrossed in his work on the scroll that he found time for little else. It was a painstaking process, especially deciphering the more blackened portions. Through experimentation, he concocted a special wetting agent made of "rosemary essence mixed with some kind of alkali."[87] The solution helped reveal the obscure text, but the timing was critical. The characters only became visible when the strip was not fully dry and then only briefly. He had to continually repeat the process, deciphering only a few words each time. Days and weeks passed as

---

[85] Harry, *The Little Daughter of Jerusalem,* 213.
[86] Ibid., 214.
[87] Ibid., 250.

Shapira carefully transcribed his manuscript, all the while becoming increasingly convinced of the importance of what he possessed.

The more he worked, the more enthusiastic he became. Shapira began to imagine how this discovery might change his station in life, relieving him of the drudgery of selling souvenirs. This scroll would bring him untold fame and fortune. If it proved to be genuine, everyone would want it, and who knew the price they would pay for such a treasure! And aside from the financial gains, Shapira felt his work would earn him a place in the ranks of the learned, validating once and for all his erudition in Semitic studies. Above all else, he longed for appreciation and respect from the academic world.

As he was nearing the completion of his transcription, he had the opportunity to show them to Carl Reinicke, the pastor of the Lutheran Church of the Redeemer of Jerusalem. The pastor was surprised to learn that Shapira had put them away for so long. [88] Reinicke's favorable response further encouraged Shapira, but he knew that more than a positive review from a protestant pastor would be needed. He sought the affirmation of the scroll's authenticity from the academic community. He determined to present his scroll to authorities in Europe where he had established himself as a purveyor of valuable manuscripts. This manuscript was unlike the others he had sold to the Royal Library at Berlin or the British Museum. Before he entered into negotiations for the sale of the leather strips, he would need the positive endorsement of the scroll's authenticity by top scholars in the field. If he could find support from the right people, and if they were as convinced of its extreme antiquity as he was, then he could name his price.

In May of 1883, having completed his new transcription of the fragments, an unexpected visitor arrived in Jerusalem. Professor Paul Schroeder arrived from Syria where he served as German consul of Beirut, a post to which he was appointed the previous year. Schroeder was a talented and respected linguist, having earned his doctorate from the University of Halle in 1867 with a dissertation on the Phoenician language. In 1869 he published a book on the Phoenician language that included grammar and writing samples. [89] Jerusalem banker Samuel Bergheim entertained Shapira and Schroeder in his home, during which time the linguist examined Shapira's manuscript. [90] Schroeder was

---

[88] When Lic. Dr. Reinicke, a German pastor in Jerusalem, heard about the fragments being stored in a vault "he was not a little astounded to hear that curious strips now had been concealed like a buried treasure for almost five years." Guthe, *Fragments of a Leather Manuscript*, 5.

[89] Paul Schröeder, *Die phönizische Sprach. Entwurf einer Grammatik, nebst Sprach-und Schriftproben* (Halle: Buchhandlung des Waisenhauses, 1869).

[90] According to the account provided by Myriam Harry in *The Little Daughter of Jerusalem*, this would not be the last time Schroeder saw the manuscript. In her telling, a close relationship soon developed between Schroeder (referred to as Hartwig in her book) and her father. She reported that "the two men discussed the famous MS. in the schoolroom upstairs [at Aga Rachid]" (Harry, 257); and that "the professor [Schroeder] had been convinced of the authenticity of the MS., and had even carried back a few fragments in order to submit them to other Oriental experts, and he promised to arrange terms with the Berlin Museum for the purchase of the archaeological prize. In the event of the fund at the disposal of the authorities not proving adequate, a direct appeal was to be made to the Kaiser's privy purse" (Harry, 260). It was Schroeder who had advised Shapira to place Augusta in a girls' school in Berlin (Harry, 164). Shapira and Augusta accompanied the Schroeder family on a European vacation to Switzerland, soon after which Schroeder's son and Shapira's daughter were engaged (Harry, 262).

impressed. He informed Shapira that he did not doubt the authenticity of the manuscript. To the contrary, he informed Shapira that he thought it to be unquestionably genuine and valuable. Schroeder was well qualified to assess the manuscript. He told Shapira that in his judgment the beautiful Phoenician writing, the purity of the Hebrew grammar, and the outward appearance were all in favor of the scroll's authenticity.

With Schroeder's positive appraisal of the manuscript, Shapira sat down at his desk to write to the brilliant German Protestant theologian and orientalist Hermann Strack. Strack and Shapira had several things in common. Both were Prussian, Strack by birth and Shapira through the grant of the consulate in Jerusalem. Both were considered experts in Talmudic and Jewish literature. Shapira was Jewish by birth but a Christian convert, and Strack had established the Berlin chapter of the Institutum Judaicum whose mission was to convert Jews to Christianity.[91]

Since 1877, Hermann Strack had been an assistant professor of Old Testament Exegesis and Semitic Languages at the University of Berlin.[92] He was also a former student of Moritz Steinschneider. Shapira felt that Strack's favorable assessment of his manuscript would enhance his case, so on 9 May 1883 he dispatched a 10-page letter to Strack from Jerusalem.[93] Having heard of the passing of Strack's father, Shapira began his letter by expressing his condolences. He then wrote, "You will excuse me dear professor if I shall trouble you now with a very long letter. I hope you will read it with interest in spite of your having so little time to spare, overburdened as you are with such abundance of work of high scholarship." Hoping he had buttered up the scholar sufficiently, Shapira made his pitch. He continued, "I am going to surprise you with a notice and a short description of a curious manuscript written in old Hebrew or Phoenician letters upon small strips of embalmed leather and seems to be a short unorthodoxical book of the last speech of Moses in the plain of Moab."

Shapira then told Professor Strack the story of how he came to possess the "curious manuscript" and how, with great difficulty, he began to transcribe it. He informed Strack that from the very beginning he noticed some "very interesting variations" between the scroll and the words of "our Bible." He told the professor that "the letters are of the oldest form—nearly the same as that of the Mesha-Stone," and added that despite the similarities, several letters in the scroll represented unattested forms.[94] He also mentioned the similarities and differences between the letters on the scroll and those on ancient coins and the Siloam Inscription.

---

[91] Hermann Strack established the Berlin chapter of Institutum Judaicum. Franz Delitzsch established the Leipzig chapter of the same organization. The organization was founded in 1724 in Halle, where Konstantine Schlottmann taught.

[92] Strack was born in 1848. This means he had been a professor at Berlin since he was 24 years old. He had just turned 35 when Shapira wrote to him.

[93] M. W. Shapira, letter to Hermann Strack, Jerusalem, 9 May 1883, British Library *Add. MS. 41294.*

[94] There are three letters that appear in the manuscript that were, and even now are, unattested— ט כ ק. See Heide, "The Moabitica and Their Aftermath," 222. See also Guthe, *Fragments of a Leather Manuscript,* 22.

"The ink," Shapira went on to say, "is nearly undestroyable, neither by rubbing, nor by washing with water or spirits," an unusual "thing in oriental manuscripts." Shapira then asked an obvious question, one he suspected someone like Strack might be asking at this point. "Now you will ask why I have been quiet about this until now?" He admits that it was because of Schlottmann's angry rebuke. He wrote, "I confess that when I received Professor Schlottmann's letter, I began to totter in my opinion," mainly, he continued, "for the general reason that the professor gave, that it contradicts our Bible." He informed Strack that this caused him to become "irresolute," and he pondered the possibility that Schlottmann might be right in his assessment that the scroll was a forgery. But he then argued with himself that if it was forged, "who could have been such a learned and artful forger? And for what purpose? As the money I paid for the manuscript was not worth the speaking of."

"Nevertheless," continued Shapira, the "reverence I always had for our Bible, which did not agree with the narrative of our manuscript, made still the manuscript somewhat doubtful in my eyes, and that was the reason I did not publish anything about it until now." Then he revealed to Strack what caused him to have a change of mind and to bring the manuscript forth:

> A short time ago a book called, *Einleitung in das Alte Testament* [Introduction to the Old Testament], by Friederich Bleek in Berlin, 1860, came into my hands, and what a change came over my mind after studying the above book. I see now that most of the variations between our manuscript and the Bible are of such a character as are already used by many eminent scholars as proof that our Deuteronomy was not written by Moses or about his time. All such passages are not to be found in our manuscript.

Shapira went on to make his case by sharing several of the notable variations between his scroll and the Bible, one of which was the preference for the generic term *Elohim* where the canonical text used *Jehovah*. He continued:

> Shall we suppose that the manuscript belonged to a sect or school who believed only that the 10 comments are from God, or should we be allowed to say that the manuscript belonged to Jews who dwelt in the east of the Jordan where the manuscript is supposed to have been found? And that they believed only in Elohim although the western Jews must have long before, known and used the word יהוה?[95] Again, as there are in the 1st verse and the last word, mentioned על פי יהוה [according to the mouth of Jehovah] and never in the midst of the book, could we suppose that the first and last verses were added by a Jehovistic scribe who copied an Elohistic manuscript?[96]

Shapira then provided his opinion as to the age of the scroll. "You will ask me dear professor what I suppose to be the date of our manuscript? To this I will

---

[95] Here, Shapira uses the Hebrew letters for God's name.
[96] The Hebrew על פי יהוה is a phrase that means "according to the word of Jehovah." Shapira's reference to "Jehovistic scribe," and "Elohistic manuscript" are terms that relate to the academic views of the Documentary Hypothesis. This will be covered in chapter nineteen.

say, judging from the form of the letters, one will be inclined to give this unorthodoxical manuscript such an early time, as between the Mesha Stone and the Siloam Inscription, or about the 6th century B.C., but one must be cautious … The question will of course be for scholars to decide (if agreed to my suggestion.)"

He then appealed to Strack to inspect the manuscript, saying, "I will also ask your pardon for all of my daring suggestions and ask you to give me your candid opinion about it should you or your friends find it so interesting as I flatter myself it to be." Shapira signed the lengthy letter and, in a postscript, informed Strack of Dr. Schroeder's favorable endorsement of the scroll. He concluded:

"Prof. or Dr. Schroeder who is now German Genr. Consul at Beirut is now here and has seen a few strips and thinks that the MS is unquestionably a genuine one. His chief proofs are: the beautiful Phoenician writing, as well as the pure grammatical Hebrew, and the outward look of it, and the old linen found in some pieces in the back. M. W. Shapira"

Shapira wanted to know for sure that the scroll was authentic, and the only way to determine that was to allow the best and brightest orientalists to examine it. Strack's reply, dated 27 May, informed Shapira that it was not worth his while "to bring such an evident forgery to Europe." Rejection was one thing, but the fact that Strack discounted the scroll's authenticity before seeing it was another matter altogether. Shapira decided to ignore the advice and made travel arrangements for June. Like it or not, European scholars would have the opportunity to judge the scroll.

The German Scholars

Shapira packed his manuscript in his handbag and set out for Berlin. After studying it only briefly, Strack stubbornly refused to change his preconceived view that it was a forgery. However, Shapira had more options in Germany. He would take his scroll to Leipzig and show it to his friend Hermann Guthe.[97] At the end of June 1883, the year before Guthe was appointed professor of Old Testament Exegesis at the University of Leipzig, the two Hebraists were reunited.

Shapira checked into the Hotel Hauffe in Leipzig on Friday evening, 29 June. The next day he paid a visit to his good friend Hermann Guthe. He took with him the leather strips. Shapira was confident that Guthe would be more receptive than Strack. After a cordial exchange of greetings, Shapira got straight to the reason for his visit. He informed Guthe that he had brought to Germany a "curious leather manuscript on which certain pieces of our Deuteronomy were written in ancient Phoenician letters." He further told him that he had first visited Professor Strack, who did not even bother to scrutinize it.[98] Shapira told Guthe that he wished for a "number of knowledgeable scholars" to examine the manuscript carefully and then publish their opinions about its worth, and of course, their assessment as to its authenticity.

From first sight, Guthe was inclined to consider the strips authentic, but he expressed doubt as to whether any scholar would make such a daring claim without achieving a "consummate understanding of the entire manuscript through equally precise examination of all parts thereof."[99] He added that such an investigation would not be possible given the immediacy of Shapira's desires, but he declared himself "willing to inspect the manuscript in his lodging at the Hotel Hauffe."[100]

---

[97] Hermann Guthe, born in 1849, was 34 years old when he inspected the manuscript. He was educated in Göttingen and Erlangen. In 1884 he became a professor of Old Testament Exegesis at Leipzig University.

[98] Shapira informed Guthe that "he had shown this to Herr Professor Strack in Berlin; but since he, due to an eye condition, could not attend to scrutinizing it." Guthe, *Fragments of a Leather Manuscript*, 2.

[99] Ibid. Based on a letter from Eduard Meyer to Georg Ebers written on 8 July 1883 we know that Guthe was inclined to consider the manuscript authentic. Meyer wrote, "Guthe told me about it on Sunday and was inclined to consider the matter real." Letter from Eduard Meyer to Georg Ebers, 8 July 1883, "Der Briefwechsel zwischen Georg Ebers und Eduard Meyer (1874–1898)," Vorbemerkung von G. Audring. https://www.geschichte.hu-berlin.de/de/bereiche-und-lehrstuehle/alte-geschichte/forschung/briefe-meyer/ebers.

[100] Guthe, *Fragments of a Leather Manuscript*, 2.

Guthe related that he went with Shapira that afternoon to the hotel and, with "manuscript before my eyes, let Shapira report to me about it."[101] Guthe was aware that Dr. Schroeder, for one, believed it was both authentic and very ancient. A mutual friend, Dr. Carlo Landberg, who had just returned from Syria, had learned about the scroll from Schroeder and shared the information with Guthe.[102] Due to Shapira's need for a quick turnaround on the examination, the two agreed to enlist Dr. Eduard Meyer, a German historian from the University of Leipzig, to facilitate the work.[103] Meyer was away on Saturday, but Guthe excitedly informed him on Sunday that he thought the manuscript Shapira had brought to Leipzig was authentic. Meyer said he initially laughed at him, but Guthe was insistent and encouraged Meyer to join him that day at the Hotel Hauffe. And so, on Sunday morning, 1 July, the two young German scholars made their way to the hotel. After examining the strips closely in the presence of Shapira, the two were "utterly certain" of the manuscript's authenticity.[104] They rearranged the furniture in Shapira's room to make the best use of the light. Then Guthe and Meyer devised a method to inspect the leather strips.

At first, they worked together, noting the external characteristics of the leather fragments. As they examined the manuscript, Shapira provided the backstory, sharing many details with the two scholars. In all, there were sixteen leather strips containing 42 columns of text. A closer look revealed that the strips comprised two copies of the same body of text, each matching the other with a fair degree of exactness. It appeared that originally there were two scrolls measuring approximately 3.5 meters (11.5 feet) each, with text arranged in 21 columns. The discussion turned to possible reasons for the existence of two copies, but with no solution forthcoming, the investigation continued.

They observed that the individual panels of texts—the ancient "pages"—contained vertical score marks running from top to bottom. At first, these seemed to be guides for the writing, though the scribe had not stayed strictly within the boundaries. Additionally, the leather was creased to produce an accordion-style "book," folded so that text side touched text side and backside touched backside. The examiners puzzled over this manner of folding; it made sense for several reasons but seemed odd since they knew of no other manuscript being folded instead of rolled. They also considered its size. The scroll strips were only a few

---

[101] Ibid.

[102] Dr. Carlo Landberg was 35 years old in 1883. He had graduated in Stockholm in 1869 and studied languages in Italy, Uppsala, and Paris. He studied Arabic in Syria and even spent time traveling among bedouin tribes. In 1882 he earned a Doctor of Philosophy degree in Leipzig. Landberg confirmed Shapira's claim to Strack about Schroeder's positive endorsement of the manuscript's authenticity and antiquity. Guthe reported, "From this information it is doubtlessly certain, 1) that Dr. Schroeder from Beirut saw the manuscript in Jerusalem and is inclined to take it for authentic—Dr. C. Landberg, who has just arrived here from Syria, heard this judgment from Dr. Schroeder's own mouth and imparted it to me." Guthe, *Fragments of a Leather Manuscript*, 5.

[103] Eduard Meyer was a brilliant young scholar, only 28 years old. He was educated at Gelehrtenschule des Johanneums, University of Bonn, and the University of Leipzig. Since 1879 he was at Leipzig.

[104] See, letter from Eduard Meyer to Georg Ebers, 8 July 1883, "Der Briefwechsel zwischen Georg Ebers und Eduard Meyer (1874–1898)," Vorbemerkung von G. Audring. https://www.geschichte.hu-berlin.de/de /bereiche-und-lehrstuehle/alte-geschichte/forschung/briefe-meyer/ebers.

inches in height, whereas the scrolls with which they were familiar were many times larger. The condition and coloring of the leather varied. The face of the manuscript was light brown in some places, in other places a darker brown, and yet other sections had turned nearly black. The leather strips also exhibited different degrees of preservation. The worst areas were the outer edges, where the leather would crumble if not handled with extreme care. Some columns were still connected to others along the seams, but five "pages" of the manuscript were not.

They recognized the lettering as a type of ancient Hebrew, otherwise known as Phoenician, though the form of some letters differed from what was known from coins and monuments such as the Mesha Stela, the Eshmunazar II sarcophagus, and the Siloam Inscription.[105] In areas where the leather was lighter in color, the black letters were easy to read, but it was difficult to decipher the writing on the darker panels. Shapira told them that he had achieved some success by wetting the darker areas with a mixture of spirits, but Guthe and Meyer thought it best to consult an expert on how to reach the desired outcome without harming the manuscript. They sent word to Dr. Franz Hofmann requesting his attendance the following day at the Hotel Hauffe for an urgent matter. Meyer also sent a telegram to his friend and colleague Adolf Erman, a distinguished orientalist in Berlin, sharing the news of the exciting project and inviting him to come and see the manuscript that Shapira had brought to Leipzig.[106]

Monday morning, the second day of July, Dr. Hofmann examined the manuscript for approximately two hours and offered his opinion on the safest way to enhance the readability of the text without damaging the manuscript. They discussed several options and conducted experiments to determine the most suitable method, carefully trying oil, ether, and alcohol. In the end, they decided to apply alcohol lightly with a brush. Dr. Hofmann recommended testing the blackened substance on the back of the fragments at a later time, but before he left, and sensing Guthe and Meyer's excitement about the manuscript, he informed them that in his examination he "found nothing suspicious."[107] Erman's expected reply by telegram from Berlin arrived on the same day, addressed to "Dr. Ed. Meyer in Leipzig Münzgasse 18.—komme Dienstag früh Schapira abkeuhlen—[coming Tuesday morning to cool off Shapira.]"[108]

---

[105] According to Meyer in a letter to Georg Ebers dated 8 July 1883, "the writing is wonderful, stands between Mesa [the Mesha Stela, ninth century BCE] and Esmun'azar [Eshmunazar II sarcophagus, fifth century BCE], is different from the Siloah scripts, and with shapes that the most skilled paleographer could not invent so beautifully and correctly … The orthography is very real." Letter from Eduard Meyer to Georg Ebers, 8 July 1883, "Der Briefwechsel zwischen Georg Ebers und Eduard Meyer (1874–1898)," Vorbemerkung von G. Audring. https://www.geschichte.hu-berlin.de/de/bereiche-und-lehrstuehle/alte-geschichte/forschung/briefe-meyer/ebers.

[106] Adolf Erman was educated at Leipzig and Berlin and had recently become associate professor of Egyptology at the University of Berlin. He was 29 years old in 1883.

[107] Ibid.

[108] Telegram from Adolf Erman to Eduard Meyer, 2 July 1883, "Der Briefwechsel zwischen Eduard Meyer und Adolf Erman (1881–1930)," Unter Mitwirkung von Yasser Sabek und Sascha Winkelmann bearbeitet von G. Audring Vorbemerkung. https://www.geschichte.hu-berlin.de/de/bereiche-und-lehrstuehle/alte-geschichte/forschung/briefe-meyer/erman.

Guthe and Meyer sorted the sixteen strips, separating the panels into two distinct but matching manuscripts. They designated seven strips representing one manuscript (A, B, D, E, F, G, and H) and then divided the strips between themselves for close examination. Guthe assumed responsibility for fragments A and B, both consisting of a single column of text; fragment D, consisting of three columns; fragment E, consisting of four columns; and three of the five columns from fragment G. For his part, Meyer took the balance of the selected strips—fragment F, consisting of four badly preserved columns; two of the five columns from fragment G; and the two columns of fragment H.

Seven Examined Strips Equal One Copy

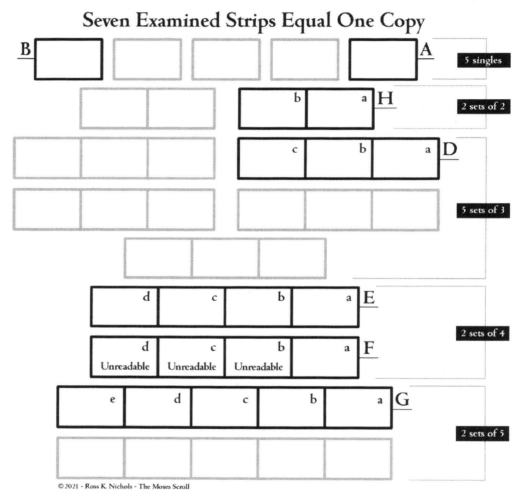

Figure 7

As promised in the telegram, Adolf Erman arrived at the Hotel Hauffe on Wednesday, 3 July 1883. Guthe and Meyer showed the scroll fragments to Erman, who "fell into archaeological delight and declared that he would eat all of the strips if they were not genuine."[109] The three young scholars realized that the authorities in Berlin would need to be likewise convinced before any official statement concerning the manuscript's authenticity was announced. Germany had already been embarrassed once with the Moabitica, and Shapira's name was tied to that as well. Shapira informed them that he would be going to Berlin after the examination was complete. Together, they quickly wrote a detailed description of the manuscript and dispatched it to three of the most distinguished scholars who they knew would need to concur with their assessment: Theodor Nöldeke, Christian Friedrich August Dillmann, and Eduard Sachau.[110] They also knew that they would need to prepare Karl Richard Lepsius, head of the Royal Library at Berlin. Guthe and Meyer agreed to do everything in their power to have a German translation as well as a comparison of the scroll fragments and the biblical text in time for the Berlin meeting. Erman agreed to work on Lepsius and departed for Berlin promising to update his friends about anything he learned.

Guthe and Meyer began work immediately on their respective strips, working independently for the most part, and struggling to read and transcribe the texts. Both found that they could read little without the assistance of the best possible lighting and the aid of magnifying glasses. Even with these, some of the letters were still impossible to decipher. They established a consistent method to denote illegible or missing letters in their reproduction of the manuscript. They also decided to use a vertical line to indicate the end of each line of text. This would help Guthe later when he prepared his publication. There were times during their work that the excitement was too much to contain. For instance, when Meyer noticed that the scroll spelled words without the later *matres lectionis,* he "roared with delight."[111] The two scholars were also amazed that the contents of the manuscript so closely endorsed what critical scholars had hypothesized concerning the earliest form of the Pentateuch.

On Wednesday, 4 July, Erman wrote to Meyer to inform him that he had spoken to Lepsius and that he was enthused, but he "urgently wishes that others don't get involved—not even [Friedrich Theodor] Althoff at first. He wants to try with the minister directly. So, please write to everyone you have written so far that they feign ignorance of the matter, as I know old L. [Lepsius], a lot depends

---

[109] Letter from Eduard Meyer to Georg Ebers, 8 July 1883, "Der Briefwechsel zwischen Georg Ebers und Eduard Meyer (1874–1898)," Vorbemerkung von G. Audring. https://www.geschichte.hu-berlin.de /de/bereiche-und-lehrstuehle/alte-geschichte/forschung/briefe-meyer/ebers.

[110] Theodor Nöldeke was a German orientalist and scholar specializing in Old Testament and Semitic languages. He was professor at University of Strasbourg from 1872. Christian Friedrich August Dillmann was a professor of theology at Berlin from 1869. Eduard Sachau was a specialist in Oriental languages and Semitic philology and professor at the University of Berlin from 1876.

[111] The Hebrew language has 22 letters, all of which are consonants. At a certain stage in the development of the language, some letters were used to indicate vowel sounds. Linguists use the Latin term matres lectionis, "mothers of reading" for these "vowel letters." Meyer's excitement was due to the fact that Shapira's manuscript did not contain these. He saw this as an indication that the text before him was produced prior to this developmental stage and it was therefore proof of its antiquity. He recounted that he "roared with delight" in, letter from Eduard Meyer to Georg Ebers, 8 July 1883, "Der Briefwechsel zwischen Georg Ebers und Eduard Meyer (187–898)," Vorbemerkung von G. Audring. https://www.geschichte.hu-berlin.de/ de/bereiche-und-lehrstuehle/alte-geschichte/forschung/briefe-meyer/ebers.

Moses W. Shapira's Deuteronomy Manuscript:

19th Century Scholars Labeled & Examined 20 Columns in 7 Fragments

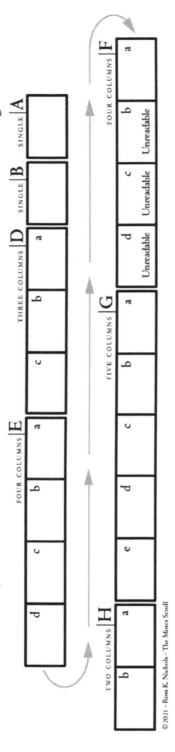

© 2021 - Ross K. Nichols - The Moses Scroll

Figure 8

On Saturday, 30 June 1883, Moses W. Shapira of Jerusalem, famed antiquarian and agent for the British Museum, visited Hermann Guthe in Leipzig, Germany. He took with him a curious manuscript consisting of leather strips inscribed with ancient Phoenician letters. Shapira informed Guthe that he wanted European scholars to scrutinize his manuscript and publish their assessments of its authenticity and worth. Guthe agreed to inspect the document and solicited Eduard Meyer's assistance to facilitate the work. On Sunday, 1 July 1883, Guthe and Meyer met Shapira in his room at the Hotel Hauffe and, over the next five days, meticulously studied the document. Shapira's manuscript consisted of forty-two columns of text written on sixteen leather strips of varying lengths. Some of the strips contained multiple connected columns of text, while others were single columns. The two German scholars observed that the total number of strips represented two copies of the "same text, doubled." Accordingly, they separated the strips into two parallel manuscripts, each measuring approximately 3.5 meters (11.5 feet) in length. Guthe and Meyer selected one of these two copies for careful study and transcription. They also compared the two sets of fragments and found them to "completely agree with each other up to a few small variations." The chosen manuscript (represented in this chart) consisted of twenty columns of text written on seven strips. These seven pieces were labeled (A, B, D, E, F, G, and H) and divided between Guthe and Meyer. Guthe was responsible for fragments A and B, each consisting of a single column of text; the three columns of fragment D; the four columns of fragment E; and columns c, d, and e of fragment G. Meyer was responsible for the four columns of fragment F; columns a and b of fragment G; and columns a and b of fragment H.

on it. Shapira must turn to him, he has good prejudice for him." Later the same day, Erman wrote Meyer again stressing the need for utmost discretion. He told Erman, "Lepsius is apparently afraid that others will get involved. 'If two horses pull on something, it will stop,' he said and urgently asked to keep it secret … so in order not to irritate the old sensitive secret councilor [Lepsius] (on whom everything here depends) silence must be commanded towards him [Guthe].… Nöldeke, Dillmann etc., etc. will of course have to come up afterwards.… Let's be wise like serpents, and *false* like doves! Without that, nothing can be done here." Erman knew that the fact that they had already advised Nöldeke, Dillmann, and Sachau must be kept between them for the present. He added, "I pretended not to know whether Dillmann, Sachau, Nöldeke, etc. had been written to."

By the end of Thursday, Guthe and Meyer had completed the task, and on Friday they double-checked their work and made necessary revisions. Although thunderstorms on Friday reduced the available light, making the final checks more difficult, the initial work was done to their satisfaction. The plan was in motion. Guthe would begin immediately to prepare a publication that would summarize their findings, and Shapira would set out for Berlin for a review of his manuscript. Shapira knew that among those who would be present was at least one who believed in the authenticity of his manuscript, Adolf Erman, and according to Erman it seemed that Lepsius was enthused about what was headed his way.

On Friday, 6 July, Erman wrote Meyer again. He informed him that Sachau went to Lepsius Thursday morning and this upset Lepsius. He further told Meyer that he was hopeful that Lespsius would find comfort in knowing that Althoff did not know about the manuscript. "You have probably not yet written Ebers," said Erman, but "if you do, just add openly that he is supposed to pretend ignorance. He knows Lepsius's peculiarities. I'll go to Schrader,[112] Dillmann, Sachau, as soon as I can. Monitoring Lepsius/Shapira will be difficult because Lepsius won't tell me how things are. It would be good if Guthe stayed in touch with Shapira, so that we can let go of our reserves of academics in time."[113]

Saturday morning, 7 July 1883, Erman wrote again to Meyer. He informed him that he had talked with Schrader and "of course he is full of doubts, but as always he's behaving very sensibly. Dillmann, on the other hand, is supposed to declare everything nonsense *a priori*. You all seem to have spoken to Lepsius." Erman then shared a few points of objection that Dillmann and Schrader were already talking about from the paper they had received from Leipzig, but, he went on to relate, "Schrader will examine the matter seriously. On the whole," continued Erman, "as far as I can judge, it is not nice, decidedly below par. My main hope is Lepsius, but he is afraid and can easily be frightened." In closing,

---

[112] Eberhard Schrader was a German orientalist. Over his career he held chair at Giessen in 1870, Jena in 1873, and from 1878 was a professor of Oriental languages at Friedrich Wilhelm University in Berlin.

[113] Postcard from Adolf Erman to Eduard Meyer, 6 July 1883, "Der Briefwechsel zwischen Eduard Meyer und Adolf Erman (188–930),"Unter Mitwirkung von Yasser Sabek und Sascha Winkelmann bearbeitet von G. Audring Vorbemerkung. https://www.geschichte.hu-berlin.de/de/bereiche-und-lehrstuehle/alte-geschichte/forschung/briefe-meyer/erman.

Erman let Meyer know that he had to be careful about meeting with Shapira because if Lepsius found out … "you know how he is."[114]

On Sunday, 8 July, Meyer wrote to Georg Ebers to inform him of what had been happening in Leipzig. He excitedly told him of Shapira's arrival with the manuscript, freely using exclamation points throughout his letter as he described the "mass of leather strips on which there is nothing less than Deuteronomy chapters 1–11 and 27–31 in a copy completely different from ours and in wonderful old Phoenician script!" He went on to relate what they had learned from Shapira about the provenance of the strips, how it had been rejected a few years earlier by Schlottmann and "old Delitzsch," how Shapira had set it aside but had recently "gained more and more conviction of its authenticity." He told Ebers that Shapira had come to Leipzig in order for Guthe to advise him on how to win the judgments of the scholars. He admitted that at first he laughed when he heard the story, but became utterly certain about the genuineness of the manuscript after he examined it for himself. He told of Hofmann's inspection, and of Erman's great zeal in the matter. He also reported of the current work going on behind the scenes, the letter to Dillmann, Sachau, Schrader, and Nöldeke, and of the enthusiasm of Lepsius, but also that the latter was upset that the others already knew of the manuscript. "Erman," he continued, "asked me to write to you specifically that you want to pretend to be completely ignorant" of the matter, and of course, "it goes without saying that under no circumstance should anything go to the newspapers prematurely."

Meyer informed Ebers that Shapira was in Berlin with plans to meet with Lepsius on Monday, 9 July. "As for the purchase, he [Shapira] is extremely clever and knows exactly what the matter is worth, but he vacillates between the self-interest of earning a colossal sum and the ambition to make a good name for himself, to serve science, etc." Meyer went on to say that the matter now depended on "how it is handled in Berlin." He then described the manuscript in detail, highlighting some of the more notable features, and then said, "The content is glorious, an endorsement of criticism that could not be grander."[115] On Tuesday, 10 July, Ebers enthusiastically replied. "That's really colossal! But, dear friends and people, children, be careful! Where Shapira appears, it smells a bit sticky … be doubly cautious … doubly suspicious. I'm so happy for you, but I'm also a little afraid." Ebers told his protégé that he wished he could have been with him to share in the excitement. As to Schlottmann, Ebers said, "as a burned child, Schlottmann naturally shies away from fire, even if it is not at all and could only be fire. It's the same with other colleagues, because, even in this heat, they get cold when they think of Schlottmann's fate." Here Ebers was referring to the damage done to Schlottmann's reputation as a result of his involvement in the

---

[114] Postcard from Adolf Erman to Eduard Meyer, 7 July 1883, ibid.

[115] Letter from Eduard Meyer to Georg Ebers, 8 July 1883, "Der Briefwechsel zwischen Georg Ebers und Eduard Meyer (187–898)," Vorbemerkung von G. Audring. https://www.geschichte.hu-berlin.de /de/bereiche-und-lehrstuehle/alte-geschichte/forschung/briefe-meyer/ebers.

Moabitica affair. But then he added, "The Moabitica are scarecrows, which keep clever sparrows away from the good fruits, if there are such."

Ebers continued, "If Guthe and you do not object to the text, and Erman considers the material object to be genuine, I am reassured … if Erman declares the strips genuine, only philological considerations will now be able to decide." He concluded his comments on the manuscript saying, "I wish with all my heart that we are dealing with something genuine here. How would I like to grant my friend Guthe and you the triumph of having recognized a diamond in the pebbles which the overly wise rejected. It is no art to declare suspicious things wrong, but it takes courage and certain knowledge to publicly declare that what is tainted with smell of the fake is still genuine. Good luck!"[116]

Meanwhile in Berlin, Shapira, having learned the day before of where the highly anticipated meeting was to take place, made his way to the home of Karl Richard Lepsius. Not only was Lepsius the head of the Royal Library at Berlin, but he was a famed discoverer and researcher in Egyptology, having himself coined the phrase "Book of the Dead." He was also a skilled linguist. Lepsius invited his most eminent colleagues. These included the Hebrew chair professor August Dillman, the distinguished orientalists professors Eduard Sachau and Adolf Erman, and Dr. Moritz Steinschneider, a former teacher of Hermann Strack.

While Shapira waited expectantly in a nearby room, the team of German scholars sequestered themselves with the manuscript. Adolf Erman quickly realized that he was the only one in the room who believed in the authenticity of the manuscript. He had hoped that Lepsius, given his earlier enthusiasm, might sway the opinion of the others, but he remained silent as one scholar after another brought forward their reasons for rejecting the genuineness of the strips. The meeting lasted only ninety minutes, and during that hour and a half, one thing seemed obvious; the decision was made before the meeting even started.

After the meeting, the scholars exited their chamber and shared little information with Shapira. Some later reports confirm that an offer was made to Shapira for the manuscript, but the amount extended by the Berlin scholars was unacceptable. Afterwards, Shapira, without making it known, went to visit Erman. Not knowing exactly what he should and should not say, he simply advised Shapira to hold on to the manuscript "until the publication was out and the question was resolved." Shapira agreed and informed Erman that he would take the scroll to England. Perhaps the British would appreciate its value and pay him what it was worth.[117]

After Shapira left, Erman sat down and wrote a letter to Meyer informing him that the experts had rejected the manuscript's authenticity. He told Meyer that he felt very "lacking in courage," and then related some of the arguments against the

---

[116] Letter from Georg Eber to Eduard Meyer, 10 July 1883, ibid.

[117] According to Harry, it was Professor Schroeder who encouraged Shapira to take his scroll elsewhere. She said, "Professor [Schroeder] urged Mr. [Shapira] to try his fortune in Paris, or, better still in London, where he was already so well known. Besides, the English were remarkable for the predilection for all that was associated with the study of Hebrew." Harry, *The Little Daughter of Jerusalem*, 264.

strips. He said that they had given their reasons and that he had offered counters to some of their arguments, but even these were dismissed. In the end he began to think that they were right, admitting in one place, "I have to admit, I can't find the certainty with which I believed in authenticity in Leipzig. The thing looks horrible—which of course is not yet proof of the falsehood since Shapira with his purifications may have been to blame.... In any case, I would not buy it until the authenticity is verified. Better no antiquity than one that is in doubt."[118]

On Monday, 16 July, Meyers replied to Erman's letter. Among other things, he said to Erman that he and Guthe would be "careful not to go too fiery. Subjectively, I am completely convinced of the truth, but in order to decide about it, the judgment of one or two is not enough, even if they have tried to keep their eyes open as much as possible. But I was very annoyed by the way the Berliners judged the thing. It was really unnecessary to write long letters to them … beforehand if they had not even looked at the matter for themselves. Obviously Sachau and Dillmann wanted to get rid of the scientifically very uncomfortable MS and at the same time the responsibility for any advice regarding the acquisition as much as possible."[119] After the exciting first week of July 1883, Meyer went back to his study of the Assyrian monarchy that he was working on before the Shapira affair interrupted him, Guthe set out to produce his book on their week-long examination, and Shapira was on his way to London. Whether the Berliners knew of Shapira's next destination is unknown, but if they did know, they made no effort to notify the British of their assessment of his manuscript. In fact, so far as the Berlin scholars were concerned, the matter was closed.

---

[118] Letter from to Adolf Erman to Eduard Meyer, 10 July 1883, "Der Briefwechsel zwischen Eduard Meyer und Adolf Erman (188–930)," Unter Mitwirkung von Yasser Sabek und Sascha Winkelmann bearbeitet von G. Audring Vorbemerkung. https://www.geschichte.hu-berlin.de/de/bereiche-und-lehrstuehle/alte-geschichte/forschung/briefe-meyer/erman.

[119] Letter from Eduard Meyer to Adolf Erman, 16 July 1883, "Der Briefwechsel zwischen Eduard Meyer und Adolf Erman (188–930)," Unter Mitwirkung von Yasser Sabek und Sascha Winkelmann bearbeitet von G. Audring Vorbemerkung. https://www.geschichte.hu-berlin.de/de/bereiche-und-lehrstuehle/alte-geschichte/forschung/briefe-meyer/erman.

The English Scholars

Moses Shapira arrived in London hoping for better success. His reputation for acquiring valuable manuscripts was well attested in Britain. Between 1877 and 1882 the British Museum had purchased an estimated 300 manuscripts from Shapira. Among them were 145 Karaite documents, making it the world's most extensive collection of texts from this Jewish sect.[120] Here, Shapira knew nearly everyone who was anyone when it came to biblical studies, and if there were some he did not know, they probably had heard about the famed antiquarian and bookseller. After all, he was an agent of the British Museum. His business cards said the same; even the sign outside of his popular Jerusalem shop carried this title.

On 20 July 1883, Moses Wilhelm Shapira arrived unannounced at 1 Adam Street in London, headquarters of the Palestine Exploration Fund (PEF). He carried his "small glazed bag" that contained potentially the most significant biblical discovery of all time.[121] In Berlin, two distinguished German scholars had spent a week examining the scroll and were now hard at work preparing to publish their findings. So far as he knew, Guthe, Meyer, and Erman all agreed with him that the manuscript was authentic. He was confident that once they announced the results of their work, the world would at long last learn the significance of his Moabite manuscript. With chin held high and a strong sense of confidence, Shapira pushed open the door of this prestigious office.

Sir Walter Besant, secretary of the PEF, greeted Shapira. Besides his duties at the PEF, Besant was a novelist and historian. He was also active in Freemasonry. Besant was a Past Master of Marquis of Dalhousie Lodge and one of the founders of the first Masonic research lodge—Quatuor Coronati Lodge No. 2076.[122] During his time at the PEF, Besant had supervised the photography of the Moabite Stone. These photographs were distributed to scholars the world over, bringing the Moabite treasure to the forefront of the academic community.[123]

---

[120] Fred Reiner, "C. D. Ginsburg and the Shapira Affair: A Nineteenth-Century Dead Sea Scroll Controversy," *The British Library Journal* (1995), 112. For an extensive list of many of the "manuscript collections assembled by Shapira," see Reiner, "C. D. Ginsburg and the Shapira Affair," 123–124 n 12.

[121] Journal of William Simpson, dated 23 January 1884. In this journal entry, Simpson described the satchel that carried the scroll fragments as "a small glazed bag—the small 'carpet-bag' of the period." The entry is quoted in full in Reiner, "C. D. Ginsburg and the Shapira Affair," 115.

[122] Besant, *Autobiography*, 239–240.

[123] Ibid., 161.

Now, a new discovery from the land of Moab was about to come his way. This one would prove to be just as significant—perhaps more so.

Shapira decided to present the scroll more confidently than he had up to this point, expressing his views with clarity and conviction. Deep down, he knew the scroll was genuine. No longer would he approach prospective buyers by requesting their opinion; instead, he would go about the work of convincing his audiences with proof. After all, he was as qualified to pass judgment on the authenticity of a scroll as nearly anyone else.

After being welcomed into the PEF office, Shapira made his move. He informed Besant that he had brought a document to London that would "make students of the Bible and Hebrew scholars reconsider their ways,"[124] further asserting that the contents of his bag "would throw a flood of light upon the Pentateuch."[125] Besant looked closely at his visitor and asked to see the document. Shapira hesitated; he was not ready to show off his wares just yet. He told Besant that the document he brought with him was written "on sheepskin, in characters closely resembling those of the Moabite Stone, and with many and most important variations."[126] The secretary again asked to see it. Shapira reached into his bag and pulled out one of the leather strips, being careful to show Besant one on which the Phoenician characters were dark and clear on the light background. Besant was familiar with the Mesha Stela and noted the similarity between these ancient letters and those on that famous Moabite artifact. Besant later recalled, "It was written in fine black ink, as fresh after three thousand years as when it was first laid on, and in the Phoenician characters of the Moabite Stone."[127] Besant marveled at the manuscript and suggested that this discovery should be made known to the world—precisely the reaction that Shapira had hoped for. He knew that by impressing Besant he might be able to arrange another meeting and that if the right people deemed the manuscript genuine it could fetch an inestimable sum. Shapira requested the audience of Captain Claude Conder, promising that if such a meeting could be arranged he would gladly bring his manuscript and a handwritten account of how he came to possess the ancient document.

The military exploits of Claude Reigner Conder were numerous, and he had recently been promoted to the rank of captain. He had also made valuable contributions to biblical studies thanks to his surveys of Palestine, the results of which frequently appeared in the quarterly publications of the Palestine Exploration Fund. The decorated English soldier was an accomplished explorer and knowledgeable antiquarian. Shapira and Conder had known each other since

---

[124] Ibid., 162.

[125] Ibid., 162.

[126] "The Shapira Manuscripts," *Palestine Exploration Fund Quarterly Statement* (Oct. 1883), 195. This work, referenced frequently in our story, is helpful as it covers the first appearance of Shapira in London at the offices of the Palestine Exploration Fund and Shapira's account of how he came to possess the manuscript in a letter to Captain Conder and Walter Besant. It also includes a translation of the scroll that appeared in *The Times* as published by Christian David Ginsburg, as well as the assessments of the scroll by A. Neubauer, A. H. Sayce, Charles Clermont-Ganneau, Claude Conder, and Christian David Ginsburg.

[127] Besant, *Autobiography,* 162.

the Moabitica affair. Conder, an able artist, had taken a keen interest in the Moabite statues and had visited Shapira's shop to make colored sketches of them, which he forwarded to the headquarters of the PEF.[128] While he ultimately came to accept that the earthenware treasures were forgeries, Conder maintained a positive view of Shapira. In an 1881 article in a PEF publication, Conder took Shapira's side in an academic debate on the meaning of the Siloam Inscription. Shapira was right, and Conder was right in saying so. What Shapira needed now was a highly respected person who considered "his opinion worthy of consideration." Conder had done so before, and he had no reason to doubt that the famed captain still held his opinion in high regard. Besant agreed to meet Shapira again on Tuesday, 24 July, at the PEF headquarters. Besant would ensure that Captain Conder was present, and Shapira agreed to bring the manuscript and his written account of how he acquired it.

Anticipating a positive response by Conder, Besant decided ahead of the planned meeting to prepare for the next steps in unveiling Shapira's scroll to others who would doubtless want to participate in such important viewings and discussions. On Monday, 23 July 1883, Besant crafted an invitation on paper bearing the PEF letterhead. It read, "Mr. Shapira of Jerusalem has brought to England an Old Hebrew Manuscript apparently of great antiquity containing the text of Deuteronomy with many important variations. He will bring the manu-script to this office on Thursday next the twenty-sixth … at 12:00 A.M. and will be very glad if you can meet him in order to see it."[129]

The next day, Tuesday, 24 July, Shapira arrived with the Deuteronomy manuscript. True to his commitment, he also brought a handwritten account of how he came to possess the document and agreed to release the statement for publication in *The Times*. The report told the story from the time Shapira first learned of the manuscript some five years earlier from certain bedouin in the home of Sheik Erekat. He told of the bedouin fleeing from their enemies and how, in the process, they came upon the cave containing the leather strips. He indicated that Conder would be able to validate the exact time of the events east of the Jordan because of his familiarity with the region. He described how he came to possess the entire manuscript piece by piece through a series of meetings with his bedouin contact. Shapira explained that after working for several weeks, he produced a transcription of the manuscript and sent it to Professor Schlottmann. He did not fail to admit that the latter had called the scroll a fabrication. He wrote about how after receiving the note from Schlottmann, he placed the strips in a bank vault for several years, but then around Easter of the present year "began to reconsider" the professor's objections. Shapira came to realize that these were partially due to his own mistakes in "deciphering the writing." He mentioned that when he showed

---

[128] Claude R. Conder, "Notes on the Drawings," *Palestine Exploration Fund Quarterly Statement* (1873), 79–80.

[129] Besant's invitation is included in British Library *Add. MS. 41294*. The invitation clearly reads "12:00 A.M.," but it is confirmed in a later note by Besant that the meeting took place at noon, not midnight.

the leather strips to Dr. Schroeder in May of 1883, Schroeder had "pronounced them genuine" and offered to buy them. He included in the statement that he took the strips to Leipzig, originally intending to have them photographed, and that while there, "professors saw them. Dr. Hermann (sic) [Erman][130] believed in them, as did Professor Guthe, who intends to write about them."[131]

Besant and Conder carefully looked over the manuscript and listened intently as Shapira recounted the story of his Moabite scroll. The meeting seemed to go very well, but the next test was soon to come. Besant informed Shapira that he had sent an invitation for a meeting on Thursday, 26 July. In attendance would be a giant in the field of Hebrew manuscripts—Dr. Christian Ginsburg.

Christian David Ginsburg was born in Warsaw on Christmas Day, 1831. His published works on the Hebrew Bible first appeared in 1867, and by 1880 he had begun his life's work, a monumental study on the Masorah, a field in which he was considered the world's authority.[132] Ginsburg was 52 when he was invited to see Shapira's manuscript at the office of the Palestine Exploration Fund. He already enjoyed recognition as one of the most outstanding scholars of the Hebrew Bible. His prowess was unsurpassed and everyone knew it, including Ginsburg.

Shapira and Ginsburg had been acquainted for more than a decade before the meeting at the PEF office. They shared much in common and had established a close relationship as a result. First, they were both Jewish by birth and Christian converts by choice. Both were highly skilled in rabbinic literature, as well as the Bible. They shared a love of the Hebrew language—the earlier the better—and their paths had crossed because of archaeological discoveries. Both had explored the region of Moab, and each had involved himself with the Mesha Stela, Moab's greatest treasure. Shapira's acquisition of Karaite manuscripts had benefitted Ginsburg immensely, the latter having published articles on the subject.[133] These shared interests had brought Ginsburg to Shapira's shop when he was in Jerusalem.

Ginsburg's trust in Shapira's knack for finding valuable manuscripts must have inspired a sense of expectancy about what brought Shapira to London this time. When Ginsburg received his invitation to the meeting, he invited others. Besant would later write, "Ginsburg considered that the invitation included his friends, and so the whole of the British Museum, so to speak, with all the Hebrew scholars in London turned up."[134]

---

[130] Shapira referred to Erman as Professor Hermann. Other investigators have missed this. He obviously means Erman. Few have closely examined the letters of Erman. Some have suggested that he is either lying in this report, or that he is confused since Guthe's first name is Hermann. The truth of the matter is that Hermann Guthe and Eduard Meyer did believe in the authenticity of the manuscript, just as Shapira said. The letters contained in the estate of Eduard Meyer prove this as we showed in the previous chapter!

[131] "The Shapira Manuscripts," *Palestine Exploration Fund Quarterly Statement* (Oct. 1883), 196.

[132] The Masorah is a body of scribal notes that form a textual guide to the Hebrew Scriptures. These notes were compiled from the seventh to the tenth centuries CE. In 1897 Ginsburg published his magnum opus on this subject as *Introduction to the Massoretico-Critical Edition of the Hebrew Bible.*

[133] C. D. Ginsburg, "The Karaites: Their History and Literature," in *Proceedings of the Literary and Philosophical Society of Liverpool* (1861–1862), 155–170.

[134] Besant, *Autobiography,* 163.

At the designated hour, a small party of savants filled the office of the PEF. They had come to behold the much-anticipated unveiling of Shapira's ancient Deuteronomy scroll. Sir Walter Besant, Captain Conder, Dr. Ginsburg, and a Mr. Bullen were in attendance. Ernest A. Wallis Budge, keeper of Egyptian and Assyrian antiquities at the British Museum, and Professor William Aldis Wright, a well-known writer and editor, were also present.[135] Between 1870 and 1872, Wright had edited the three volumes of the *Catalogue of the Syriac Manuscripts in the British Museum.* Since 1870 he had also served as secretary of the Old Testament Revision Company. Thomas Hayter Lewis, professor of architecture at the University College of London and a chairman of the PEF, was also invited. The famous Scottish artist William Simpson was at the meeting as well. His illustrious career had already spanned decades as both an artist and a correspondent, much of which he did in the service of the *Illustrated London News.* He also was a member of the PEF Executive Committee. His work as a reporter proved useful at the meeting since he wrote an account of the evening. A month later, Simpson would sketch Shapira in the British Museum. His sketch is one of only two known surviving "pictures" of Moses Shapira.

All attention was on Shapira. A hush fell over the guests standing around the table where his bag sat. Hardly anyone batted an eye as Shapira announced that the British Museum could purchase the scroll for the price of one million pounds sterling – an astounding figure, which, according to some currency conversion models is well over 100 million dollars in 2021![136] Shapira then reached into the bag and withdrew the leather strips, and as William Simpson would later recall, he "threw them in a very jaunty manner on the table, round which we stood."[137] Besant later observed, "Shapira unfolded his manuscript amid such excitement as is very seldom exhibited by scholars."[138]

Shapira was in his element. The enthusiasm shown by the group led him to believe that soon his dreams would come true. He told them the story of the scroll and highlighted its more noteworthy features. Of course, he pointed out some of the variant readings as well. Like a showman, he pinched off a small piece of the manuscript to illustrate the nature of the leather and then passed the fragment around the table. Simpson whispered to Bullen that the value of the "bit he tore off" must be about 500 pounds if the whole is worth a million!

But Shapira was not finished with what Simpson later called his "grand performance." When the discussion turned to the more challenging parts of the leather strips to read, Shapira pulled a bottle of his specially-made spirits from his bag. With a brush, he demonstrated before their eyes how letters appeared where

---

[135] The attendee list only provided Mr. Budge. I learned the full name from Fred Reiner, "Tracking the Shapira Case: A Biblical Scandal Revisited," *Biblical Archaeology Review 23.2* (May/June 1997), 4.

[136] See, for instance, (https://www.uwyo.edu/numimage/currency.htm), which estimates the current value at $118,998,274!

[137] From William Simpson's journal entry on 23 January 1884, reported in Reiner, "C. D. Ginsburg and the Shapira Affair," 115.

[138] Besant, *Autobiography,* 163.

prior to wetting nothing was visible. In the excitement of the demonstration, the bottle was accidentally knocked over, spilling the secret concoction onto the manuscript. Shapira calmly stood the bottle upright and continued as if nothing had happened.

Most of the invitees participated in the discussion. From his place at the table, Moses Shapira felt confident that those present were convinced of his scroll's authenticity. Feeling that he had done his absolute best, Shapira stepped back and quietly watched as some of England's brightest minds discussed the scroll. He overheard one of them say that this was "a remarkable illustration of the arts as known and practiced in the time of Moses." Another, "a professor of Hebrew, exclaimed with conviction, 'This is one of the few things which could not be a forgery and a fraud!'"[139] These and many other comments pleased Shapira. He already believed that his Moabite treasure was genuine, but to have his beliefs confirmed by such a distinguished assembly of scholars was music to his ears.

The meeting lasted nearly three hours. Everyone agreed that Dr. Ginsburg should be in charge of the manuscript for as long as necessary to do a more thorough examination. Shapira concurred. They would store the fragments in the British Museum, where the Hebrew savant would carefully scrutinize them. Ginsburg's stamp of approval would settle the matter once and for all.

Shapira gathered up the pieces and handed them to Ginsburg. As the guests departed, Shapira smiled, knowing that his friend would soon announce to the world what he already knew. Outside the office at 1 Adam Street, Shapira watched as Ginsburg carried away the precious bundle. It was only a matter of time now.

---

[139] Ibid., 163.

The Hero of the Hour

Within days of the meeting in the office of the Palestine Exploration Fund, Shapira and his Moabite scroll began to create quite a sensation. Writing under the pen name Myriam Harry, his younger daughter, Maria Rosette, would later describe the honor, recognition, and fame that her father suddenly received as word spread of the scroll's arrival in London. "Directly he set foot in one of the best hotels, he was besieged by interviewers, reporters and photographers. He was the hero of the hour, ladies showered letters on him, his portrait appeared in every paper, and accounts of his life in Palestine, his travels and his researches were published everywhere. Paragraphs dilating on his wonderful erudition found their way into current periodicals, his shop in Jerusalem was represented as a palace."[140]

In London, Moses Shapira took up temporary residence at the Cannon Street Hotel. The five-story Italianate edifice, modeled on sixteenth-century Renaissance architectural style, was opened in 1867 as the City Terminus Hotel. It was situated directly across from the Cannon Street Station, the city's central railway terminus. Now, more than a month since he left Jerusalem, Shapira and his scroll were finally getting the attention they deserved. He wrote home to inform his wife and daughter about the latest developments and the wealth that would soon pass into their hands. Once Ginsburg completed his assessment of the scroll, rendering his verdict publicly in newspapers worldwide, Shapira would receive his asking price of one million pounds sterling. He was certain of it. Rumors about efforts to secure the sum had already begun to circulate. He told his family that there would be "no more need to spend long days in the stuffy shop, engraving texts on olive-wood covers for prayer books and albums! Good heavens, no! He would sell off the whole stock," or perhaps "make it a free gift" to his shopkeeper.[141]

Shapira's older daughter was already in Berlin, engaged, as it turned out, to the son of Paul Schroeder, the eminent professor who had vouched for the scroll's authenticity. Mrs. Schroeder had taken a liking to Augusta Louisa Wilhemina Shapira when she and her husband visited the Shapira family. Initially, the Shapiras were concerned that marriage into a German family of such high status would be difficult since it would require a large dowry beyond their means. Still,

---

[140] Harry, *The Little Daughter of Jerusalem,* 264.
[141] Ibid., 261.

everyone agreed that when the manuscript finally sold—and *it would sell*—the Shapiras' financial and social status would be greatly enhanced and the matter would be moot. The professor had helped Shapira arrange the meetings with scholars in Berlin but had also been the one who encouraged him to take the scroll to England to pursue a purchase rather than wait on his countrymen to make an acceptable offer. As the professor informed Shapira, "the English were remarkable for their predilection for all that was associated with the study of Hebrew."[142]

Shapira was confident that his family would soon be among the wealthiest in Jerusalem. The British scholars' positive reception of the scroll assured him of it, but this was of secondary importance for Shapira. Maria would later reveal, "What weighed far more with him than any pecuniary consideration was the fact that his reputation would now be established beyond any doubt, and that at last he would 'leap to fame.' … His vast knowledge as a Hebraist, which he acquired at the cost of twenty years of unremitting labor and research throughout Palestine, would be blazoned abroad and would amaze the world."[143]

Moses Shapira wanted to be at Ginsburg's side as he evaluated the manuscript. While he was permitted to visit from time to time, Ginsburg preferred to be alone to make a fair and thorough examination of the scroll fragments. To minimize interruptions, Ginsburg requested that he and Shapira coordinate meetings at mutually convenient times. Shapira reluctantly agreed. He knew that the sooner Ginsburg was able to confirm the scroll's authenticity, the sooner the British Museum would secure the money and pay him. He tried to be patient, but Ginsburg rarely obliged Shapira even when he attempted to follow the agreed-upon protocol. The scholar spent all his time poring over the manuscript, refusing interruptions from anyone.

A week after Ginsburg took the manuscript to the British Museum and began his examination, the story started to hit the papers. Friday, 3 August 1883, notices appeared in *The Times* as well as *The Jewish Chronicle*. In an article entitled "A New Version of Deuteronomy," *The Jewish Chronicle* stated:

> A very curious Phoenician copy of Deuteronomy, or at least a part of that book, has been brought to London. A number of Semitic savants met the other day in the office of the Palestine Exploration Fund, where the document was to be seen. The word *document* ought not perhaps to be used, for it consists of a number of small pieces of parchment, in a very decayed and dirty condition. On some of them Phoenician letters are distinctly visible, while on others spirits of wine must be passed with a camel hair pencil before the letters can be seen. The writing has been to a certain extent deciphered, and is part of the Book of Deuteronomy: it is said to be as old as the Moabite stone, which is generally supposed to date back to about 900 before the Christian era.

---

[142] Ibid., 264.
[143] Ibid., 260.

It need scarcely be stated that if this turns out to be correct, these pieces of leather will possess a high value, not only in money, but also in a literary sense, for they contain some curious variations in the reading, among which we have an extra commandment, which is, "Thou shalt not hate thy brother in thy heart"—by joining the first and second commandment into one, this becomes the tenth in the Phoenician version. In chapter vii. 20, instead of "hornet" the copy gives "leprosy."[144] There is also an important variation in chapter xxviii, in relation to the "Blessings," and the death of Moses is omitted.

This singular relic of the past has been brought to this country by Mr. Shapira, of Jerusalem, who was introduced to the meeting by Mr. Besant, and he explained how he became possessed of it. Five years ago he received information that some Arabs near Diban, in Moab, the same locality where the Moabite stone was discovered, had a rare talisman to which they attributed all the good luck which befell them. Mr. Shapira, thinking it might be something ancient, employed some Arabs to aid him, and he described their character as "people who would steal their own mother-in-law for a few piasters." By this means the talisman was carried off, and from a cave in the Wadi Mojib it now appears in the Strand, subject to the anxious scrutiny of men learned in Hebrew and Assyrian writing.

The previous reputation of "Moabite Pottery," which had the name of Mr. Shapira connected with it, naturally tends to make people careful in their judgment on Moabite manuscripts. After the Moabite stone was accepted as authentic, other Moabite stones were found which had to be rejected; and savants are now inclined to be skeptical of anything coming from the eastern side of the Dead Sea. Before this copy of Deuteronomy can pass as genuine, it will have to undergo a very minute scrutiny, and be subjected to a careful examination. It is now under this process, and Dr. Ginsburg's report as well as that of others who are engaged on it, will be looked for with great anxiety by all Biblical scholars. Mr. Shapira talks of a million sterling as the value of this discovery. Purchasers at that sum will probably be scarce.

The reporter did not divulge his source, but as Shapira read the article he wondered who might have provided the information. On the one hand, he was pleased to see that *The Times* and *Jewish Chronicle* talked about his manuscript and that the first public release suggested a possible date as early as 900 BCE. But he was disturbed to read the writer's reluctance to present any real hope of its authenticity. Perhaps he was overreacting, but when he read, "if this turns out to be correct," the *IF* seemed larger than all the other words in the sentence. To make

---

[144] The canonical version reads "hornets"—צרעה in Deuteronomy 7:20, where Ginsburg proposed a reading of "leprosy"—צרעת in the Moses Scroll. However, neither Ginsburg nor Meyer was certain of the reading. Both recorded the first letter as ה, and final two letters as עת. Based on the certainty of the final two letters, the word is not "hornets." If the text did read "leprosy," it should be noted that leprosy in the Bible, צרעת, is not what is known as Hansen's disease today.

matters worse, it appeared that his past involvement with those "other Moabite stones" and the writer's statement that "savants are now inclined to be skeptical of anything coming from the eastern side of the Dead Sea" troubled him. Shapira wondered why so much of the article was devoted to casting doubt on the scroll's authenticity and making him suspect so early in the ordeal. Of course, he realized that Ginsburg must subject the artifact to "a very minute scrutiny," but the tone worried him. So much so that he felt compelled to write to Ginsburg. From his room in the Cannon Street Hotel, Shapira penned a lengthy defense against his role in the Moabitica affair.

The letter, dated 6 August 1883, began, "Dear Dr.! The known article of the 4th of August, mentions again the sad business of the Moabite pottery and I think it will be right to let you know dear sir how little I am to be blamed even if the pottery should be unquestionably forgeries." Shapira continued, "My business with antiquities begins from the end of the year 1871." He told Ginsburg that at that time he received "some squeezes and 2 stones with inscriptions through the agency of Mr. Bergheim, all of which proved false." Shapira told Ginsburg about other pieces that came into his shop, and how he "became very cautious."

He continued, "In April and May 1872 some small pieces of pottery were brought to me." These also raised Shapira's suspicion, and he told Ginsburg that he "doubted very much their genuineness, but Captain Conder and Mr. Drake thought them genuine and persuaded me to buy more of them." Shapira's letter told of how other inscribed jars came into his shop and how Captain Conder sent news of the discoveries to London. Meanwhile, the German pastor Lic. Weser notified Professor Schlottmann of the discoveries in Moab. England expressed doubts, but word out of Berlin via a telegram expressed "high interest." Weser was advised to secure more of the Moabitica items and to try to visit the places where these artifacts originated. Shapira went on to tell Ginsburg that after the Germans learned that he (Shapira) was connected to the source, they encouraged him to buy as many as possible and to name his price. Berlin's obvious interest in the items drove the price up to ten times what it was in the beginning. Nonetheless, sometime around the end of 1872 Shapira made the requested list and fixed a price, "which was accepted by telegram." The purchase agreement came with the condition that Shapira take the artifacts to Berlin in the summer and with the added stipulation that he not sell them to anyone else. Shapira traveled to Berlin to discuss how he would deliver the purchased items. He then returned home, packed them with great care, and took them to Berlin in August.

Shapira stressed in his letter that he had not wanted to accept any money until the authorities in Berlin could examine the Moabite artifacts. After four weeks of scrutiny by the German buyers, Shapira said they bought a second portion. They then urged him to go back and acquire as many more as he could. The Germans also asked Shapira to visit the places and caves where those items were found, and if possible, to try to understand more about the Moabitica. Shapira told Ginsburg that he had received many purchase offers but refused to sell them until

Professor Schlottmann published a book about them as he had promised to do, or until officers of the PEF had a chance to visit the excavation sites. Finally, Shapira informed Ginsburg that in his August 1873 trip to Berlin he had "pointed out … some jars which I believed were imitations of the others and forgeries, but no one wished to hear me. Now, you will understand dear Dr., why my greatest enemies —M. Ganneau and Kautzsch—could write nothing against my honesty."

The 3 August articles were the first of many to appear in *The Times, The Jewish Chronicle,* and *The Athenæum,* London's prestigious literary magazine. It soon became hard to keep up with all the reports about the events at the British Museum and about the scroll and its owner. Other outlets picked up a number of those articles, and the story spread across the globe. Shapira and his scroll made world news, and soon everyone was anxiously awaiting the next report from London. Hardly a story lacked mention of the one million sterling riding on Ginsburg's final decision, and he seemed to know it. If he had any opinion regarding whether the manuscript dated to 900 BCE or was a modern forgery, he was careful not to give so much as a hint.

The day after *The Times* and *Jewish Chronicle* introduced the subject to the public, Ginsburg was quoted in *The Athenæum* as saying, "The writing of the Shapira MSS. seems not to be a picked alphabet, but current, and this is in favour of the genuineness of the document. It is pretty clear that, whatever the age of the leather, the writing must either date from somewhere about 800 BC or from AD 1880."[145] The wording was clever. On the one hand, Ginsburg included a statement that the lettering was "in favour of the genuineness of the document," but also said the writing either dated from the ninth century BCE or had been added to the leather strips within the previous few years. With this statement, he had hooked everyone who was following the unfolding investigation. It would be up to Ginsburg to determine which was the truth. The world could thank him later.

On the same day that Ginsburg's statement appeared in *The Athenæum,* the manuscript was undergoing an examination by chemist and mineralogist Dr. Walter Flight. A letter dated Saturday, 4 August 1883, reported Dr. Flight's assessment of the blackish substance on the leather strips. He wrote to Bond:

> As regards the strips of skin, brought home by Shapira and alleged to be a very early manuscript of Deuteronomy, I have not much to say. The black colouring matter, taken from the back and front of the skins, does not appear to be asphaltum but rather wax, like bees-wax, of a very impure dirty kind. It leaves an ash amounting to 10 to 15 percent. It readily melts and, when destroyed by further heating, does not emit the smell of asphaltum. It is very variously acted upon by different solvents: hydrogen-peroxide is almost without action; cold alcohol has hardly more action; and cold ether much the same action; spirit of turpentine has a considerable solvent action; benzol has much action; and so has chloroform, still more so. But the most

---

145 "Literary Gossip," *The Athenæum,* no. 2910, 4 August 1883, 147.

active solvent of all is carbon-bisulphide. I believe, if the surface should be cleaned and all the character laid bare that chloroform would be the best agent to employ and that all the writing could thus be exposed clearly.

Believe me, yours truly, Walter Flight

Ginsburg began transcribing and translating the manuscript and decided to publish the results in installments. The first appeared in *The Times* on Wednesday, 10 August 1883, and in *The Athenæum* the following day. Friday, 12 August, *The Jewish Chronicle* followed up on its entry from the previous Friday with an article titled "The New Manuscript of Deuteronomy." Readers wanted to know more about the scroll and the man who brought it to England. In that article the writer called it a "remarkable MS. of Deuteronomy," and then informed the readers that Mr. Shapira, the gentleman who was responsible for bringing it to London, was "well known for the large number of MSS. he had obtained from the Arabs of South Palestine and brought to Europe." The article then described some of the more notable and valuable texts that Shapira had delivered in the past. Regarding the Moabitica affair, the article mentioned that Mr. Shapira "appears to have been more sinned against than sinning in this matter," slightly softening the more accusatory tone from the previous week. It went on to provide some details about the leather strips. The proposed date of 800 BC, it said, "seems to be in a way justified by the appearance of the leather folds which are black and impregnated with the odour of funereal spices." It gave the strips' approximate sizes and shared that each strip "contains about ten lines" of text.

The Jewish Chronicle treated its readers to a sampling of the new manuscript. It juxtaposed certain readings from the Shapira manuscript and the Authorized Version for contrast and comparison. The "omissions are even more striking than the variations," the writer told the readers, and went on to give a few examples. He also mentioned another feature involving the use of the Divine Name, the Tetragrammaton, or four-lettered name of God. The reporter did not know all the details but reported, "The Tetragrammaton does not occur throughout, 'Elohim' being used instead." The Decalogue, as it appeared in the manuscript, was also released in that week's flurry of press coverage, and so was this promise from Ginsburg: "In the next issue I hope to give the other portions of the text in their proper sequences, commencing with the beginning of Deuteronomy."

A mere two weeks had passed since Shapira presented his manuscript to the assembled savants at the PEF office on Adam Street, and now the whole world was aware of the curious leather strips. There was a sense of expectancy for the next piece of news out of London.

On Display before the World

As the second week of Ginsburg's analysis came to an end, and with public interest on the rise, two of the leather strips were placed on display in a poorly-lit glass case in the King's Library of the British Museum. Each day, between the hours of ten and four, under the watchful eye of an assigned guard, crowds of people visited the exhibit to cast their eyes upon the celebrated scroll fragments.

On Monday, 13 August, British Prime Minister William Gladstone took the opportunity to examine the display. Not only was Gladstone interested in biblical matters, but it also seems that he was invested particularly in the work and research of Christian David Ginsburg. An article appearing in *The Times* on Friday, 3 August 1883, referred to Ginsburg as the "well-known Semitic scholar [who received] a grant of £500 from the Prime Minister towards the production of his important work on the Massorah."[146] The *London Standard* reported that during his visit the prime minister discussed the scroll with Ginsburg and Shapira. Gladstone reportedly commented on the similarity of the script of the fragments with those of the Mesha Stela and the Siloam Inscription, indicating his familiarity with details if only from an informed lay perspective. The reporter also added:

> The battle which is now waxing hot among orientalists will be the renewal of the old war of the Moabite Stone. The question is partly one of paleography. Obsolete words and words regarded as late Hebrew appear. Among those who hold that the manuscript is genuine, the divergency of opinion as to the date is very great. Some 8th century, some the time of the captivity, while a third party places it to be the Maccabean period.[147]

Ginsburg, now well into his assessment of the strips, had not indicated his opinion as to their authenticity, not even to Prime Minister Gladstone. He simply went about his work, publishing his translation, stringing people along, and leading them to believe that the lack of any word of forgery from him must mean that he thought it genuine. And this is precisely what people believed. Meanwhile, Ginsburg's work began to elicit opinions from other scholars who, despite having not seen the scroll, felt obliged to opine and thereby get in on the attention that

---

[146] Estimated at nearly $60,000 in 2021.
[147] *The London Standard,* 14 August 1883.

Figure 9–The King's Library of the British Museum.

the Phoenician fragments were attracting. On the same day that the British prime minister viewed the scroll, two scholars would weigh in against its authenticity.

Adolf Neubauer, Hungarian-born former Austrian consul of Jerusalem and Oxford scholar, stated his doubts concerning the scroll's authenticity without equivocation.[148] His article began, "From the very outset, when I did not as yet know a word of the contents of Mr. Shapira's Moabite Deuteronomy (as I must call it, since it was discovered in the land of Moab, and is reported to be written in characters similar to those on the Moabite Stone), I held it to be a forgery." To bolster his position, Neubauer made a point of bringing up the infamous Moabite pottery and his declaration of them as forgeries. Since he had been right then, he wanted to go on record now and label the Moabite Deuteronomy a fraud as well. Based on Ginsburg's articles that he had read in multiple press releases, Neubauer set out to demonstrate his reasoning. He challenged the "forger's" word choices, showing that Old Testament readings did not support some of them, but rather that they were a form of Hebrew such as one finds in the later Jewish literature of the Targum and Talmud. He cited examples from the Decalogue that he learned from Ginsburg and criticized the "forger's" inclusion of certain "ungrammatical" usages. He sarcastically wrote, "Evidently the Moabite writer did not make use of Dr. Driver's excellent work on the Hebrew tenses."[149]

---

[148] Neubauer published his criticisms in *The Academy,* 18, 25 August and 8 September 1883. See also "The Shapira Manuscripts," *Palestine Exploration Fund Quarterly Statement* (Oct. 1883), 198–200.

[149] S. R. Driver, *A Treatise on the Use of the Tenses in Hebrew and Some Other Syntactical Questions* (London: Oxford University Press, 1874).

Aside from Neubauer's sharp critique of the grammatical errors and divergence from the authorized texts, he also found faults in the story of the scroll's discovery as related by Ginsburg in the press. He observed that the person responsible for the new Deuteronomy had made a very shrewd move. He intended to pass the scroll off as an early recension of the text by his use of *Elohim* instead of *Jehovah,* a clue that scholars had identified as a supposed Elohistic source writer in the books of the Pentateuch. This "is certainly the cleverest thing in the new Deuteronomy, as it turns the fragments into an Elohistic text," claimed Neubauer. "Unfortunately, the Moabite Moses [had] blundered" because, according to what was published in *The Times,* the name Jehovah appears twice in the scroll. Shapira also wondered about this and had mentioned it in his 9 May 1883 letter to Strack. He suggested that the original manuscript may have represented the work of an Elohistic scribe at some early time before the name Jehovah was known and used to refer to the Hebrew God. He also proposed that the first and last lines, which contained the name, may have been appended to the original document later by a "Jehovistic" scribe. Shapira, too, was unsettled as to why the name was lacking in the body of his scroll, but he did not view it as a blunder of "the Moabite Moses." In his eyes, it may have been proof of an earlier recension of the text.

Neubauer went on to note a few other discrepancies between the Moabite scroll and the "Authorized Version," incongruities that to him were evidence of fraud. His last sentence underscored his opinion clearly: "I am convinced from the text itself that the whole is a forgery."

The same day, Archibald Henry Sayce also made his opinion known.[150] Sayce was a British Assyriologist, researcher, lecturer, and brilliant linguist, known to be competent in twenty modern and ancient languages. His opinion, too, was based on Ginsburg's articles in *The Times* and *The Athenæum.* Still, one wonders if his negative assessment was in any way influenced by past debates with Shapira in academic journals over the reading of the Siloam Inscription. At the time, Captain Conder had sided with Shapira's view against the "hastily" published views of Sayce. It was to the Siloam Inscription that Sayce directed one of his criticisms of the Shapira scroll. While commenting on the similarity of the letters, he said, "Now the discovery of the Siloam inscription has shown that these were not the characters used in Judah (and therefore presumably in the northern kingdom of Israel) in the pre-exilic period. Consequently, if the fragments were genuine, they would belong to a Moabite and not to a Jewish Book of Deuteronomy, and the opening verse of the book would contain the name of Chemosh, and not of Yahveh or Jehovah." Sayce also found it difficult to believe the story of an ancient scroll's discovery in a cave near the Dead Sea. He put it this way: "It really is demanding too much of Western credulity to ask us to believe that in a damp climate like that of Palestine any sheepskins could have

---

[150] "The Shapira Manuscripts," *Palestine Exploration Fund Quarterly Statement* (Oct. 1883), 200–201.

lasted 3,000 years, either above the ground or under the ground, even though they may have been abundantly salted with asphalt from the Vale of Siddim itself."[151]

Claude Conder had not yet published his opinion of Shapira's scroll. He was among the first to see it when Shapira arrived in London, initially with Walter Besant and later as part of the small group of savants at the office of the PEF. During most of that meeting he had offered only passing comments and questions, but as the meeting came to a close he reportedly remarked to Besant, "I observe that all the points objected to by German critics have vanished in this new and epoch-making *trouvaille*.[152] The geography is not confused, and Moses does not record his own death."[153]

This point of geography was noted by Shapira as well. The order of travel contained in the canonical Deuteronomy is, on the other hand, confused. The narrative leads one to believe that the author of the early chapters of Deuteronomy was unfamiliar with the lay of the land across the Jordan. This is not a matter of modern readers simply being ignorant of the geography of the ancient world. When Shapira took the manuscript to Leipzig, he felt that Hermann Guthe might especially appreciate this aspect of his scroll. Guthe would later write, "Shapira came to Leipzig in order to receive counsel from me as to what there was to do in the matter; the text of the manuscript offered something peculiar in the topographical (more correctly, arguably, geographical or ethnographical) regard, and thus he believed that its contents might also especially concern my special studies about Palestine."[154]

Shapira described this issue in detail in his letter to Strack:

> No displaced passages are to be met in our manuscript especially in a topographical point of view. The order of the last journeys and battles are in the best order. So, first through Seir, then through the wilderness of Moab, then through Moab which seems to lay between the brook Zered and Arnon. Then through the passage over Arnon, the battle with Sihon and taking his land unto Jabbok, the passages over Jabbok to the land of Ammon, the battle of Jezer and through the forced battle with Og, King of Bashan. Then the returning southward to the Plains of Moab opposite Beth Peor, then a love affair with the daughters of Moab and the women of Midian and the sacrifice to Peor, and lastly the battle with the Midianites.[155]

---

[151] In response to Sayce's objection, the 22 August edition of the *Daily News* reported, "Mr. Sayce has, indeed, expressed the opinion that it is utterly unreasonable to suppose that in a climate so damp as that of Palestine any sheepskin could possibly have lasted for nearly 3,000 years.... But according to Mr. Shapira's account, the manuscripts were found in caves at a considerable altitude from the ground, protected moreover by an external covering, which, we may presume, was coated with asphalte. Under these circumstances it is scarcely possible to say how long a sheepskin might endure, even in the climate of Palestine." John Marco Allegro, *The Shapira Affair* (New York: Doubleday & Company, Inc., 1965), 58.

[152] *Trouvaille* is a French term meaning a "lucky find" or "windfall."

[153] Conder's remarks are recorded in Besant, *Autobiography,* 163–164.

[154] Guthe, *Fragments of a Leather Manuscript,* 2.

[155] This is found in Shapira's letter to Hermann Strack dated 9 May 1883, British Library *Add. MS. 41294.*

However, it seemed that beyond any clarification offered by accurate geography, for Conder the most significant barrier to accepting the authenticity of the fragments was that a leather scroll could survive in a cave in Moab. He confided in Besant, "I know, I believe, all the caves of Moab, and they are all damp and earthy. There is not a dry cave in the country."[156] A week after Sayce published his opinion, Conder would write, "A more improbable set of assumptions could hardly be conceived, yet the difficulty of the great age which is necessary to suppose leather to be able to attain without rotting in a damp cave is even more fatal to this clever forgery."[157]

As a result of Ginsburg's published glimpses, the scholarly world was beginning to make decisions about the scroll, but Ginsburg kept his opinion to himself. William Simpson, who was among the savants at the unveiling of Shapira's scroll, wrote the following in his journal as the world waited for Ginsburg to pronounce his verdict:

> From that meeting [26 July] the pieces of leather … were removed to the British Museum, where Dr. Ginsburg has been busily engaged transcribing the characters into their Hebrew equivalents, and also in translating the whole into English. This is now nearly completed and will be presented to the Trustees of the Museum. Dr. Ginsburg has been very reticent while so engaged, and has not expressed any opinion as to the genuineness of the manuscript; but he is understood to be making a report on it for the Trustees, to guide them as to whether they should enter into negotiations with Mr. Shapira for the purchase of the document. In this report Dr. Ginsburg will have to express his notions regarding its authenticity, and consequently all interested in Biblical matters are waiting anxiously to learn what such an authority will have to say, and whether the learned Dr will date them 800 B.C. or 1800 A.D. The pieces of skin have become very much darker since they were first exhibited at the Office of the Palestine Exploration Fund. On the few parts of the leather where the characters could be easily seen they have now become so darkened that it is with difficulty they can be made out.[158]

Nevertheless, Shapira remained optimistic. His scroll was on display before the world and every major newspaper was writing about it. The most outstanding scholars in the world were discussing the new Deuteronomy, and those who had studied it the closest had yet to make known their assessments. Public opinion was on his side. As the world awaited the final judgment, Shapira retired to the Cannon Street Hotel, and from the little desk in his room he wrote a letter home to tell Rosette and Maria about his meeting with the prime minister. He knew that by the time the letter arrived they would have already read all about it in the

---

[156] Besant, *Autobiography,* 164.
[157] "The Shapira Manuscripts," *Palestine Exploration Fund Quarterly Statement* (Oct. 1883), 206.
[158] From the journal of William Simpson, contained in British Library Or. MS. 14705. The text is reproduced in Fred Reiner, "C. D. Ginsburg and the Shapira Affair," 116–117.

papers, but he wanted to share his version anyway. He reiterated his confidence in the positive outcome, expressed his love for them, and then slipped into bed for some much-needed sleep.

Thou Dost Protest Too Much

Forty-five days after first laying eyes on Shapira's manuscript in the Hauffe Hotel in Germany, Hermann Guthe wrote the foreword to a 95-page booklet that explained his assessment of the sixteen leather strips.[159] The work was titled *Fragments of a Leather Manuscript Containing Moses' Last Words to the Children of Israel*.[160] Guthe divided his exposition into five sections: I. Foreword, II. Description and Origin of the Manuscript, III. The Text of the Leather Manuscript and of Deuteronomy, IV. The Character of the Text, V. Remarks on the Text. The booklet also featured a hand-drawn table containing Guthe's presentation of the letters "taken from the most readable columns of the manuscript, namely the fragments D and E." Although Guthe and Meyer had examined the fragments in July, the booklet would not appear until September, and even then would receive little notice. Nonetheless, the German scholars were the first to complete a thorough examination of the Moabite scroll.

Charles Clermont-Ganneau watched with skepticism from a distance as news reports continually appeared in the papers. His moment arrived when the French minister of public instruction dispatched him to London on "a special mission to examine Mr. Shapira's manuscripts, at present deposited in the British Museum, and which have, for some time past, excited such great interest in England."[161] Admittedly, for Clermont-Ganneau the trip was only to confirm his suspicions from afar about the supposed authenticity of Shapira's Torah manuscript. The purpose was to dispel any doubt in the minds of those who truly believed in the genuineness of the leather strips. The Frenchman had previously achieved notoriety as a detector of frauds. Of particular significance were his "decisive disclosures with regard to the fabrication of spurious Moabite potteries," the entire collection of which was connected with Moses Shapira.[162] In that discovery he stopped short of identifying Shapira as the forger, pointing the finger of blame instead at the Arab Selim al-Qari. Now he was investigating another possible

---

[159] The foreword was dated "Leipzig, 14 August 1883."

[160] Golde's unpublished translation of, Hermann Guthe, *Fragmente einer Lederhandschrift enthaltend Mose's letzte Rede an die Kinder Israel* (Leipzig: Druck und Verlag von Breitkopf & Härtel, 1883).

[161] "The Shapira Manuscripts," *Palestine Exploration Fund Quarterly Statement* (Oct. 1883), 201. The account in this chapter is based primarily on the account of Monsieur Clermont-Ganneau contained in this edition of the *Palestine Exploration Fund Quarterly Statement*, pages 201–205.

[162] Clermont-Ganneau, "The Shapira Manuscripts," *Palestine Exploration Fund Quarterly Statement* (Oct. 1883), 201.

forgery, but this time it was the antiquarian and bookseller Shapira who was under the microscope.

Charles Clermont-Ganneau arrived in London on 15 August 1883 and went straightway to the British Museum. In the antiquities department he met 70-year-old Dr. Samuel Birch. Birch had been in the museum's employ for nearly half a century and was known as an antiquarian and expert in Egyptology. Without delay, Dr. Birch obligingly took his French acquaintance to the manuscript department, where Dr. Ginsburg and Mr. Shapira were "engaged in studying the fragments" together. Although unnecessary, Dr. Birch made introductions as a matter of courtesy and then dismissed himself from the three men.

The meeting was awkward. Clermont-Ganneau had all but ruined Shapira's reputation. The Moabitica affair remained one of the chief causes for doubts surrounding his scroll's authenticity, and here standing before him was the man responsible! Ginsburg didn't hold the French savant in high regard either; he had written previously about his quest for fame, lack of discretion, and affinity for taking credit where credit wasn't due. All three knew that despite their discomfort, they must handle the meeting with care. Trust vanished from the room, which seemed to grow increasingly crowded from the minute Clermont-Ganneau entered. After what seemed an eternity, Clermont-Ganneau requested an opportunity to examine the fragments. Ginsburg reluctantly permitted the Frenchman to take a quick look at the fragments on the table, but then confessed that he was uncertain whether he could grant such a request. Sensing that Dr. Ginsburg "feared some encroachment" on his part, Clermont-Ganneau sought to reassure him that he was happy to acknowledge Ginsburg's hard work to this point. He further indicated that he would not publish his assessment immediately. For the present, he only wished to concern himself with the "external and material state of the fragments," agreeing to conduct his examination in Ginsburg's presence. Dr. Ginsburg said that given the nature of his present work on the scroll, a more comprehensive review by Clermont-Ganneau might not be convenient. He informed the Frenchman that he would provide an answer on Friday, 17 August.

Meanwhile, the public anxiously awaited Ginsburg's verdict. What was taking so long? If it were a forgery, surely he would have announced it by now. On Thursday, 16 August, the *Liverpool Daily Post* reported: "Dr. Ginsburg is still busily engaged at the British Museum in deciphering Mr. Shapira's latest antiquarian find; and the reticence Dr. Ginsburg displays leads many to put faith in the original assertion that these scraps of leather are hundreds of years older than the Christian era. It is argued by these believers that, if the skins had been forgeries, such an acute scholar as Dr. Ginsburg would have been able long before this to have detected the fraud."[163]

On Friday, Clermont-Ganneau returned to the museum where he was informed with "great regret" by Edward Augustus Bond, the principal librarian,

---

[163] *Liverpool Daily Post,* 16 August 1883.

that Mr. Shapira had "expressly refused his consent" for him to inspect the fragments. The Frenchman would describe his feelings about this refusal in a piece published before the week ended. He wrote, "There was nothing to be said against this; the owner was free to act as he pleased. It was his strict right, but it is also my right to record publicly this refusal, quite personal to me; and this to some extent is the cause of this communication. I leave to public opinion the business of explaining the refusal. I will confine myself to recalling one fact, with comment. It was Mr. Shapira who sold the spurious Moabite potteries to Germany; and it was M. Clermont-Ganneau who, ten years ago, discovered and established the apocryphal nature of them."[164]

Clermont-Ganneau had traveled to England expecting to be extended the courtesy, as he put it, "which was accorded to other scholars, and to persons of distinction, of making me acquainted with these documents." He felt this was due him, given his "labours in connection with Semitic inscriptions generally" and his acknowledged "authority upon the question" at hand. When none was afforded him, though he was offended, he set about the work that had brought him to London—to disprove the scroll's authenticity once and for all. Unlike before, this time he would not excuse Shapira.

The angered French scholar would have to prove his preconceived opinion based on observations gained by his momentary look at the strips two days earlier, supplemented by what he could learn at the dimly-lit display case in the manuscript department. It must have been injurious to his pride to stand alongside the crowds of unintelligent folk, knowing that most, if not all of them, were unable to recognize a single letter on the sheepskin. This was especially so knowing that not far from the "crowd of curious pressing round these venerable relics," Ginsburg and Shapira sat comfortably at a well-lit desk, working in much better conditions. He would report that he was "devoted to this unpleasant task both Friday and Saturday."

The public's pressure for a published decision was now taking a back seat to the fact that Clermont-Ganneau was working on his own announcement and that at any moment he would go to press with his views. Until Clermont-Ganneau's arrival, Mr. Bond was perfectly willing to allow Ginsburg to proceed at his own snailish pace. The attention the British Museum was attracting had been favorable for Bond as well as for Ginsburg. Likely suspecting that Clermont-Ganneau's report would bring discredit upon all involved parties, he wrote to Ginsburg, his subordinate, offering his own appraisal and perhaps insinuating that the doctor should make a declaration of forgery. In his letter of Friday, 17 August, he wrote, "For myself I regard the account of the first discovery of the fragments as altogether unsatisfactory and consider that the condition of the manuscripts is incompatible with exposure to atmosphere for the long period indicated by the character of the writing." He added, "I am also of the opinion that the setting of

---

[164] Clermont-Ganneau, "The Shapira Manuscripts," *Palestine Exploration Fund Quarterly Statement* (Oct. 1883), 202.

the text in widely separated columns between ruled lines is a later character than the period indicated by the writing, and I have little doubt that your critical examination of the manuscripts in respect of the text will lead to the same conclusion as that of their external condition."[165]

The same day, *The Times* published the second of Ginsburg's two articles about the scroll. Bond left to spend the weekend in the country, and Clermont-Ganneau spent the entire day in front of the display case. The Frenchman finalized his report on Saturday. He concluded, just as he suspected before ever laying eyes on the fragments, that they were the work of a modern forger.

On 18 August, from 42 Great Russell Street,[166] Monsieur Clermont-Ganneau put his cleverly devised theory to paper. The day after learning from Mr. Bond that Shapira had refused him access to the scroll fragments, the Frenchman wrote the following: "In these circumstances, the object of my mission became extremely difficult to attain, and I almost despaired of it. I did not, however, lose courage, and I set to work with the meagre means of information which were at my disposal: (1) The hasty inspection of two or three pieces which M. Ginsburg had allowed me to handle for a few minutes on my first visit; (2) the examination of two fragments exposed to public view in a glass case in the Manuscript Department at the British Museum—a case very ill-lighted and difficult to approach, owing to the crowd of the curious pressing round these venerable relics. I devoted to this unpleasant task both Friday and Saturday, and had the satisfaction of obtaining an unhoped-for result."[167]

Clermont-Ganneau had taken Shapira's refusal personally, complaining that this made the object of his mission "extremely difficult to attain." He admitted being near despair but not lacking courage as he "set to work with the meagre means of information" at his disposal. However, those means surprisingly yielded plenty for the French scholar. Hermann Guthe had spent an entire week carefully scrutinizing the fragments and another five weeks producing a scholarly report to express his opinion. Guthe stated in his exposition, "A conscientious scholar would rather not pass such a judgment until he had achieved a consummate understanding of the entire manuscript through equally precise examination of all the parts thereof; that would be a work not to be achieved in a few days, but would rather demand weeks or even months."[168] As far as we know, Clermont-Ganneau was unaware of his German colleague's previous work or his opinion that a "consummate understanding" required more time of a conscientious scholar than he was willing or able to devote to his assessment. Besides, he was not hiding the fact that before he arrived in London to inspect the leather strips he already

---

[165] Allegro, *The Shapira Affair*, 62. Based on Bond's letter to Ginsburg, Allegro suggests that "Bond had given his expert the clearest possible hint on how he expected him to direct his judgment."
[166] The British Museum is located on Great Russel Street.
[167] Charles Clermont-Ganneau, letter dated 18 August 1883, published in *The Times* on 21 August 1883. Republished in "The Shapira Manuscripts," *Palestine Exploration Fund Quarterly Statement* (Oct. 1883), 202.
[168] Guthe, *Fragments of a Leather Manuscript*, 2.

harbored "doubts as to their authenticity." He only needed to confirm those doubts, which was why he had come in the first place.

Clermont-Ganneau's assessment, written on Saturday, 18 August, was meant for publication and distribution as soon as possible.[169] The thought of being denied a proper seat at the inspection table where Ginsburg had worked for nearly three weeks was in his mind as he wrote.

> These are my conclusions: The fragments are the work of a modern forger. This is not the expression of an *à priori* incredulity, a feeling which many scholars must, like me, have experienced at the mere announcement of this wonderful discovery. I am able to show, with the documents before me, how the forger went to work. He took one of those large synagogue rolls of leather, containing the Pentateuch, written in square Hebrew character, and perhaps dating back two or three centuries—rolls which Mr. Shapira must be well acquainted with, for he deals in them, and has sold to several of the public libraries of England sundry copies of them, obtained from the existing synagogues of Judea and of the Yemen.

> The forger then cut off the lower edge of this roll—that which offered him the widest surface. He obtained in this way some narrow strips of leather with an appearance of comparative antiquity, which was still further heightened by the use of the proper chemical agents. On these strips of leather he wrote with ink, making use of the alphabet of the Moabite Stone, and introducing such "various readings" as fancy dictated, the passages from Deuteronomy which have been deciphered and translated by M. Ginsburg, with patience and learning worthy of better employment.

Clearly, he intended the last sentence to be a slight against his academic colleague. With these words Clermont-Ganneau suggested that Ginsburg had wasted his time on the scroll—one that should have been easily recognized as a forgery. He then described his theory about how the forger produced his deceptive Deuteronomy and what he believed had led him to detect the fraud:[170]

> That which put me on the scent was the presence—ascertained by me at first sight—on the fragments of an important detail, of which I had not at first understood the full significance. The lines of Moabitish writing are arranged in the shape of columns, separated by vertical creases in the leather—that is to say, by creases perpendicular to the general direction of

---

[169] The conclusions of Clermont-Ganneau are reproduced here from "The Shapira Manuscripts," *Palestine Exploration Fund Quarterly Statement* (Oct. 1883), 202–205.

[170] Despite its length, I have included the full summary of Clermont-Ganneau's evidence. I feel it is necessary to grasp the theory put forward by the French scholar, especially since many have followed his theory or a form thereof, the most recent being Chanan Tigay, *The Lost Book of Moses.* See especially page 319, where Tigay describes his inspection of a manuscript that Shapira sold to the British Museum, designated Oriental 1457. Tigay reports, "I removed the scroll from the box and unrolled it, then leaned over to look at the slip with a magnifying glass. There they were: three vertical lines etched into the shiny leather in exactly the pattern one sees in Torah scrolls. If I had any doubts before, they were now gone. I had not only found a Shapira scroll from which the lower margin had been removed, but a piece of leather he had removed from a Torah scroll and written on. There could be no more doubt. Shapira was our forger."

writing. On the right side and left of each of these folds I had noticed two vertical straight lines, drawn with a hard point, as guides for the vertical margins, starting from the upper edge of the strip, and extending to the lower edge, which they do not always reach. The Moabitish forger had not paid much attention to these extremely fine lines, which have scratched the leather in an almost invisible but indelible manner; and the lines of Moabitish characters, instead of being confined by this drawing, have no relation to it. Sometimes they pass over the lines, sometimes they rest on the inner sides of them, both at their beginning and ending. The forger was obviously guided in observing the limits of his space, not by the vertical

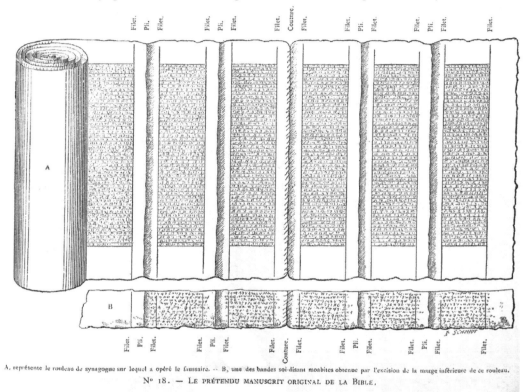

Figure 10–Illustration of Clermont-Ganneau's theory.

marginal lines, but by the intermediary creases. If, however, we compare these strips of leather with one of the synagogue rolls of which I spoke just now, the explanation of this mystery will be made plain to us at once.

These rolls consist of large pieces of leather (generally sheepskin) sewn end to end, forming enormous strips, which may be 30 or 40 mètres [98–131 feet] in length, and with a breadth of 16 centimètres [6¼ inches] or more.

The text of the Pentateuch, in the square Hebrew characters, is arranged in regular parallel columns containing some fifty lines each. At the top a horizontal margin is left, and at the bottom another horizontal margin, everywhere wider than the upper one, both extending for the entire length of the roll. This lower margin, to take an example, on a roll in the British Museum coming from Jerusalem and bearing the number 1460, measures 8 centimètres [3 inches] in height. The columns of the text separated by intervals, which in the roll instanced by me by way of comparison, measure about 4 centimètres [1½ inches], are marked out with the stylus. The horizontal marks along which the square Hebrew characters are brought into line are confined on the right and left by two long vertical lines, traced in the same manner, which, for the most part, cross the first and the last horizontal line, and jut out into the upper and lower margin. This is not all. Between each column and the next one, the leather has a vertical crease which runs from top to bottom of the roll. It is these ends of the vertical lines drawn with the stylus and the peculiar creases which divide them which we meet with on the long narrow Moabitish strips whereon the forger has written his Moabitish characters.

There is more yet. I have said that the large pieces of leather of the synagogue rolls were sewn end to end. Now, among the Moabitish strips, I saw at least one where this seam still exists. I need not point out how interesting it would be to examine the character of the thread. Finally, one sees that on the Moabitish strips one of the two edges, either the upper or the lower, is fringed and ragged. It is the original edge of the roll which furnished the raw material to the forger. The second edge, on the other hand, is sharply cut with a penknife or scissors; it is the cutting made by the forger immediately under the last line of the square Hebrew characters.

I advise all the impartial scholars who would thoroughly inform themselves as to this gross imposition, and to whom may be permitted an examination which is denied to me (I know not, or rather, I know very well why), to take the suspected strips, and to lay them against the lower edge of one of the synagogue rolls preserved at the British Museum. The trick will stare them in the face. I will also beg my more favoured fellow students to be kind enough, in order to throw complete light upon a problem (which is no longer one to me), to make certain important investigations, especially the following:

(1) To ascertain whether, by chance, there does not remain on the upper portion of the strips traces of the tails of the square Hebrew letters, especially of the final letters which, as we know, descend below the normal line.

(2) To see if the back of the leather does not materially differ in appearance from the face of it, and whether it has not been left in the raw state, as on the synagogue rolls.

(3) To take the average height of all the strips, in order to obtain from them the greatest height, which will enable us to determine the height of the original margin of the roll (or the rolls) that supplied the forger. I can at once

affirm that on this roll the column of square Hebrew characters were from 10 to 11 centimètres [3.9–4.3 inches] in breadth, and were separated by blank intervals of about 4½ centimètres [1¾ inches] in breadth.

(4) To ascertain the description of the leather, and above all of the thread in the seams.

Nothing is more easy than to effect the experimental examination which I suggest. Let there be given me a synagogue roll, two or three centuries old, with permission to cut it up. I engage to procure from it strips in every respect similar to the Moabitish strips, and to transcribe upon them in archaic characters the text of Leviticus, for example, or one of Numbers. This would make a fitting sequel to the Deuteronomy of Mr. Shapira, but would have the slight advantage over it of not costing quite a million sterling.

Who is the forger? That is a question which it does not concern me to answer, nor even to raise. I will merely call attention to the fact that he can only be a person familiar with Hebrew, and who has had before his eyes exact copies of the Moabite Stone.

One word in conclusion. It would be interesting to learn whether the forger has completely destroyed the synagogue roll from which he has cut the strips required for the imposition. Certainly elementary prudence would have required the annihilation of the *corpus delicti*.[171] Nevertheless, the Hebrew text remaining intact, after the abstraction of the lower margin, and these synagogue rolls having a fixed market value, it is not impossible, although it would have been at a serious risk, that the forger should have tried to make something by it, and to "kill two birds with one stone." If ever a synagogue roll should be met with without a lower margin, it will be well to try if, by chance, the Moabitish strips would not fit it.

Clermont-Ganneau, 42 Great Russell Street, 18 August

With these words, the Frenchman wished to distance himself from any potential accusations of a hastily determined position in his forthcoming public statement. However, he had given himself away by admitting that he possessed doubts before arriving in London. One can almost hear echoes of a line from Shakespeare's *Hamlet* calling, "Monsieur Clermont-Ganneau, thou doth protest too much, methinks!"[172] Clermont-Ganneau's report would not appear in *The Times* until 21 August, but the day was not yet over.

---

[171] The body of evidence that constitutes objective proof that a crime has been committed.
[172] Act III, scene iii.

ℸ

Thrice Denied in Two Days

On Saturday, 18 August, the same day that Monsieur Clermont-Ganneau recorded his conclusions about Shapira's manuscript, Captain Claude Conder also felt obliged to come forward with his own statement since reports about the scroll fragments frequently mentioned his name.[173] The celebrated soldier-scholar wrote that although he had not seen the fragments before they arrived in London, he had since had the opportunity to examine them and compare them "with other manuscripts, true and forged," which he had seen in the East. Based on his assessment he stated, "I had no hesitation in concluding that the supposed fragments of Deuteronomy were deliberate forgeries."

To support the reason for his quick recognition (to which we were not privy until now), he recounted visits to Moab in 1881 and 1882. During these trips east of the Jordan he had frequent conversations with "Bedawin" on the subject of antiquities. He heard nothing in these discussions about "the supposed find of Mr. Shapira's manuscript." He did, however, hear reports of fake pottery being buried, only to be unearthed by unsuspecting Europeans and represented as authentic antiquities. He reported that some of the faked pottery were inscribed with letters similar to those on Shapira's scroll. He wrote, "Some fragments of similar pottery [by which he meant the faked pottery mentioned previously] have been shown to me by Mr. Shapira, and I understand that the Arabs represented these as having been found with the manuscript." It is worth noting that in this last statement he seemed to suddenly remember hearing something about a manuscript that he had not recalled a few sentences earlier.

Next, he applied his expertise in tribal names and territories to other portions of Shapira's story: "In the present instance, it would be satisfactory to know the name of the tribe which discovered the manuscript. The only name yet given is that of Sheikh Mahmûd Arekat, who is not a Bedawin chief, but a fellah chief of Abu Dis, near Jerusalem. The names of the Moabite chiefs and tribes I have certainly ascertained, and could say whether the district east of Aroer on Arnon belongs to any of them or not."

Next, he ventured briefly into some of the characteristics of the scroll:

---

[173] Conder's remarks concerning his views of Shapira's manuscript, dated Guilford, August 18, appear in "The Shapira Manuscripts," *Palestine Exploration Fund Quarterly Statement* (Oct. 1883), 205–206.

The use of square Hebrew by the Jews we have now traced in Palestine to a period earlier than the Christian era, and we know that the Palmyrenes and other trans-Jordanic peoples were using similar alphabet about that time. The manuscript under consideration is therefore (if it be genuine) more than 2,000 years old. I do not think any archaeologist will suppose that leather, as limp and supple as that on which this manuscript is written, could exist for such a length of time in the damp atmosphere of a country which has a rainfall of 20 inches. Having explored many hundreds of caves and tombs, I know well the mouldy smell of such excavations, and the rapid decay of frescoes not more than 600 years old on their walls. We know that the Accadians and Assyrians used papyrus and parchment, but not a fragment of their books is known to remain. The tattered fragments of our oldest Hebrew manuscript are not older than the seventh century A.D., and the condition of the famous oldest Samaritan roll at Shechem (a document which I have three times examined, and which, from the character of its letters, is not older than, perhaps, the sixth century A.D.) contrasts in an extraordinary manner with that of Mr. Shapira's leather leaves, supposed to be at least 1,400 years older, as does the faded colour of the letters with the very distinct black ink of the Shapira manuscript. It is only in the dry, rainless Theban desert that really ancient papyri (some 3,000 to 4,000 years old) have been found, or are likely to have survived, and the condition of such papyri before they are unrolled is very different from that of the supple leather of the new manuscript, which, however, is not unlike the forged manuscripts which have been offered for sale at Nâblus....

A more improbable set of assumptions could hardly be conceived, yet the difficulty of the great age which it is necessary to suppose leather to be able to attain without rotting in a damp cave is even more fatal to this clever forgery.

CLAUDE R. CONDER, R. E. Guilford, August 18

Meanwhile, on the same day that Captain Conder and Monsieur Clermont-Ganneau penned their opinions against the authenticity of the Moabite manuscript, the second of Ginsburg's three installments appeared in *The Athenæum*. Again, there was not so much as a hint about a possible forgery. Readers of Ginsburg's much-anticipated postings were still inclined to accept the manuscript as a genuinely ancient relic.

Nevertheless, Tuesday, 21 August 1883, would present the world with another view of the now-famous manuscript fragments. This time, *The Times'* columns would not be filled with the translations and teasing comments of Dr. Ginsburg but rather the straightforward negative views of the new Deuteronomy penned by Conder and Clermont-Ganneau. In the same paper, immediately following these reports, the editor said, "In first calling attention to the subject we pointed out the strong antecedent presumption against the genuineness of the fragments, a presumption resting upon the extreme improbability that leather should be found in excellent preservation after the lapse of twenty-seven centuries when skins known to date from the seventh century of our era are falling to pieces, upon the dexterity with which ancient relics are forged, and upon the magnitude of the gains they may reasonably hope to secure in case of success." The article closed, "We have not concealed the view we are disposed to take of the manuscript, but we have placed all that is known about it before the public, which will form its own opinions pending the final decision of the learned."

News quickly spread about the condemning remarks of these two respected experts published on that fateful Tuesday morning, first in the streets of London then in other places near and far. The appearance for the first time of outright declarations of forgery came as a shock to nearly everyone.

In the Wednesday, 22 August edition of the *Daily News,* in an article titled "Mr. Shapira's Deuteronomy," an unnamed expert reported, "A few days ago the present writer had an opportunity of more closely examining a portion of the manuscript which certainly wore the appearance of antiquity." The writer then proceeded to report various arguments for and against the authenticity, considering internal and external evidence. He also noted, "The portions of Mr. Shapira's manuscript exhibited last Friday and Saturday have been this week withdrawn from view." This means that the display was removed very soon after Clermont-Ganneau turned in his report on Saturday evening, 18 August. The writer then briefly mentioned the theory of the Frenchman, and added, "This assertion will no doubt be fully inquired into, but the portion of the Deuteronomy manuscript examined by the present writer was written on leather of a thicker character, differing very considerably from that usually employed in synagogue-rolls. Moreover, it is questionable whether on a purely speculative business it would have been worthwhile to mutilate and spoil a valuable roll. M. Clermont-Ganneau's evidence is also vitiated by the strong prejudice which he confesses he had previously entertained."[174]

On the same day, the *Standard* published a lengthy piece, which began, "The solemn farce of the 'Shapira Manuscripts' seems rapidly drawing to a close." It then criticized the scholars for taking so long to detect the forgery. Obviously expressing a great deal of frustration, the writer said, "Indeed, our only wonder has always been how a fraud so transparent could for a single hour have imposed on the credulity of the experts who for the last three weeks have been wasting their learned leisure in discussing the authenticity of these scraps of dingy leather."

Ginsburg, whose third and final installment had appeared that day in *The Times,* still offered no word of his final assessment of the scroll. He knew that he had to act quickly. The same article was set to appear in *The Athenæum* on Saturday, 25 August, and so, at the end of that second version he added the following: "I have designedly abstained from making any remark or calling

---

[174] *The Daily News,* 22 August 1883.

attention to any anomalies in the Hebrew text, as my report, which is to appear next week, will contain a full account of all the peculiarities of the MS. and the conclusion I have arrived at about its genuineness."[175] The public would have to wait to read Ginsburg's assessment of the scroll he had worked on for more than three weeks, but Mr. Bond needed to know his judgment right away, and so, on Wednesday, 22 August 1883, Ginsburg wrote to Bond detailing his conclusion.[176]

The manuscript of Deuteronomy which Mr. Shapira submitted to us for examination is a forgery.

As the interest which it has excited is so great, and as the public are waiting to hear the result of our investigation, I shall endeavor to give my reasons for the conclusion I arrived at in as popular a manner as the essentially technical nature of the subject will admit.

The writing of the manuscript exhibits the oldest alphabetical characters hitherto known. The letters greatly resemble those on the Moabite Stone, *circa* B.C. 900. The document, therefore, pretends to be about B.C. 800–900. This conclusion cannot be set aside by the supposition that extremely archaic forms may have been retained in some districts, either in the east or west of the Jordan, and that the manuscript may therefore only claim to be of about B.C. 200–300. The pretence to extreme antiquity is confirmed by the fact that the text of Deuteronomy in its present form was substantially the same *circa* B.C. 300. This is attested by the Septuagint version of the Pentateuch, which, as is generally admitted, was made about that time. As the Shapira manuscript pretends to give an entirely different recension, it presumably claims to exhibit a text prior to B.C. 300.

The evidence which to my mind convicts the manuscript as a modern forgery is of a twofold nature—viz., external and internal.

I. The narrow slips of leather on which it is written are cut off from the margin of synagogue scrolls. According to an ancient practice, the Jews in all parts of the world read the Sabbatical lessons from the Pentateuch from manuscript scrolls. Owing to partial defacement or damage, these scrolls frequently become illegal, and are withdrawn from public use. And although the Jews as a rule guard these sacred relics against profanation, and deposit them in receptacles abutting on the synagogues, still the communities in the East, and especially in South Arabia, are driven by poverty to part with them. Hence almost every public library in Europe, and many private collectors, possess such disused parchments or skins belonging to different ages, ranging from the eleventh to the nineteenth century. On the 24th of November, 1877, the British Museum bought a number of these scrolls from Mr. Shapira, which he brought from Yemen. The remarkable part about

---

[175] "The Shapira MS. of Deuteronomy," *The Athenæum,* no. 2913, 25 August 1883, 244.

[176] As in the case of Clermont-Ganneau's published findings, those of Ginsburg are quoted here in full. The reader will notice immediately the similarity between the two reports. This same report would appear in *The Times* on the following Monday, 27 August. It was also published later in "The Shapira Manuscripts," *Palestine Exploration Fund Quarterly Statement* (Oct. 1883), 207–209.

these scrolls is that (1) some of them are written on similar rough sheepskins to the material on which the Deuteronomy slips are written; (2) the lower margin of some of these scrolls (Comp. Oriental, 1452; Oriental, 1453; Oriental, 1454; Oriental, 1459; Oriental, 1465) is the same width as the height of the Shapira slips; and (3) one of these scrolls—viz., Oriental, 1457, has actually such a cut-off slip fastened to the beginning of Genesis—and this scroll was bought from Mr. Shapira in 1877, the very year in which he declares that he obtained the inscribed slips.[177]

II. The columns of these scrolls are bounded on the right and left by vertical lines drawn with a hard point. These lines not only extend from the top to the bottom of the written portion, but reach to the very end of the leather, right across the upper and lower margins. Now, the Shapira fragments exhibit these lines with the dry point, but not as boundaries to the margin, for the writing on them extends on each side beyond the lines, thus confirming the theory that they originally formed the ruled margins of legally written scrolls. What is still more remarkable is the fact that the uninscribed slip already mentioned has also these guiding lines, and that they correspond to the inscribed Shapira fragments.

III. The upper and lower margins are very rough, ragged, and worn in the old scrolls, as will be seen in scroll Oriental, 1456, and Oriental, 1457. Now, many of the Shapira slips are only ragged at the bottom, but straight at the top, thus plainly showing that they have been comparatively recently cut off from the scrolls, since they have not had time to become ragged at the top.

IV. Some of the slips show plainly that they have been covered by a frame which inclosed the writing, and that this frame was filled with chemical agents. The result of this is to be seen in the fact that, while the inscribed part has thereby been rendered perfectly black and shiny, the part of the leather covered by a frame is of a different and fresher colour, and exhibits the shape of the frame.

As to the internal evidence, it will be seen from the following analysis of the documents that there were no less than four or five different persons engaged in the production of the forgery, and that the compiler of the Hebrew text was a Polish, Russian, or German Jew, or one who had learned Hebrew in the North of Europe.

I. Taking for granted that because the canonical text already contains two recensions of the Decalogue, no insurmountable objection would be raised against a third recension, provided it exhibited the Biblical precepts, the forger manifestly made the Ten Commandments the groundwork of his text. Accordingly, he not only modelled the Decalogue after the pattern of

---

[177] This is the piece on which Chanan Tigay based his conclusion. See Tigay, *The Lost Book of Moses,* 319. It should be noted that Ginsburg said, "This scroll was bought from Mr. Shapira in 1877, the very year in which he declares that he obtained the inscribed slips." All of our accounts say that Shapira obtained the inscribed slips in 1878, not in 1877 as Ginsburg claimed.

Leviticus xviii and xix, but derived his additions from those chapters. Thus the refrain 'I am God thy God,' which he inserted ten times, is simply a variation of the longer refrain 'I am the Lord your God,' which occurs exactly ten times at the end of ten precepts or groups of precepts in Leviticus (xviii, 2, 4, 30; xix, 2, 3, 4, 10, 25, 31, 34). Again, what is here the Seventh Commandment is made up of Leviticus xix, 12, while the additional Tenth Commandment is simply Leviticus xix, 17.

II. Though Deuteronomy xxvii, 11–14 orders that the representatives of the twelve tribes are to place themselves on Mount Gerizim and Mount Ebal, in order to recite the blessings and the curses for the observance and the transgression of certain precepts, yet the maledictions only are given (verses 15–26). This manifestly suggested to the forger the idea of supplying the benedictions. In accordance with his plan, therefore, he not only filled up the gap with ten beatitudes, but made these ten benedictions harmonise with his version of the Ten Commandments.

III. Equally manifest is his design in altering the maledictions contained in the canonical text of Deuteronomy xxvii, 15–26. The additions, omissions, and insertions in the Shapira slips are palpably so framed as to yield ten maledictions to range the Ten Commandments according to the forger's version of them.

To impart to the document the appearance of antiquity, the forger not only imitated closely the archaic writing of the inscription on the Moabite Stone, but adopted the expressions which are to be found on this lapidary document.[178] Thus, for instance, in the Decalogue, which I have already shown, forms the central point of the forged text, the forger not only separated the words, but put a full stop after every expression, exactly as it is on the Moabite Stone. The only exceptions being in the particles *eth,* which is the sign of the accusative, and *lo,* which is the negative. That the forger used the Moabite Inscription as a model is, moreover, to be seen from the following facts. He exchanged the word rendered "before time" in the Authorised Version (Deut. ii, 12) for the word *meolam*—"from of old," because it occurs in this ancient inscription. Again, in describing the Moabite territory, the forger mentions Moab, Aroer, Jahaz, and the Arnon, because these four names are to be found on the Moabite Stone; but he omits Paran, Tophel, Laban, Hazeroth, and Dizahab (which occur in Deut. i, 1) simply because they are not to be found in the Moabite Inscription.

V. My reason for concluding that the compiler was a Jew from the North of Europe is that certain errors in spelling which occur in this document can only be accounted for on this hypothesis. Thus the Jews in Poland, Russia, and Germany pronounce the undagesched *caph* and the guttural letter *cheth* alike. Hence, when the compiler of the text dictated to

---

[178] Engraved or inscribed in stone.

the scribe the word *chebel,* the latter spelled it *kebel,* with *caph;* and *vice versâ,* when the compiler told him to write the expression which denotes "of their drink-offerings," and which is written with a *caph,* the copyist spelled it with *cheth.* In the North of Europe, moreover, the Jews pronounce alike the letters *teth* and *tau.* This accounts for the otherwise inexplicable spelling in this document of the word rendered "frontlets" in our Authorised Version.

VI. The compiler of the text, who was a tolerable adept in writing Hebrew, could not have been familiar with the Phoenician characters exhibited in these slips, or he would assuredly have read over the transcript and have detected those errors. He would especially have noticed the transposition of the two letters in the predicate applied to God, which, instead of saying He was "angry," declares that He "committed adultery."

From the facts that the slips exhibit two distinct hand-writings, I conclude that there were two scribes employed in copying them. These, with the compiler of the Hebrew text and the chemist who manipulated the slips, account for my remark that there were four or five persons engaged in the forgery.

CHRISTIAN D. GINSBURG

On Thursday, 23 August, a writer from the *Echo* expressed the views of many who felt that the question of the scroll's authenticity had not been given a fair trial: "Whatever the final verdict—by no means pronounced as yet—upon the Shapira Manuscript may be, one point is left in no uncertainty at all. From the moment that the discoveries—so-called—were declared to the world there was an eagerness in many quarters, quite inconsistent with the true spirit of criticism or scholarship, to stigmatize them as forgeries." The writer went on to give examples of an impatient revolt against discoveries, "that may, or may not, be disagreeable to the egotism of the learned world."

Ginsburg's conclusions would not reach the public until *The Times* published them on Monday, 27 August 1883, but Shapira read them ahead of their appearance in the papers. With the wind knocked out of him from the public accusations by Conder and Clermont-Ganneau on Tuesday, the news of Ginsburg's rejection on Wednesday felt like a fatal blow to Shapira. From his hotel room he wrote the following to Ginsburg on Thursday, 23 August: "Dear Dr. Ginsburg! You have made a fool of me by publishing and exhibiting things that you believe them to be false. I do not think I shall be able to survive this shame, although I am yet not convince[d] that the MS is a forgery unless M. Ganneau did it. I will leave London in a day or two for Berlin. Yours truly, M.W. Shapira."[179]

Nevertheless, despite Shapira's desperate tone, he was not giving up. It seems that he intended to express in the strongest terms his displeasure with Ginsburg and his utter disbelief at what he viewed as a betrayal. In the upper left-hand

---

[179] This letter from Moses Shapira to Dr. Ginsburg, dated 23 Aug. 1883, is contained in British Library *Add. MS. 41294.*

corner of this note, one can make out a few grammatical points, penned by Shapira. Ginsburg had made a fool of him, but the week was not yet over. Even as Shapira was shocked by the threefold rejection of the scroll, so was the public.

Since the press first published reports about the Moabite manuscript fragments on 3 August, nearly three weeks had gone by with no indication from Dr. Ginsburg that this newfound Deuteronomy was anything other than a faithful ancient witness. Newspapers worldwide had chronicled the news from the British Museum's manuscript department, and the public had assumed that the leather strips were genuine. The incredulous reports by Conder and Clermont-Ganneau that appeared in Tuesday's paper had taken nearly everyone by surprise. Some even suspected an underlying prejudice, particularly on the part of the fraud-finding Frenchman. It would be several days before they found out that Ginsburg shared Clermont-Ganneau's negative appraisal.

On Monday, 27 August, the long-awaited and much anticipated report from Dr. Ginsburg appeared in *The Times*. In addition to Ginsburg's report to Bond, the editor wrote, "We publish this morning Dr. Ginsburg's report on the Shapira Manuscript. It is to the effect we anticipated from the first. The manuscript is pronounced to be beyond all question a forgery." The paper also included a promise from Ginsburg for "another and fuller report on the linguistic features of the slips he has been engaged in examining." And then, adding insult to injury, the public was made aware of Shapira's note to Ginsburg, which had apparently been leaked, saying that he may not survive this shame. The writer concluded his article with this observation:

> He is so disappointed with the results of his bargain that he threatens to commit suicide. This, we venture to think, he will not do. He has survived the Moabite pottery fraud, and he will probably survive this new one. His wise course will be to return to Jerusalem, to follow up the fraud, and to endeavor to trace it to its origin. The story in its entirety will be so strange that it will be received with a welcome which will go far to make up to him for his present disappointment. If he has no story to tell, we can only profess ourselves sorry for him; consolation we have none to offer.

However, Shapira would never return to Jerusalem.

7

The Greater Sin

Rosette and Maria grew concerned after several days of silence from London. Shapira's last letter said he expected to sell the manuscript soon, but then the communication stopped. Rosette tried to remain optimistic in her attempts to explain her husband's sudden silence. She told Maria, "He's certain to send us a telegram. From what he said in his last letter, the MS. was to be offered for sale just about now, and you may depend upon it, he is telegraphing the result, that we may hear it as quickly as possible."[180] But days went by with no communication by telegram or letter, and though they hoped for the best, worry soon occupied their every thought. When word finally came from London, it was not the good news they had hoped to hear.

The report of Clermont-Ganneau's disputation of the scroll's authenticity arrived in Jerusalem. According to rumors, the Frenchman's uncompromising declaration of forgery had led to its removal from the manuscript department display "where it had been guarded by detectives."[181] The Holy City, which just a week earlier was so willing to congratulate the Shapiras on their successes, seemed now to be just as willing to look away as the shopkeeper's wife and daughter made their way through the narrow alleyways. With each day that passed, Rosette and Maria became more troubled by the stream of reports about scholars who had declared the fragments a forgery, and the lack of any word from Moses only heightened their distress. Adding to the worry was news out of Germany that the school fees of the elder Shapira daughter, Augusta, had gone unpaid, and all the negative reports about the scroll and its owner had caused her fiancée's family to treat her differently. Without the prospects of the scroll's anticipated sale—and a growing stigma attached to the Shapira name—it seemed unlikely that the engagement would endure.

Dr. Schroeder, who had so strongly expressed his belief in the unquestionable authenticity of the manuscript, feared that the negative press might cost him his position at the university. He began to "assure everyone that from the first he had had misgivings." Schroeder penned a harsh letter to Mrs. Shapira, going on record that he "had never put much faith in the so-called Deuteronomy." He continued,

---

[180] Harry, *The Little Daughter of Jerusalem,* 267.
[181] Ibid., 272. The 27 August 1883 edition of *The Leeds Mercury* included the following notice: "Meanwhile the manuscript which has occasioned so much stir in the learned world has been removed from the British Museum, and is no longer in the care of the British government."

"You will understand that if he cannot disprove all the accusations brought against him, we cannot possibly receive [Augusta] into our family, with its irreproachable record."[182] Rosette knew that Schroeder had believed in the genuineness of the manuscript, but his denial at this point was not what was on her mind. Her concern was for Augusta and Maria, and of course for Moses. Why did he not write? All she could do was hope and pray.

Shapira left London soon after Ginsburg revealed his opinion about the scroll. On 23 August he had mentioned in his note to Ginsburg that in a day or two he would be leaving for Berlin. It is most likely that he left London before Ginsburg's verdict was published in *The Times* on Monday, 27 August. One can only assume that he went to Berlin shortly after writing to Ginsburg, just as he said. Augusta was there, enrolled in a boarding school and desperately in need of funds. We simply can't say for sure. What we do know is that Ginsburg's report on his assessment of the scroll was not the end of bad news for Shapira and his scroll.

On Tuesday, 28 August, *The Times* published news out of Berlin reporting that the Germans had supposedly known all along that Shapira's manuscript fragments were forgeries. Everyone reading this news had one burning question. If the Germans had decided against the authenticity of the manuscript on 10 July, why were they only now sharing this news? It wasn't like the examination of Shapira's manuscript at the British Museum was being done in a vacuum. People began to suspect that something was amiss. A publication of the Palestine Exploration Fund later said this: "It only has to be added that it is now said that the German Professors in Berlin to whom Shapira showed the skins, immediately discovered that the writing was a forgery. That may be so, but no one thought fit to publish his opinion until there was no longer any doubt on the subject existing among English scholars."[183] The meeting with the scholars in Berlin had taken place on 10 July in the home of Richard Lepsius, head of the Royal Library. The tardy report, as told by a writer for *The Times,* said:

> [Lepsius] at once convened a committee of the most learned of his colleagues to examine into their [the fragments'] nature and value…. The committee met at the house of its convener, Professor Lepsius, on the 10th July last; while Mr. Shapira, of Jerusalem, was waiting in expectant trepidation in an adjoining room, spent exactly one hour and a half in a close and critical investigation into the character of the goatskin wares. At the end of the sitting they unanimously pronounced the alleged codex to be a clever and impudent forgery. There was some thought of calling in a chemist to look at the matter from his particular point of view; but so satisfied were the committee with the general internal evidence against the presumption of the

---

[182] Harry, *The Little Daughter of Jerusalem,* 272–273.
[183] "The Shapira Manuscripts," *Palestine Exploration Fund Quarterly Statement* (Oct. 1883), 206.

antiquity of more than 2000 years claimed for the strips, that they deemed it unnecessary to call for further proof.[184]

But truth be told, they didn't bother to let Shapira in on their little secret. No one informed him that in an hour and a half they unanimously determined his leather fragments to be a "clever and impudent forgery," not even Adolf Erman, who was in the room and was a supposed ally to Shapira's cause. As Erman admitted in his letter to Meyer, "I feel very lacking in courage ... Shapira visited me when it was all over, I did what had to be done under these circumstances and advised him to keep [the manuscript] until the publication [of Guthe] was out and the question had been resolved."[185] Furthermore the British wondered if rumors were true that the Germans offered to buy it. Why would they have offered to buy the manuscript if they were "so satisfied" it was a forgery?

The Times correspondent in Berlin wanted to confirm the rumors that the Germans had made an offer to purchase the fragments, "notwithstanding their verdicts," but that the price offered was not acceptable to Shapira.[186] The German scholars admitted that they had indeed put forward a proposal, but according to them, this was so it could serve as "an example of what could really be in the way of literary fabrication."[187] As to why they didn't inform the British scholars that they had deemed the scroll to be a "clever and impudent forgery," Neubauer reported to *The Athenæum* that it was because they were on vacation.[188] Hermann Strack would later suggest a reason for silence on the part of the Germans: "Nothing of this was then made public, because no one in Berlin for a moment supposed that the codex in question would be the object of further discussion."[189] One lone scholar, Franz Delitzsch, claimed that when the manuscript reached London he shared his assessment with "some English friends," informing them that he had already read it several years earlier. But it remained unclear who those friends were.[190] If the message reached any of his English friends, they elected to keep the matter secret or disregard the warning. No one ever mentioned hearing anything whatsoever from anyone in Germany regarding the authenticity of the scroll. It is also interesting to note that none of those who offered excuses for the silence on the part of the German scholars were in the meeting! Moses Wilhelm Shapira had presented his leather strips to the best scholars in Germany and England. They had all come to the same conclusion.

---

[184] *The Times*, 28 August 1883.

[185] Letter from to Adolf Erman to Eduard Meyer, 10 July 1883, "Der Briefwechsel zwischen Eduard Meyer und Adolf Erman (188–930)," Unter Mitwirkung von Yasser Sabek und Sascha Winkelmann bearbeitet von G. Audring Vorbemerkung. https://www.geschichte.hu-berlin.de/de/bereiche-und-lehrstuehle/alte-geschichte/forschung/briefe-meyer.erman.

[186] Mansoor, "The Case of Shapira's Dead Sea (Deuteronomy) Scrolls of 1883," *Transactions of the Wisconsin Academy of Sciences, Arts, and* Letters (1958), 18–25, 193 n 49.

[187] *The Times*, 28 August 1883.

[188] A. Neubauer, "The Shapira MSS." *The Athenæum*, no. 2915, 8 September 1883, 306.

[189] *The Times*, 4 September 1883, letter from Dr. Hermann L. Strack dated 31 August 1883.

[190] Franz Delitzsch, "Schapira's Pseudo-Deuteronomium," no. 36 (7 Sept 1883), 846.

As the scholarly world lined up to declare their condemnation of Shapira's manuscript, each claiming he knew it was forged all along, Shapira arrived in Amsterdam. On Tuesday, 28 August, he wrote a lengthy letter to Edward Augustus Bond, chief librarian for the British Museum, countering many of the points Ginsburg had proffered as evidence of forgery. His previous note to Ginsburg, as well as this note to Bond, revealed Shapira's state of mind. Despite the growing number of opinions against the authenticity of the manuscript, he remained convinced. He would do his best to convince someone of the same.

Shapira began, "You will excuse my troubling you again with my bad English, but the thing seems to me to be of such big importance that I chose to write again begging you to let the MS be examined by several scholars and archaeologists of different schools or doctrines. The sin of believing in a false document is not much greater than disbelieving the truth. The tendency of showing great scholarship by detecting a forgery is rather great in our age." Shapira's plea for another look at the manuscript indicates that he suspected a bias on the part of Ginsburg. He also rightly pointed out that detecting forgeries was a method whereby one might advance his career.

Shapira then directly countered the arguments of Ginsburg. First on the list was Ginsburg's theory that the forger, or part of Ginsburg's hypothetical team of forgers, was a Polish Jew. The specificity of Ginsburg's theory clearly intended to narrow the search for the guilty party. What Polish Jew might Ginsburg have had in mind as the forger? Strangely, Ginsburg himself was a Polish Jew, born in Warsaw! But this was no confession of forgery by Ginsburg.

Shapira provided several paragraphs intended to show the absurdity of the Polish Jew theory. Ginsburg's point was that certain misspellings in the manuscript were due to mispronunciations by one member of the forgery team dictating to the scribe and the scribe recording what he heard. Shapira composed a lengthy refutation, arguing that this was an impossibility and that even a "schoolboy" would not make such confusions in writing.

An example of one of Ginsburg's arguments was, "In the north of Europe, moreover, the Jews pronounce alike the letters *teth* and *tau*. This accounts for the otherwise inexplicable spelling in this document of the word rendered 'frontlets' in our Authorized Version." Shapira countered this in several ways. First, this word is repeated in prayer by religious Jews three times daily. Not even an "ignorant Jew if he only knew to read a little Hebrew would have mistaken and miswritten that word." He then made the point that even though the word appears three times in the Bible (Exod 13:16; Deut 6:8; 11:18), no one even knows what it means. He said that the translation of "frontlets," was "by imagination." Shapira argued that this word, as it appears in the Bible, may not even be of Hebrew origin. Additionally, the word in question is difficult to read in the manuscript, a point that Ginsburg and Guthe both noted in their transcriptions. Finally, Shapira asked why a Polish Jew and the forgery team would only make the *teth* and *tau* mistake in a single word and not throughout the entire scroll.

Shapira demonstrated an erudite knowledge of Hebrew as he countered other points of Ginsburg's statement.[191] At the end of the letter he said, "I am not convinced that the manuscripts are false. Nevertheless, I do not wish to sell it even if the buyer should take the risk for himself (I have such offers), unless to authorities."[192] Clearly, this letter shows that Shapira still believed in the genuineness of his manuscript. It was no longer about the money. He had tried the path that might lead to what Meyer had called "a colossal sum," but now he wanted only to save his good name.

As August of 1883 gave way to September, the scroll was still in the news. Dr. Ginsburg had achieved a celebrity status that his regular work never would have afforded him. There was talk of a forthcoming work by Ginsburg, a "much more elaborate document than the popular report which was published in the daily papers, and will deal with the linguistic problem presented by this ingenious forgery."[193] As confirmation of Shapira's words, and like Clermont-Ganneau, Ginsburg's scholarship was deemed greater for having detected a forgery. Ginsburg wrote to his daughter Ethel on 3 September:

> My darling Ethel … The excitement about the ms. has by no means ceased. You will probably have heard that last Saturday, the *Spectator,* the *Saturday Review* & other periodicals had still articles on the subject. I do not think that the month which I spent on the ms. is time thrown away though it is a forgery and though the deciphering of it has nearly blinded me. Though I was sure the first week of my examination that it was a forgery yet the extraordinary cleverness and skill displayed in the production of it as well as the fact that a company were engaged in it made it absolutely necessary thoroughly to make it out, to translate it and to publish it before I gave the verdict and before publishing the report. By so doing I made it impossible for this clever band of rogues to practice any more impositions. Mr. Shapira has disappeared and the ms. is still here. I do wish you could come up to town to see it for it is so wonderfully clever. If I could afford it, I would give £200 for it.[194] There is such a demand for my report that the British Museum have decided to reprint it with the original and my translation.[195]

A controversy ensued over who discovered the forgery. Clermont-Ganneau's report had hit the papers before Dr. Ginsburg revealed his verdict. In his letter to his daughter he said that he was sure it was a forgery in the first week, but this seems unlikely since the prime minister's visit was into the third week of his

---

[191] Many of these points deserve careful consideration but are of such a technical nature that they should be discussed in a different format. This writer intends to address these points more fully in a series of articles.

[192] Letter from Shapira to Bond, dated 28 Aug. 1883, from Amsterdam, is contained in British Library *Add. MS. 41294.*

[193] "Literary Gossip," *The Athenæum,* no 2914, 1 Sept 1883, 275.

[194] According to some currency conversion models, this would be nearly $24,000 in 2021! It is astonishing that Ginsburg would pay that much money for a manuscript that he had declared a forgery.

[195] British Library *Add. MS. 57486.*

PUNCH'S FANCY PORTRAITS.—NO. 152.

MR. SHARP-EYE-RA.

SHOWING, IN VERY FANCIFUL PORTRAITURE, HOW DETECTIVE GINSBURG
ACTUALLY DID MR. SHARP-EYE-RA OUT OF HIS SKIN.

Figure 11

evaluation and apparently he said nothing to the effect at that time. Clermont-Ganneau had not made any friends with the press or the public when he arrived on the scene and quickly declared the scroll a fraud. On Monday, 27 August, *The Daily News* "commented caustically on the Frenchman 'whose special function it is to discredit Mr. Shapira's antiquities.'"[196] A few days after Ginsburg wrote to his daughter, *The Manchester Guardian* shared the sentiment of many regarding Clermont-Ganneau, saying that he had "shown the hand of the critic a little too soon for British notions of fair play."[197] It would remain unclear to the public if one of the two had influenced the other, but in the end, Ginsburg was recognized as the one who caught Shapira. The *London Charivari,* or *Punch,* a British magazine for satire and humor, published a caricature showing a hook-nosed Shapira grasping his scroll in one hand and Dr. Ginsburg smiling and gripping his other arm, finger dripping with ink. The irony is that both men were of European Jewish descent, but Shapira was depicted according to racial, even anti-Semitic, stereotypes.[198]

---

[196] *The Daily News,* 27 August 1883.

[197] *The Manchester Guardian,* 6 September 1883.

[198] One wonders how much anti-Semitism played into the treatment of Shapira in the nineteenth century. We find in the accounts of the time at least some possible indication of this. Besant, for example, recalling Shapira's first visit to the offices of the PEF, said, "Some years later a certain Shapira, a Polish Jew converted to Christianity but not to good works." See Besant, *Autobiography,* 161. Yoram Sabo shows that the attacks against the character of Shapira have not been restricted to non-Jews, observing that in the Moabitica affair "it should be noted that everyone who referred to Shapira as a forger was Jewish (the nineteenth-century *Jewish Press,* Herschel Shanks, *The Hebrew Encyclopedia,* Haim Be'Er, Yaakov Meshorer, and others) while those who abstained from doing so, then and now, were not Jewish (Clermont-Ganneau, Schlottmann, Allegro, Conder, and others). Is the fact that Shapira was an apostate what influenced this distinction?" See Sabo, "Between Apostate and Forger," 23.

FACSIMILE OF THE SHAPIRA MS.

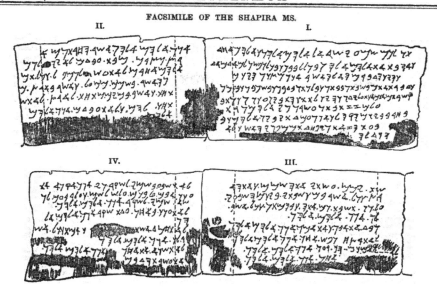

Figure 12–Reproduction of a portion of the Shapira manuscript
as it appeared in The Athenæum.

The papers continued to run stories about Shapira's suddenly discredited manuscript. On 8 September 1883, *The Athenæum* published a facsimile of four columns of text.[199] The facsimile was based on the work of William St. Chad Boscawen. Commenting on the drawing of the scroll pieces, Ginsburg expressed his indebtedness to a Miss Tennant and Mr. Boscawen, "whose large practice in copying Assyrian inscriptions specially qualifies him for such delicate work. The facsimile was made under my strict superintendence, and I can therefore vouch for its accuracy."

On 31 August 1883, Hermann Guthe's book was published in Leipzig, but notice of its publication would not reach the press in England until news of it appeared in the 8 September edition of *The Academy,* No. 592, in an article titled "The Shapira MSS. of Deuteronomy." His verdict was also that the manuscript was forged, but not based on the same criteria as Ginsburg and Clermont-Ganneau. After briefly covering the contents of the work, the report says, "Herr Guthe's attention does not seem to have been turned to the decisive evidence first disclosed by M. Clermont-Ganneau—that the pieces of sheepskin have evidently been cut off a modern synagogue roll. His condemnation of the forgery is based upon internal evidence … In his preface he states that his conclusions have received the general approval of Prof. Nöldeke, of Strassburg, and Prof. Kautzsch, of Tübingen."

---

[199] The column of text was from the fragment designated as E among the "numbered" strips and contained the Shema and the Ten Words. See, "Facsimile of the Shapira MS.," *The Athenæum*, no. 2915, 8 September 1883, 305.

On 1 September, Eduard Meyer wrote to Georg Ebers and said, "Guthe's brochure was also published yesterday; it should have come out eight days earlier before Neubauer's and Ganneau's comments were published. The latter is absolutely right about the appearance of the handwriting; he thinks the leather strips are the lower pieces of a Torah scroll."

Guthe concluded his publication with the following comments:

> The examination of the text has led to the certain realization that the manuscript is a forgery.... It is not the artistry of a gifted craftsman to which we must, as must others attribute this forgery. Its originator is at least a dilettante in the area of Old Testament science, scarcely a representative thereof by profession—his work must, then, in any case count as a witness of arguably good facilities.... He shows, namely, in the last part of his work, a quite good handling of Hebrew expression, has language understanding, as the application of interpuncts in the Decalogue proves, has certain epigraphical knowledge, is familiar with multiple results of Pentateuch criticism, was able to giftedly recognize doublets in our Bible text, but betrays, in his critical operations, the complete lack of a firm method.[200]

Despite his decision against the authenticity of the manuscript, Guthe expressed uncertainty on several points because there was simply nothing with which to compare a manuscript that "pretends" to be this old.

One is left to wonder what happened. Did Guthe succumb to pressure from senior scholars in Berlin. Was he, like Schroeder, concerned that coming out favorably towards the authenticity of a manuscript, against the view of his older colleagues, might jeopardize his standing in the academic community? And what about Meyer? What did he mean when he said to Ebers of Clermont-Ganneau's theory, that he "is absolutely right about the appearance of the handwriting?"[201] Did he maintain his belief in the genuineness of the manuscript? In the letter that Erman sent him on the day that the Berlin scholars had declared the manuscript a forgery, Erman had advised Meyer, "In any case, publish, but enclose yourself in terms of authenticity." Was Erman suggesting to Meyer and Guthe how they should summarize their findings? In Meyer's reply to Erman, he said, "Thank you very much for your letter. You already know from Guthe that we do not see the matter any differently than you and that we will be careful not to go too fiery."

Perhaps Guthe and Meyer realized that if you can't beat them, it might be best to join them. Meyer also said, though, that he remained convinced of the manuscript's authenticity. It is interesting that Meyer's name does not appear on the booklet. One wonders why. He is obviously mentioned within, but few clues of their excitement over the manuscript made it into print. Yoram Sabo draws attention to Meyer, pointing out that "Meyer's letters are the only nineteenth-

---

[200] Guthe, *Fragments of a Leather Manuscript,* 38.

[201] Letter from Eduard Meyer to Georg Ebers, 1 September 1883, "Der Briefwechsel zwischen Georg Ebers und Eduard Meyer (187–898)," Vorbemerkung von G. Audring. https://www.geschichte.hu-berlin.de/de/bereiche-und-lehrstuehle/alte-geschichte/forschung/briefe-meyer/ebers.

century testimony from anyone who has studied the Shapira scrolls in depth, which supports the theory that they are not false." [202]

Aside from Meyer, there undoubtedly were others who continued to believe that the manuscript was authentic, but Shapira had rightly said that "the tendency of showing great scholarship by detecting a forgery is rather great in our age." Scholars had come forward from every corner to declare that they had known all along the scroll was a fraud. This would continue for some time. Almost everyone wanted to go on record as having perceived the falsity of Shapira's leather strips from the start. One critic after another made his claim, and many assumed that Moses Shapira was the ingenious creator.

On 28 August, Shapira had written a twelve-page letter to Bond arguing for the authenticity of his manuscript and requesting of Bond to have the manuscript examined by other scholars. One question that has evaded an answer is why was Shapira in Amsterdam?

---

[202] Yoram Sabo, *The Scroll Merchant, In Search of Moses Wilhelm Shapira's Lost Jewish Treasure* (Israel: Hakibbutz Hameuchad Publishing House Ltd. 2018), (Hebrew), 93. Yoram Sabo is one the foremost authorities on Shapira, a self-proclaimed Shapiramaniac. He has been studying the Shapira affair for more than four decades. He was first introduced to the Shapira affair in 1979 through the book by John Marco Allegro. Since that time, he has been on a quest to understand the story and help others do the same. Besides his book (Hebrew only), he has written articles, and produced and directed a film on Shapira, *Shapira and I: Ruth Films*, 2014. On 15 February 2020, the author and Dr. James D. Tabor met with Yoram Sabo in his home in Israel. He was very helpful and generous. We have maintained a cordial relationship with Yoram and look forward to meeting with him on future trips to Israel.

ل

The Venice of the North

Shapira was not the only visitor to Amsterdam at that time—far from it. The Netherlands was hosting the International Colonial and Export Exhibition, a sort of world's fair, and people from around the world converged on the Venice of the North.[203] Improved transportation was making the world smaller, and between the opening day of the Expo on 1 May and the end of October 1883, when the event ended, an estimated 1.5 million people had explored the extensive exhibits.

It was a glory to behold. Buildings were erected to house the exhibits of many nations. The exhibits showcased not only the "great Dutch tradition of trade … and the magnificent public works" of Amsterdam, but also many of the unique cultures of the world. There were galleries for the arts, examples of the latest "modern" machines, including a steam crane, a telephone, and a centrifugal pump, along with restaurants, beer halls, and bazaars from dozens of nations near and far. The fairgrounds, "a mixture of education and amusement," were set up behind the National Gallery and covered 220,000 square meters.[204] The cost of staging this event was enormous, but in the end, wealthy investors contributed much of the upfront money, the government providing funds as well. In addition to the sheer amusement of the exhibits, there were also intellectual offerings, some of which appealed to those interested in religion and religious customs.

From his hotel in Amsterdam, on 28 August Shapira wrote his lengthy letter to Bond begging him to "let the manuscript be examined by several scholars and archaeologists of different schools and doctrines." But Shapira was not holding his breath. Rather than depend on Bond, or anyone else for that matter, to find several other scholars to examine the manuscript, he would seek them out himself. The International Colonial and Export Exhibition was not the only significant event taking place in the Netherlands. In Leiden, just thirty-five kilometers southeast of Amsterdam, the single greatest assemblage of orientalists would soon arrive for the Sixth International Congress of Orientalists, scheduled for 10–15 September.

---

[203] For information on the International Colonial and Export Exhibition held in Amsterdam from 1 May to 31 October 1883, see Molendijk, Arie L., "Religion at the 1883 Colonial and Export Trade Exhibition in Amsterdam." *Zeitschrift für Neuere Theologiegeschichte / Journal for the History of Modern Theology* 11.2 (2004), 215–245.

[204] About fifty-four acres. Molendijk, "Religion at the 1883 Colonial and Export Trade Expedition," 221.

The first Congress of Orientalists was held in Paris in 1873, and since its inception was considered an assembly of the greatest minds in the field. At the close of the fifth congress in Berlin on 17 September 1881, it had been decided to hold the next congress in Leiden in 1884. The date, however, was changed in view of the International Colonial and Export Exhibition to be hosted in Amsterdam in 1883. With government approval and the consent of the fifth congress, the meeting was moved to 10–15 September 1883 to coincide with the Expo. What better time for the Netherlands to host this event? Plans were made for the participants of the Congress of Orientalists to visit the Colonial Exhibition and to be received by the Amsterdam municipal authorities.[205]

On 10 September 1883, the Congress of Orientalists held its opening ceremony. "The Congress was chaired by the Old Testament scholar Abraham Kuenen."[206] The preface of the published proceedings mentioned that use was made of "some articles on the Congress, especially those of M. Clermont-Ganneau in the official journal."[207] The French scholar also "discussed Semitic epigraphy from the comparative point of view" at the conference.[208] Others, associated with the Shapira affair were in attendance, including, Professor Schlottmann, Dr. C. Landberg, and Professor Sayce. Christian D. Ginsburg's name is listed as a member, and Professor Eberhard Schrader, who viewed Shapira's manuscript in the home of Lepsius, was President of the Semitic section of the Congress.[209]

We do not know if from the time Moses Shapira left Jerusalem in May he had planned to be in the Netherlands for this event, but perhaps this highly publicized gathering was what attracted him to Amsterdam. Either way, one can hardly imagine Shapira not sitting in on some of the lectures in Leiden. Among the attendees he was likely to find some unbiased scholars who would consider the merits of his Phoenician fragments. One can also be certain that the recent news out of London, only a month earlier, was a frequent topic of conversation among the scholars as they socialized in the evenings at the bars, beer halls, and restaurants.

Shapira had taken several valuable manuscripts to Amsterdam, among them "a Yemenite prayer book, a fifteenth-century commentary on the Book of Exodus, a fourteenth-century medical text complete with botanical lexicon, and the book of Genesis with Arabic translation."[210] He also would have had with him two columns of the Moabite scroll on a single strip of leather, the piece that was pulled

---

[205] M. J. de Goeje, ed., *Actes du Sixième Congrès International des Orientalistes ten en, 1883 à Leide, Part I: Compte-Rendu des Séances*, Leide (Brill) 1884–1885, vol. I, 44, 212–218.

[206] Molendijk, "Religion at the 1883 Colonial and Export Trade Expedition," 238–241.

[207] Ibid.

[208] "The Oriental Congress at Leyden," *The Athenæum*, no. 2917, 22 Sept. 1883, 369.

[209] On Schrader, see, "The Oriental Congress at Leyden," *The Athenæum*, no. 2916, 15 Sept. 1883, 340. For Schlottmann, Landberg, and Sayce see "The Oriental Congress at Leyden," *The Athenæum*, no. 2917, 22 Sept. 1883, 369.

[210] Tigay, *The Lost Book of Moses,* 304.

after Guthe and Meyer had assessed the scroll but before Ginsburg made his examination.[211] Fifteen leather strips remained at the British Museum.

It is safe to assume that Shapira spent some of his time in Amsterdam exploring the Expo exhibits. There, among the crowds, he would have been able to escape the spotlight and scrutiny of the "scoffing atheists" who had refused to acknowledge the authenticity of his manuscript.[212] We know for certain that Shapira was still selling manuscripts to the British Museum during his stay in Amsterdam. Among the museum's archives we have a record of sale detailed by Dr. Charles Rieu, dated 15 October 1883. It says, "Dr. Rieu has the honor of reporting to the trustees that the following four Hebrew MSS. have been offered by Mr. Shapira for £25.00.[213] The above manuscripts have been selected as the most valuable of the set of 20 offered by Mr. Shapira and the price demanded, being moderate, Dr. Rieu begs to recommend this purchase."[214]

By the beginning of November, the International Colonial and Export Exhibition had ended, but the attacks on the genuineness of Shapira's manuscript persisted. In a publication covering a meeting of the Society of Biblical Archaeology in November 1883, the following report appears:

> The Rev. A Lowy, at the request of the President, made some remarks on the well-known forgeries called the Shapira MS. He stated that in the month of August when he saw a reproduction in *The Athenæum* of some portions of the alleged ancient text, he had no hesitation in mentioning before a large audience that a most daring fraud had been committed by some unscrupulous speculators. The forger had eliminated from the text nearly all the *vavs* and *yods* which serve as *matres lectionis,* in order to bring his work in harmony with the ancient Phoenician inscriptions.[215] But he had forgotten to be consistent. For example, Sihon was written with a *yod* after the *samekh.* The interpolations were suggested by the Samaritan system of garbling the text of the Pentateuch. The innovations introduced by the forger were ridiculous.[216]

---

[211] Guthe reported, "The manuscript consists of sixteen leather strips." See Guthe, *Fragments of a Leather Manuscript,* 3. Thereafter, everyone mentions only fifteen.

[212] On "scoffing atheists" see Reiner, "C. D. Ginsburg and the Shapira Affair," 126.

[213] According to some currency conversion models, this amount is estimated to be equivalent to nearly $3,000 in 2021.

[214] In Yoram Sabo's film *Shapira & I,* Yoram, Andrea Stern (film producer, London) and Stephanie Clark (archivist at the British Museum) read these entries. Also covered in Tigay, *The Lost Book of Moses,* 304–305.

[215] This is a technical point. The writer means to suggest that the person who wrote the scroll sometimes spelled words as they would likely appear in an ancient document by eliminating *"vavs* and *yods* which serve as *matres lectionis,"* but he "had forgotten to be consistent." The *matres lectionis* are letters which can serve as so-called vowel letters. Since the use of vowel letters was believed to be a later practice, their presence in an ancient manuscript was not expected, and so in the writer's view their inclusion in the manuscript was evidence of a forger, who, while eliminating most of them to make his forgery appear ancient, had forgotten to do so consistently.

[216] Mansoor, "The Case of Shapira's Dead Sea (Deuteronomy) Scrolls of 1883," 205 n 105.

It did not matter that the good Reverend Lowy had previously declared beyond doubt that the Mesha Stone, accepted by scholars as authentic, was also a forgery![217]

Sometime in November, Shapira moved on from Amsterdam. He went first to Bloemendaal for a short stay and then to Rotterdam where he took up residence in Adler's Guesthouse.

"Toward the end of December, Hermann Guthe issued a public correction, prompted by a review of his work by Professor Kautzsch. The correction stated, Professor Dr. Kautzsch had mentioned in the review of my brochure "Fragments of a Leather Manuscript, etc." in No. 22 of this literary newspaper after my communication (from Schapira's mouth) that Consul Dr. Schroeder in Beirut had also declared the hideous leather strips to be genuine." This is interesting since Guthe's published work, while it did report this claim "from Schapira's mouth," also reported that, "Dr. C. Landberg, who has just arrived here from Syria, heard this judgment from Dr. Schroeder's own mouth and imparted it to me."[218] Guthe continued:

> I take this opportunity to tell you what Consul Dr. Schroeder wrote to me to correct Schapira's statements. "I was granted only a fleeting glimpse of a leather strip by the lamp light on the evening of May 18th in the house of Mr. S. Bergheim in Jerusalem. I doubted its authenticity to a great extent, but I could not justify it for the time being since neither the inspection of the entire manuscript nor a precise examination of the contents of it was allowed to me. When Mr. Schapira asked me whether I thought the manuscript was genuine, I answered: that I could neither answer this question in the affirmative nor in the negative without a longer study of the entire manuscript, but that I could not derive any proof of forgery from the character of the writing alone, i.e., from the outer appearance of the characters." Although not asked to do so, I consider it necessary to bring the above to the public's knowledge and thereby correct Shapira's statements.[219]

This published correction does not address Guthe's claim that Landberg informed him that he had heard Schroeder say that he was inclined to take Shapira's manuscript for authentic. Did Guthe believe that Landberg lied? It was easy to "correct Shapira's statement," since the whole world was against him, but why didn't he correct Landberg's statement while he was at it. The two statements appear on the same page, one after the other, in his work. Perhaps Shapira's daughter was right when she said that Schroeder changed his story to reduce the chance of "losing his post at the University."[220]

---

[217] Ibid.

[218] Guthe, *Fragments of a Leather Manuscript,* 5.

[219] "Berichtigung under Nachtrage," in *Theologische Literaturezeitung*, 8. Jahrgang no. 26 (29.12.1883), col. 621.

[220] Harry, *The Little Daughter of Jerusalem,* 272.

In January of 1884, while Shapira was in Rotterdam, he made another business transaction with the British Museum. This purchase included "a medical work in Arabic and Hebrew, a copy of Genesis and a portion of Numbers with translation in Arabic, translation and comments in Talmudic law."[221] The trustees approved. This is the second known transaction that Shapira made with the museum. He was still conducting business and there were obviously people at the British Museum who knew how to contact him. He was not in hiding and he was not broke. He was selling manuscripts as a correspondent to the British Museum. Who else was he doing business with?

Also in January, the French minister of public instruction dispatched Monsieur Clermont-Ganneau back to London on a "new archaeological mission."[222] There Clermont-Ganneau requested permission to examine the leather strips up close. Bond initially denied the request because the last word from Shapira on 15 August was that he had "expressly refused his consent." As far as Bond was concerned, the ban was still in effect. He did, however, promise to write to Mr. Shapira in the Netherlands and seek his permission for Clermont-Ganneau to examine the strips. Within a few short days, Bond sent a note to Clermont-Ganneau saying, "I am happy to be able to inform you that I have received from Mr. Shapira permission to allow you to examine the manuscript in the presence of a Museum officer."[223] One has to wonder why Shapira would have authorized this inspection. Perhaps he felt that he had nothing to lose and possibly something to gain if the French savant's close inspection convinced him of the genuineness of the leather strips. The next day, the curator of oriental manuscripts at the British Museum, Dr. Rieu, made himself available for the supervised inspection.

Writing about it later, Clermont-Ganneau said, "The Moabite strips were finally in my hands and I was able to examine them at my ease; thanks be to the magnanimity of their brooding owner. I devoted three good sessions to this examination." He then went on to tell of a "rather entertaining little interlude caused by the unexpected intervention of Dr. Ginsburg who, in the grip of a visible agitation, burst into Dr. Rieu's office and disturbed for a few moments my face to face with his dear relics. He felt, it seems, the need to throw one more glance, just as I was granted the favor of a first inspection of them. Fortunately, they succeeded in calming him down and making him understand that he would have plenty of time, my little inspection over, to come back, if he wanted to, to those documents on which he had paled for many weeks."

Clermont-Ganneau then recorded his findings. He commented on the "indefinable smell of rancid oil … of the pieces of leather." He noted the traces of stitching and, in one instance, of a small knot in the thread. He maintained that

---

[221] Sabo, *Shapira & I.* Also in Tigay, *The Lost Book of Moses*, 304–305.
[222] Charles Clermont-Ganneau, *Les Fraudes Archéologiques En Palestine: Suivies De Quelques Monuments Phéniciens Apocryphes* (Paris: Ernest Leroux, 1885), 253–266.
[223] Ibid.

the forger had cut the leather strips, but seemed to backtrack slightly from his view that they were made from "intact rolls," claiming now with a closer inspection that these pieces of leather making up the whole came "from at least three rolls, perhaps four, of different sizes … not from intact rolls … from the debris of incomplete rolls, spare pieces, waste." Previously he claimed that one edge apparently had been cut with a knife since it appeared smoother than the other. But now he observed that in some of the strips the upper, as well as the lower edges were equally smooth. He puzzled over how the strips were labeled but otherwise added no further proofs to support his original theory. In fact, in his published refutation of 18 August he had advised "all the impartial scholars … to whom may be permitted an examination which is denied to me," to conduct four tests, boasting, "Nothing is more easy than to effect the experimental examination which I suggest." Four easy tests, yet five months later, when he was permitted to examine the fragments, he seemingly forgot his own advice. If the experiments he had enumerated were such an easy way to prove the fragments a forgery, Clermont-Ganneau missed an excellent opportunity to do so during those "three good sessions" in Dr. Rieu's office at the British Museum in January of 1884.

Around the end of February, Moses Shapira moved again, renting a room at L. C. Wickers's guesthouse, the Hotel Willemsbrug in the Boompjes near the Maas River wharf. On Sunday, 9 March, the office staff realized that they had not seen Shapira since Friday. Someone checked on him, but the room was locked, and Shapira did not respond when they knocked and called his name. The police were notified, and a short time later Inspector Gerald Putman Cramer arrived to investigate. The entry for 9 March 1884 in the police log, housed in the Rotterdam archives, reports the following: "After it was discovered at the office in the guesthouse of L. C. Wickers at Boompjes at the Hotel Willemsbrug that a lodge guest did not come out of his room the day before yesterday and the door was still closed, Inspector police officer, Gerald Putman Cramer went in to look. It was found that a guest named Shapira, bookdealer and agent of the British Museum robbed himself of his life by gunshot. The corpse was looked at by a medical person before it was brought to the storage known as drinkling."[224]

According to the Rotterdam city archives, on Wednesday, 12 March, two "agents of the municipality appeared before" the authorities stating that "on the 9th of this month, at twelve o'clock, in the building in the Boompjes neighborhood of this city, Wilhelm Shapira died when he was fifty-one, born in Ducchid and living in Stockhausen, a book salesman, there are no other known details except that the deceased was married."[225] Some of the details in this statement are not correct—the age, birthplace, and residence of Shapira are all wrong. Yoram Sabo suggests that Shapira may have provided this information to the hotel staff for

---

[224] The report is from the Daily Report of the Amsterdam police department. *Dagrapporten Gem. Dienst Bur. Witte de Withst. Afd.* 4a 1884. According to Sabo, *The Scroll Merchant*, 192, In the nineteenth century, in Rotterdam, the body of an anonymous drowned person would be brought to the "house of drinkling," so the family of the missing could come and identify the body.
[225] Ibid., 191.

reasons known only to him.[226] Could he have done so to avoid recognition or association with the Shapira of Jerusalem who had been covered in all the papers?

Notices of Shapira's death began to appear in the Dutch papers and then dispatched to newspapers worldwide.[227] The reports offered different and sometimes conflicting details, likely due to unconfirmed accounts provided by unnamed interviewees. The basic story was consistent, however. While in the Netherlands over approximately six months, Shapira had moved several times, beginning in Amsterdam, then Bloemendaal, and finally Rotterdam. He had only been at the Hotel Willemsbrug for a "fortnight." Several accounts described the scene inside the room. The consistent points were that there was a trunk or case inside the room that contained Hebrew and English manuscripts, brochures, letters, and some business cards "bearing the addresses of booksellers and antiquarian agents in London and Jerusalem."[228]

Besides these, and other than discovering the deceased Shapira in the room, speculations and inconsistencies abounded. Was Shapira discovered on the bed or on the floor? Was there a gun in the room? Some speculated about his state of mind, and one of the reports even alleged that the police had recently detained him in neighboring Scheidam where he was suspected of insanity.[229] Another report from the Scheidam paper said that this was wrong, correcting the story by saying that the police had merely questioned and released him. It was apparently a case of mistaken identity.[230]

It did not take long for the chief characters in the Moabite manuscript saga to feel the need to weigh in and thus ensure that they were not accused of having led to this tragic end. Clermont-Ganneau said, "This affair, which began as a comedy, was to end in a tragedy. Bloody endings are not a frequent thing in archaeological discussions. It is however by blood that this one has just ended."[231] Some news outlets also mentioned a letter that Shapira had written shortly before his death. Although we have no information about the contents of the letter, Clermont-Ganneau took a keen interest in it. He said:

> I cannot help but regret that the letter written by Mr. Shapira before his death was not published. We are not even told to whom it was addressed … the addressee of the letter, whose name it is possible to suspect, put it in his pocket. He must have had good reasons for it, but we would like to recognize that by doing so, there is something suspicious about this discretion. People who have been actively involved in this matter must feel

---

[226] Ibid.

[227] For example, *Leidsch Dagblad,* 12 March 1884; *De Tijd,* 13 March 1884; and *The New York Times,* 30 March 1884.

[228] *The New York Times,* 30 March 1884, "Dr. Shapira's Suicide, Dispatch from the Hague to the London Standard."

[229] "Kunst en Letteren," *Nieuwe Rotterdamsch Courant,* 11 Maart 1884.

[230] "Schiedam, 11 Maart 1884," *Schiedamsch Courant,* no. 2914, 11 Maart 1884.

[231] Clermont-Ganneau, *Les Fraudes Archéologiques en Palestine,* 253–266.

a certain sense of responsibility in the face of this dramatic epilogue and should be keen, it seems, to extricate themselves.

In closing, Clermont-Ganneau reported, "[My] conscience does not reproach me for anything." For the Frenchman, "if Mr. Shapira has anyone to blame for his death, they are the many whose gullibility, too late masked by a clumsy turnaround, was the real cause of his downfall … Was this what was said in this mysterious letter which was made to disappear as a promising testimony? I must admit that I would not be surprised." One can only speculate as to what Clermont-Ganneau is insinuating in regard to the "letter" he mentions several times. Perhaps he is referring to a letter found in Shapira's room. Did he leave a note? He seems to be suggesting that the note may have implicated someone. Based on his statements, Clermont-Ganneau seems to have someone in mind. We simply do not know. Most of the sources say that Shapira took his own life, but did he?

While Clermont-Ganneau may have lost little sleep over his acquaintance's death, Shapira's family was crushed. The news made its way around the world. On 31 March 1884, the *Havatzelet* newspaper reported, "The apostate[232] Shapira, a resident of our city and the proprietor of a book shop here, who is known infamously (?) regarding the forgery of Moabite jars, has recently committed suicide during his stay in Rotterdam…. The police broke down the door and came into the room and found Shapira lying dead upon his bed surrounded by a stream of blood, for he had taken his own life and killed himself with the barrel of a rifle."[233] The Shapira family must have found this report particularly distressing. The notice could not have been worse. In just a few short words, the paper referred to him as an "apostate … known infamously regarding the Moabite jars." From then on, his name would be associated with such terms, and his life of achievements and adventures denigrated as heresy and impropriety.

Moses Shapira's daughter Maria recounted the events of the day when news of her father's death reached her house. Three men, including the British consul to Jerusalem and the German banker, approached with black coats and solemn faces. She watched as "each sat down on the edge of his chair, forming a half-circle round her mother."[234] She could not hear what the men were saying, but all of a sudden her mother "gave a piercing cry and all the men closed around her … The Lord will strengthen me to bear this heavy burden," her mother said as the men left the house. She then pulled Maria close and sobbed, "Your father is dead! Your father is dead!"[235]

It would be some time before Rosette would tell her daughter, "Your father put an end to his own life, he committed suicide … he blew out his brains with a

---

[232] The word for "apostate" is a translation for a word used to describe one who converts out of the faith.

[233] Sabo, "Between Apostate and Forger," 24. The translation "rifle" need not be considered a variation of other accounts that mention a gun or revolver. The Hebrew word seemingly can mean "gun" just as easily. The question mark (?) that appears after the word "infamously" is in the original for reasons unknown.

[234] Harry, *The Little Daughter of Jerusalem,* 280.

[235] Ibid., 281.

revolver."[236] It brought even greater sorrow to know that her beloved father had died alone in this way, in Europe, and all because "the people were so wicked and so cruel that they broke his heart." The Shapiras sold nearly everything they owned, including the merchandise in the Old City's best tourist shop, raising just enough money to pay off their creditors. Rosette was able to keep her husband's manuscript collection, which she carefully packed for the journey to Berlin, where the family would seek to begin again.

We may never know some of the details surrounding the tragic death of Moses Wilhelm Shapira. What we do know is that the whole affair took place in the span of a single year. Shapira had reported that it was around Easter of 1883 when he withdrew the leather strips from the Jerusalem bank vault. Easter that year was Sunday, 25 March, or 16 Adar II on the Jewish calendar, which was Shushan Purim. Shapira would be found dead almost a year later on 9 March 1884 or 12 Adar on the Jewish calendar. Interestingly, the Torah reading for the Sabbath of his death was Ki Thissa (Exod 30:11–34:35), which ends with Moses in possession of a second set of stone tablets containing the words of the covenant. Moses Shapira also had presented to the world a second set of those words.

On 23 August, Moses Shapira had written to Dr. Christian David Ginsburg saying that he did not think he would be able to survive the shame. He didn't. Moses Shapira's remains were taken to a burial place in Rotterdam reserved for those drowned at sea. He was placed in an unmarked grave, and like his namesake, "no one knows his burial place to this day" (Deut 34:6). According to tradition, the biblical Moses, too, had died in the Jewish month of Adar.[237]

---

[236] Ibid., 284.
[237] See, for instance, the Talmud, Meg. 13b; Kid. 38a.

Following the Famous Fragments

It was painful to go through the personal belongings of Moses Shapira, but it was necessary due to bankruptcy proceedings. Rosette faced difficult decisions concerning what to auction and what to keep. She had no idea of the value of any of the items spread out before her. Admittedly, the world of biblical scholarship was always the field and interest of her husband. Her only acquaintance with his work was through the bits and pieces he had shared with her, and she had not paid very close attention. Besides, the family would need to part with nearly everything to settle debts and help provide for life in Berlin.

As she sorted through papers and manuscripts, including items recently shipped to Jerusalem from Moses' last trip to Europe, she came across two small pieces of the now infamous scroll. She immediately recognized them as such, and the sight of them brought a flood of emotion. On the one hand, her husband had believed until the very end in their authenticity, as had others. She knew this to be so. For instance, she knew of Professor Paul Schroeder's early endorsement; he had expressed his belief in them in her presence. She also knew all too well, however, that he had come to side with those who considered the scroll spurious, even if only in word, in order to protect his job. She thought long and hard about what to do with these two fragments of the manuscript that had ultimately brought her family such devastation. She remembered her husband mentioning a German scholar who had stood by him years earlier during the Moabitica affair. If she could recall his name, she would send the two fragments to him. Perhaps he could use them to vindicate her husband's reputation, and then maybe, at last, the scroll could be sold to provide the family with needed funds. When she finally remembered the name, she sent them off by post. Rosette also decided to write to the British Museum to inquire about her husband's manuscript. It was not among his belongings that had been returned, so she assumed they were still at the British Museum.

On 7 July 1884, Edward Bond wrote to Dr. Ginsburg informing him that Shapira's widow had asked about retrieving the fragments that her husband had left at the British Museum. The note said, "Dear Dr. Ginsburg, Mrs. Shapira in a letter just received asks to have sent to her a letter of recommendation of her late husband from Lepsius and a similar one written by myself which she states are in your hands. If you have them and will entrust them to me, I will forward them to Mrs. Shapira as she desires. She enquires after the Deuteronomy fragments and says she found two small pieces among her husband's papers and sent them to Professor Schlottmann. Very truly yours! E. A. Bond."[238] This note raises several questions. Why was Bond informing Ginsburg that Shapira's widow "enquires after the Deuteronomy fragments"? Were they in Ginsburg's possession at that time, or was he simply keeping Ginsburg in the loop about a matter in which he had invested so much time and interest? We do not know, and we have no record of any response from Ginsburg to Bond or from Bond to Rosette.

What we do know is that this resolves one of the mysteries of the Shapira scroll saga. During the first week of July 1883, when Hermann Guthe and Eduard Meyers studied the leather strips, it was explicitly noted, "The manuscript consists of sixteen leather strips."[239] All subsequent reports mention only fifteen. Guthe provided details that account for the difference. He mentioned five single columns (which he called "layers"), and besides the single-columned strips there were "two of two layers, five of three layers, two of four layers, and two of five layers."[240] Each of these strips of varying "layers" accounted for a portion of the total. Guthe and Meyer used seven of the strips, which they "numbered." In the final published work, Guthe and Meyer had transcribed the greater part of the whole document using those seven strips: fragments A and B were single layers, fragment D consisted of three layers, fragments E and F consisted of four layers each, fragment G contained five layers, and fragment H had two layers. Guthe's original list said there were "two of two layers," but only one of these was used in the transcription. For some reason, Shapira must have removed one of the two-layered pieces of the scroll and kept it. When he passed the manuscript to Ginsburg, he gave him fifteen leather strips (seven numbered and eight unnumbered) and withheld one strip with two layers.

Rosette had no way of knowing that Schlottmann had also turned on her husband and, in October of 1878, was the first to reject the scroll. She only remembered that he had maintained a positive view of the Moabitica when no others had. When she wrote to Bond that she had discovered two small fragments among her husband's belongings, it would have been the sixteenth strip, one of two in the collection consisting of two "layers" or columns. We have no record of any response by Schlottmann. All we have is Rosette's word that she sent him "two small pieces" of the Deuteronomy scroll.

After leaving Jerusalem in May, Shapira never returned home. Since Guthe recorded that there were sixteen strips, and everyone thereafter reported only fifteen, it seems safe to assume that Shapira had retained the missing strip containing two columns. He must have taken it to the Netherlands and shown it to prospective buyers or potential advocates for the scroll's authenticity. If this is the case, it likely would have been among Shapira's belongings that were returned

---

[238] British Library *Add. MS. 41294.*
[239] Guthe, *Fragments of a Leather Manuscript,* 3.
[240] Ibid.

"Two Small Pieces" Sent To Prof. Schlottmann

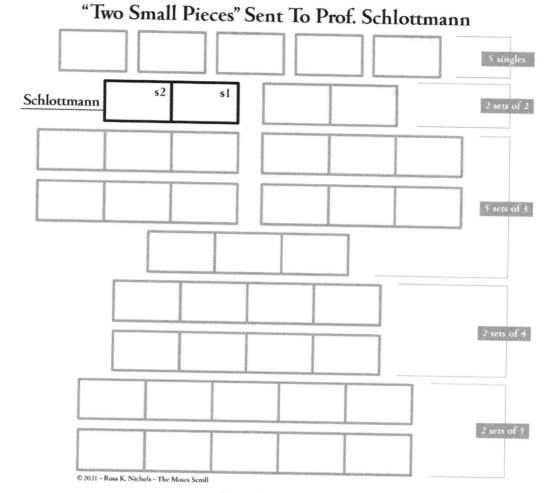

Figure 13

to the family after his death. This explains how Rosette would have "found two small pieces among her husband's papers."

Regarding the remaining fifteen leather strips, the British Museum did not return them to Widow Shapira. In fact, they were sold almost a year to the day after Bond notified Ginsburg about her request. John Marco Allegro notes in his book *The Shapira Affair*, "Sotheby, Wilkinson and Hodge, the famous auctioneers of the Strand, London, held a sale of 'The Schapira Manuscripts.' Lot 302 is recorded in their catalogue as 'Deuteronomy in Hebrew. 7 numbered and 8 unnumbered fragments, *written on leather.*' Alongside the entry is the purchaser's name, the bookseller Bernard Quaritch, and the amount he paid for his bargain, '£10. 5S.'"[241] The purchaser was plainly identified, but who authorized the sale?

Since we have a letter from Shapira's widow inquiring about the Deuteronomy fragments but no record of a response, we are left to wonder. Was there a

---

[241] Allegro, *The Shapira Affair*, 73.

response? Was an agreement made with Rosette to transfer the ownership of the fifteen leather strips that once belonged to her husband? Did she sell the manuscript through the agency of the British Museum? This is definitely a possibility. All we know for certain is that a year after Mrs. Shapira inquired about the fragments, Bernard Quaritch purchased them at an auction.

Some have suspected that Ginsburg was the ultimate possessor of the manuscript. This seems to be due to a misunderstanding. Yoram Sabo reports that on 31 July 1885, nearly two years after the affair ended for the public, *The Jewish Chronicle* published the following: "The manuscripts, which belonged to the notorious Shapira, were sold at a public auction in London by the Sotheby's auction house. The fake manuscripts Shapira hoped to sell to the British Museum two years ago were bought by Dr. Ginsburg for three shillings."[242] This story seems to have been the source of the report that appeared in *The Times* on 11 March 1914 when it published Christian David Ginsburg's death notice. The article said, "The scholar, biblical expert Dr. David Ginsburg, had passed away and was buried in Southgate Cemetery in central London. Later, it was noted that one of the most interesting events of the late scholar's life was the 'Shapira Affair' … The news writer even reported that after Shapira's suicide, Dr. Ginsburg bought the fake scrolls in Sotheby's for a few shillings."[243]

While these accounts contradict what we learn from the sales records of Bernard Quaritch, it is strange that we have persistent reports that Ginsburg owned the manuscript. We know that he was very interested in them and that the entire episode had gained him worldwide notoriety. We also know that on 3 September 1883 he had written to his daughter Ethel expressing his willingness, if he could afford it, to pay £200 for the manuscript. Ginsburg was present when the manuscript was sold to Quaritch for much less than this amount. Why did he not buy it? We know that he purchased other manuscripts at the same auction.[244] Perhaps it was because of the way it would have looked for the brilliant scholar, who declared the scroll a forgery, to then turn around and buy it. This certainly could be seen as a conflict of interest.

We also have Clermont-Ganneau's account of Ginsburg's behavior in January 1884 while the Frenchman was inspecting the fragments. "In the grip of a visible agitation, [Ginsburg] bursted into Dr. Rieu's office" for one more glance at "his dear relics." Ginsburg wanted the manuscript, but did he purchase it? And if he ever came to possess the scroll, how and when did the transaction take place?

The next mention of the scroll appears nearly two years later when Bernard Quaritch exhibited the strips in 1887 in London's Royal Hall during the Anglo-

---

[242] Sabo, *The Scroll Merchant,* 113.

[243] Ibid., 114.

[244] Shapira researcher Matthew Hamilton shared the following with me: "Ginsburg was at the auction for at least the day the Shapira MSS were auctioned. His name is recorded against the following lots [he provides the lot numbers as well as what they contained] … from the annotated auction catalogue, Ginsburg spent 3 shillings on a bundle of fragments of the Hebrew Bible, lot 297, a lot that is not listed in the catalogue as being from Shapira. It may be coincidence, but the amount corresponds to the amount noted in [*The Jewish Chronicle* article]." See "The Shapira Manuscripts," *The Jewish Chronicle,* N.S. no 853 (31 July 1885), 12.

Jewish Historical Exhibition. One of the categories listed in the catalogue for the event was antiquities. The introduction to the manuscript section described some of the more notable collections on display and then notes: "Turning from the sublime to the other extreme, attention may be drawn to the notorious 'Shapira MS.' which created such a sensation while the question of its authenticity was still *sub lite.*"[245] The entry for the Shapira manuscript read, "Fifteen fragments, supposed to be the original MS. of Deuteronomy. Discovered by the late Mr. Shapira, and valued at £1,000,000. These MSS. were, on examination by experts, declared to be forgeries; but for a time they created a great sensation."[246]

Quaritch subsequently listed the Shapira MSS in his sales catalogue with the following description:

> BIBLE. The most original MS of Deuteronomy, from the hand of Moses (? Ben Amram) as discovered by the late Mr. Shapira, and valued at £1,000,000; 15 separate fragments (7 numbered and 8 unnumbered), written in the primeval Hebrew character on strips of blackened leather, £25. Ante-Christum 1500 – A.D. 1800.

> These are the famous fragments which Dr. Ginsburg so painfully deciphered and published in *The Times*, and which led the religious world of England to sing halleluiahs. The scoffing atheists of Germany and France had refused to acknowledge them genuine.

As Fred Reiner pointed out, Quaritch's description

> [F]ails to mention that the "famous fragments" were declared a forgery by Ginsburg. One interpretation of the phrase "led the religious world of England to sing halleluiahs" is that Ginsburg's evaluation and judgment preserved the authenticity of the authorized text of Deuteronomy. The Shapira manuscript, after all, represented a conflicting version of the book and challenged the received biblical text. In addition, Ginsburg's verdict saved the British people world embarrassment by not accepting as authentic a manuscript that European authorities had declared a forgery. But the last sentence of the Quaritch 1887 description implies that the British religious community accepted what the "scoffing atheists" of Germany and France "had refused to acknowledge as genuine." In fact, Ginsburg, Clermont-Ganneau, and Strack all came to the same conclusion: that the scroll was a forgery. Perhaps Quaritch himself was not convinced and thought that the scroll might be authentic and have religious relevance.[247]

Yoram Sabo discovered that the Quaritch catalogue of September 1888 still listed the fragments for sale with the same description, noting only that in this final entry the price had been reduced to £20. He further observed that the

---

[245] *Catalogue of the Anglo-Jewish Historical Exhibition,* Royal Albert Hall, London 187. Compiled by Joseph Jacobs and Lucien Wolf. Illustrated by Frank Haes. Publication of the Exhibition Committee No. IV (London: F. Haes, 28, Bassett Road, W. 1888), 133. *Sub lite* means "in dispute" or "disputed."
[246] Ibid, 136.
[247] Reiner, "C. D. Ginsburg and the Shapira Affair," 126–127 n 68.

September 1888 listing was the last time the Shapira manuscripts appeared in the Quaritch catalogues. This means that they were sold sometime after September of 1888 but before the earliest catalogue of 1889. Past investigations led researchers to speculate on potential buyers.[248] Based on an article published by Alan Crown in 1970, it was believed for years that Sir Charles Nicholson had purchased the manuscript fragments. Crown hypothesized that Nicholson bought the scroll and it was likely consumed in a fire at the Nicholson home on 22 February 1899.[249] Another researcher, Shlomo Guil, stated that Crown's theory, though unsubstantiated, caught on and became the prevailing view.[250] If Crown's theory was right, all hopes of finding the manuscript fragments were gone. But all of that would change when Yoram Sabo revealed a bombshell find.

Sabo relates that during all his years of research on Shapira, he seldom came across anything new. Most researchers covered the known details, and often they repeated the errors of previous writers. He had a hunch that the Nicholson theory was baseless but needed proof. He learned of a researcher in Australia named Matthew Hamilton who also was interested in Shapira and decided to email him. The exchange with Hamilton convinced Sabo that a trip to Australia was warranted. On 18 November 2013 the two met on the campus of the University of Sydney. During their time together, Hamilton informed Sabo about "the most important discovery in the story of the scroll since Shapira's death."[251] Matthew Hamilton had made the discovery in November of 2011 using a complex Google search.

Before his eyes was a reference to Philip Brookes Mason, who "became the eventual possessor of the 'Shapira' manuscript." It was an unexpected discovery. In all of his research he had never come across Mason's name. Oddly enough, the source was an obituary in the October 1904 edition of the *Journal of Conchology*, published by the Conchological Society of Great Britain and Ireland.[252] The reference to the Shapira manuscript that showed up in Hamilton's online search was the text of a eulogy read at Mason's funeral by Rev. Charles F. Thornewill, his friend and associate. In his eulogy, Rev. Thornewill included this statement: "It is not generally known that Mr. Mason became the eventual possessor of the notorious 'Shapira' manuscript, which for a time deceived some of the most experienced authorities on such matters, but was at length discovered to be a remarkably clever forgery." And just like that, with a new clue—the name of the last-known possessor of the scroll fragments—the hunt was back on.

---

[248] Yoram Sabo covers the principal theories in *The Scroll Merchant*, 112–124.

[249] A. D. Crown, "The Fate of the Shapira Scroll," *Revue de Qumrân*, Vol. 7, No. 3 (27) (Décembre 1970), 421–423.

[250] Shlomo Guil, "The Shapira Scroll was an Authentic Dead Sea Scroll," *Palestine Exploration Quarterly*, 149:1 (2017), DOI: 10.1080/00310328.2016.1185895, 9.

[251] Sabo, *The Scroll Merchant*, 180. Sabo says of Hamilton that he is "no less than a genius," and that "he had studied Shapira more than anyone else I had ever met." See Sabo, *The Scroll Merchant*, 174.

[252] Tigay, *The Lost Book of Moses*, 232.

Since that time, Sabo, with permission from Hamilton, included this fact in his film and later in his book. Shortly after Sabo's film came out, Chanan Tigay also revealed the name of Philip Brookes Mason as the last known possessor of the Shapira manuscript. Tigay also learned this from Hamilton.[253] As is often the case, great discoveries are affirmed by the fact that others find them independently around the same time. This was true in regard to Mason being the last known possessor of Shapira's manuscript. While researching for her master's thesis, Patricia Francis discovered the reference as well. She seems to have been the first, having found it shortly before Hamilton, but only later published the find and then mentioned it in a larger work on Mason's extensive collection. She said, "The most significant object in Mason's collection which was not natural history was the 'Shapira manuscript.'" She then recorded a version of the affair in a single paragraph because, for her, it was a peripheral point.[254]

Since this cold-case discovery, researchers have learned that Philip Brookes Mason and Rev. Charles Thornewill were both members of the Burton-on-Trent Natural History and Archaeological Society. At a meeting of that society on 8 March 1889, P. B. Mason presented a paper titled "The Forgery of Shapira." An article appeared in the 14 March 1889 edition of the *Burton Chronicle* recounting the 8 March meeting:

> Not even the promise of a paper on the forgery of Shapira, whose alleged discovery of a manuscript of a portion of the Bible caused no little excitement some years back among biblical scholars, and for the matter of that, the general public, could induce many members of the Natural History and Archaeological Society to brave the elements on Friday evening, but the few who ran the gauntlet were well rewarded for their courage.

The article gave the content of Mr. Mason's talk, which began with his reason for choosing the topic. He justified his presentation by stressing that archaeology was a branch of their work. Since the fragments were "fabrications of what purported to be a manuscript portion of the Bible, not less than twenty-seven centuries old, and one not only venerable for its antiquity, but more valuable in itself, as it would have settled forever a burning question between two schools of critics of the Biblical text." Mason then spent most of his time at the podium reading from articles published in 1883 by those who had declared the manuscript a forgery.

The report in the *Burton Chronicle* closed by saying, "Mr. Mason is possessed of the whole of the Shapira fragments, and the audience, much to their delight were afforded an opportunity of inspecting them." So far as is known, this meeting on Friday, 8 March 1889, was the last sighting of Shapira's Deuteronomy fragments. After the Burton-on-Trent Natural History and Archaeological Society meeting on that rainy night, we lose the trail once again. Thus far, all attempts to

---

[253] Sabo, *Shapira & I* (2014). *The Scroll Merchant* (2018). Chanan Tigay, *The Lost Book of Moses,* 226–233..
[254] Patricia Francis, "Philip Brookes Mason (1842–1903): Surgeon, General Practitioner and Naturalist," *Archives of Natural History* 42.1 (2015), 126–39. See page 131 for the relevant section on Shapira.

find the scroll have proven fruitless. One present researcher, David Adkins, has proposed that the leather strips were buried with Philip Brookes Mason since he had no children. As the obituary put it, "Mr. Mason left no family, and his various collections have passed into the keeping of his widow." Careful investigation of his widow's distribution of his collections also has not provided researchers with any leads about where the scroll went next if it ever left Burton-on-Trent. Losing the trail of the Shapira manuscript in 1889, as the nineteenth century came to a close, seemed a likely place to end the story. Eminent scholars had declared it a forgery and marked Shapira as a "purveyor of spurious manuscripts." Shapira had died, his name forever associated with the often-affixed label *Forger,* and eventually the sands of time covered the story. But for a chance discovery in the Judean desert, the whole affair might have remained buried in Burton-on-Trent.

7

Ancient Scroll Discoveries

On 29 November 1873, Captain Conder and Horatio Kitchener visited Khirbet Qumran in the Judean Desert.[255] The report of their visit begins: "The ruins lie on a natural platform, 300 feet above the Dead Sea level, at the base of the cliffs. The remains are very rough." The summary of the site includes remarks about the "ruined buildings now presenting nothing beyond heaps of rough stones … a small *birkeh,* rudely lined with stones, unhewn, the joints packed with smaller stones and roughly plastered."[256] The feature that received the most attention was the graveyard. The report continues, "The peculiar feature of the site is the immense number of graves occupying the plateau and the eastern slope. There are some 700 or more in all, arranged closely together in regular rows." It was determined, based on the orientation of "20° west of north along their length," that they were not "Moslem graves." Among the graves they also saw "the remains of a skeleton with the head to the south … the bones much decayed."

Also in 1873, Charles Clermont-Ganneau visited the site as well.[257] In the same published survey, his report follows that of Conder and Kitchener. He described his "journey to the south, to examine the site of Khurbet Kumrân, and especially the cemetery." He made a passing remark about the ruins, saying only that they were "insignificant in themselves: a few fallen walls of mean construction; a little *birkeh,* into which you descend by steps; and numerous fragments of irregular pottery scattered over the soil." Like Conder and Kitchener, Clermont-Ganneau's attention was mainly attracted to "the numerous tombs (perhaps a thousand), which cover the mound and adjacent plateau." He noted, as did Conder and Kitchener, that the only reason one might suppose these were not "ordinary Arab tombs" was their orientation, since they "all have their major axis north and south instead of east and west." Clermont-Ganneau reported that he supervised the opening of one of the graves, from which was exhumed "a bit of a jawbone, with teeth adhering, which will perhaps enable anthropological conclusions to be drawn." He concluded his report saying, "It is difficult to form

---

[255] In the reports of the nineteenth-century scholars, the site name is spelled Khurbet Kumrân, whereas the generally accepted spelling today is Khirbet Qumran.

[256] The *birkeh* described is a *mikvah* or Jewish ritual bath.

[257] The accounts of the visit to Qumran in 1873 by Conder and Kitchener, as well as the report of Clermont-Ganneau's visit and remarks about the ruins, are recorded in "Khurbet Kumrân," in Claude R. Conder and Herbert H. Kitchener, *The Survey of Western Palestine* (London: Palestine Exploration Society, 1883), 210–211.

any opinion on these sepulchers, principally on account of their abnormal orientation." Beyond these observations, the three scholars known in our story had little else to report from Qumran.

The accomplishments of these and other nineteenth-century explorers have impressed modern researchers. But despite their contributions to our understanding of the Bible and Bible lands, these three famous scholars had no idea what was hidden in the caves all around them where they stood at Khirbet Qumran. Less than a decade after their unimpressive trip to Qumran, Conder and Clermont-Ganneau would both declare Shapira's manuscript a forgery. One of Conder's main objections was the improbability that a leather manuscript could survive in a cave, as Shapira claimed for his manuscript. Shapira's story of bedouin finding the manuscript in a cave high among the marled cliffs of the Wadi Mujib, wrapped in moldy linen and smelling of asphalt, with apparent traces of the black substance on the backside of the manuscript strips, seemed preposterous to nineteenth-century scholars. They doubted that such relics could survive the ravages of time and humidity, even if, as Archibald Sayce put it, "they may have been abundantly salted with asphalte from the Vale of Siddim itself." It should be evident to present-day readers that the caves around Kirbet Qumran were not among the "hundreds of caves" that Conder explored, for had he done so during his trip, Shapira's story would not have been considered improbable at all.

Eight decades after bedouin discovered the sixteen leather strips east of the Jordan, another discovery was made by bedouin in a cave south of Jericho near the Dead Sea. This story bears many similarities to one about the nineteenth-century discovery of Shapira's manuscript.[258] In the winter of 1946–47 three bedouin of the Ta'amireh tribe were shepherding their flocks near Khirbet Qumran. One of the bedouin, named Jum'a Muhammed Khalil, "had a penchant for exploring caves, for he felt confident that someday he would locate one in which a cache of gold had been stored in ancient times."[259] While the flock grazed below, Jum'a noticed two holes in the marled cliffs, one above the other. The lower opening was only large enough "for a cat to enter," but the upper one would allow a small person to pass through. Jum'a picked up a rock and tossed it into the smaller hole. He "was startled by the strange sound he heard: apparently the rock shattered an earthenware jar within. Thinking there might be a cache of gold within, he summoned the two other herdsmen to show them the curious holes."[260]

The sun was setting, and the next day the bedouin needed to take their flocks to Ain Feshkha for water, so they agreed that they would return to investigate the cave on the third day. On the morning of the third day, while Jum'a and his older cousin, Khalil Musa, slept, the youngest of the trio, Muhammed Ahmed el-Hamed, nicknamed Edh-Dhib, sneaked away to get the first look at whatever was

---

[258] The story of the discovery related here has been told many times with varying details. The narrative contained in this chapter is based primarily on the accounts presented by John Trever. See John C. Trever, *The Untold Story of Qumran* (Westwood, New Jersey: Revell), 1965.
[259] Ibid., 103.
[260] Ibid.

in the cave. He made his way up the cliff face and entered the larger opening feet first. Once inside, he noticed ten large jars against the wall of the cave. Some of the jars had lids and small handles; eight of them were empty, one contained "reddish earth," and one held two bundles wrapped in a darkened cloth and one leather roll without a wrapping. Muhammed took the mysterious bundles down to his companions. Uncertain of what he had found but thinking the items might prove to be of some value, the bedouin took them to their camp. The discovery turned out to be ancient scrolls composed in Hebrew and Aramaic—the first of what became known as the Dead Sea Scrolls!

Despite their many contributions to biblical research, Claude Conder, Horatio Kitchener, and Charles Clermont-Ganneau would not be associated with the great discoveries in the Wadi Qumran. Three other names would earn that distinction: Muhammed Ahmad el-Hamid, also known as ed-Dib ("the Wolf"), Jum'a Muhammed Khalil, and Khalil Musa, members of the Ta'amireh bedouin tribe. The cave that the tribesmen discovered would be designated Cave 1. Subsequent searches in the Wadi Qumran would prove fruitful over the next decade, during which ten more caves would yield many more ancient documents.

These first scrolls found by the Ta'amireh bedouin were sold to the Syrian Metropolitan Mar Samuel, who contacted Prof. Eliezer Sukenik of Hebrew University to get an expert opinion. Based on a small fragment, Sukenik was excited beyond words. The date was 29 November 1947 – the very day the United Nations voted for Partition of Palestine, allowing for the declaration of a Jewish State. Hostilities broke out the next day and despite the dangers, Sukenik, dressed as an Arab woman, rode a bus to Bethlehem and brought back three scrolls to examine. He was so excited he seemed to forget the war. He was convinced they were at least 2000 years old!

John Trever was the "first American to examine, study, and photograph the documents about twelve months after their accidental discovery."[261] He was in Jerusalem for the 1947–48 academic year, having received a fellowship from the American School of Oriental Research (ASOR). On Sunday, 15 February 1948, the director of the American School went to Baghdad for a two-week trip and left the young scholar as acting director *pro tem*.[262] During his time as acting director, John Trever received a telephone call that would forever change his life and the field of biblical studies.

The call was from Father Butrus Sowmy, the librarian for the Monastery of St. Mark in the Old City of Jerusalem. Father Sowmy told Trever that he had some ancient Hebrew manuscripts to show the American scholars in the hope that they might help supply the needed information for their catalogue. Trever knew that arranging a meeting would be difficult. Ever since 29 November 1947, when the United Nations decided to partition Palestine, Arabs had been guarding the Old

---

[261] Ibid., 9.

[262] The abbreviation *pro tem* is short for *pro tempore* and means "for the present, but not permanent, i.e. temporary."

City gates. Trever agreed to examine the manuscripts if Father Sowmy would bring them to the American School.

On Thursday, 19 February 1948, Father Sowmy and his brother Ibrahim arrived at the school. In Trever's description of the meeting, he noted that Sowmy had a leather satchel in his hand. "Laying it on my desk, he lifted the cover and withdrew what looked like a roll of Arabic newspapers. Removing the paper, he handed me a very brittle, tightly rolled scroll of cream-colored leather, less than two inches in diameter. Very gently I pulled back the end of the scroll and saw that it was written in a clear, square Hebrew script, not at all like archaic Hebrew."[263]

Trever barely had time for a close look before Sowmy pulled the next roll out of his satchel. This scroll was about 10½ inches long and 6 inches in diameter. He noticed that one piece of the leather scroll, consisting of two columns, had become detached due to the disintegration of the linen thread that connected the sheets of the scroll. He was growing excited as he inspected the scroll and the script. He knew of the Nash Papyrus and of Dr. W. F. Albright's proposed dating to the first or second century BCE.[264] The script on the large scroll before him, particularly the shape of a few of the letters, resembled the script of that document. Other similarities suggested that this scroll might be from the same period. He would later recall, "My heart began to pound. Could this manuscript, so beautifully preserved, be as old as the Nash Papyrus? Such a thought appeared too incredible, but the similarity to the Nash Papyrus was strong evidence leading in that direction."[265]

As Trever studied the manuscripts, the Syrians told him the story of the scrolls' origins. They related how bedouin discovered them in a cave. Ibrahim remarked that in his study of Jericho and the Dead Sea area he had become interested in the Essenes, and as a result had developed a theory. He believed, and had conveyed to those at the monastery, that the scrolls may have belonged to the Essenes, "and been deposited by them in the cave during a period of persecution, perhaps when the Romans attacked Jerusalem in A.D. 70."[266] Ibrahim continued, "Since the scrolls had been wrapped like mummies originally … they must be very ancient, for mummification had long since become a lost art."

Realizing that a careful examination would be required, the Syrians left the scrolls in the care of the American School so the scholars could make an assessment. Trever requested their patience as he sought the opinion of other scholars. He then bade his guests farewell and set to work. Trever was convinced of the antiquity of the scrolls. He discovered that the large one was a scroll of Isaiah. He wrote to his wife, "I cannot see how it [the Isaiah scroll] can very well

---

[263] Ibid., 22.
[264] W. F. Albright, "A Biblical Fragment from the Maccabean Age: The Nash Papyrus" (*Journal of Biblical Literature* LVI [September 1937], 145–176).
[265] Trever, *The Untold Story,* 24.
[266] Ibid., 25.

be a fake … It would take an artist of extremely skilled ability to produce such a manuscript in modern times. If it is genuine, it may prove to be a sensational discovery."[267] Trever decided to get the opinion of Albright, so on 25 February 1948 he wrote the following to him:

> Enclosed are some sample prints from a manuscript which I have discovered here in Jerusalem in Dr. Burrows' absence…. If you are right about your dating of the Nash papyrus, then I believe that this is the oldest Bible document yet discovered! My first thought when seeing these scrolls was to get them photographed and a copy sent to you for study. I firmly believe the script cannot be later than the 2nd Cent. A.D…. and it has some indications to show it may be earlier than the Nash Papyrus. I am so busy with the photographing of them that I can't take time now to make the careful study that they demand for more accurate dating. I am personally convinced that their age is great."[268]

On Monday, 15 March 1948, Trever received Albright's reply:

> Dear Trever, your air-letter of Feb. 25th, with its enclosures, arrived this morning and I immediately got out my magnifying glass and started in. I am now having the prints enlarged so I can study the script to better advantage. My heartiest congratulations on the greatest MS discovery of modern times! There is no doubt whatever in my mind that the script is more archaic than that of the Nash Papyrus, standing very close to that of the third-century Egyptian papyri and ostraca in Aramaic. Of course, in the present state of our definite knowledge about Hebrew paleography it would be safe only to date it in the Maccabean period, i.e., not later than the ascension of Herod the Great. I should prefer a date around 100 B.C. The script is in every respect older than that of the Dura parchment fragment…. I repeat that in my opinion you have made the greatest MS discovery of modern times—certainly the greatest biblical MS find…. You can imagine how my eyes bulged when I saw the script through my magnifying glass! What an absolutely incredible find! And there can happily not be the slightest doubt in the world about the genuineness of the MS.
>
> Cordially, W. F. Albright."[269]

Moses Shapira would have loved to receive this sort of affirmation from a distinguished scholar such as Albright, but it was not to be. Leaving the reported discovery of Shapira's scroll aside, the discovery of the Ta'amireh bedouin was not the first reported mention of scrolls being discovered in caves near the Dead Sea. We have very early sources that relate similar stories. "Bishop Epiphanius of Salamis, fourth century A.D., refers to Old Testament manuscripts in Hebrew and Greek found concealed in earthenware jars near Jericho in A.D. 217. Both Origen

---

[267] Ibid., 26–27.
[268] Ibid., 60.
[269] Ibid., 85.

(second to third century) and Eusebius (third to fourth century) refer to this find. According to Origen, a Greek version of the Psalms was among the manuscripts." Also, "Nestorian Church Patriarch Timothy (780–823) in a Syriac letter addressed to Sergius, Metropolitan of Ela, tells of books found near Jericho in a house on the rocks. Timothy goes on to say that 'more than two hundred Psalms of David' have been found among the books."[270] We can safely assume that the nineteenth-century scholars were unaware of these earlier finds, for had they been, the story of Shapira would not have been considered incredulous.

Predictably, not everyone was inclined to accept the authenticity of the newly-discovered scrolls. Among the reasons for skepticism was a previous discovery of blackened scrolls wrapped in linen, allegedly discovered by bedouin in a cave near the Dead Sea. In the last week of July 1947, when a search was underway for someone who could best judge the genuineness of the recent discovery, we find the following account: "According to Antoun Hazou, Father Vincent would have been the more logical person at the École to judge the scrolls, but he did not even want to look at them, Hazou said, because he was afraid they were fakes, something like the one Shapira had tried to sell years before."[271] Then, in the third week of August 1947, we find another person who maintained a similar reservation. "During the next few days, Metropolitan Samuel consulted Stephen Hanna Stephan, a Syrian Christian employed by the Transjordan Department of Antiquities, but he pronounced the scrolls 'late' (that is medieval), despite Samuel's recounting of the stories of Origen and 'Catholicos Timothy.' Stephan cautioned Samuel, citing the Shapira Affair."[272]

Sixty-three years after his death, Moses Wilhelm Shapira was still remembered as the one who created a clever but impudent forgery that purported to be ancient but was ultimately ruled a fake by the leading scholars of the day. But did Shapira's scroll fragments cast doubt on the authenticity of the newfound documents, or could those latest discoveries help validate the genuineness of Shapira's manuscript? In 1873, Conder and Clermont-Ganneau had stood within a stone's throw of "the greatest manuscript discovery of modern times" and missed it. Did they miss another opportunity for a great manuscript discovery in 1883? Could they have been wrong in their assessment of Shapira's manuscript? In fairness to the nineteenth-century scholars, they simply had nothing with which to compare Shapira's manuscript.

Today, visitors to Khirbet Qumran find themselves within walking distance of eleven caves that Conder never explored. If he had entered any one of them, he most certainly would have made "the greatest manuscript discovery of modern times"—the Dead Sea Scrolls. Given what we now know, we must reassess the nineteenth-century scholarly verdict in light of new evidence.

---

[270] Mansoor, *The Dead Sea Scrolls, A College Textbook and a Study Guide* (Leiden, Netherlands: E.J. Brill, 1964), 3.
[271] Weston Fields, *The Dead Sea Scrolls: A Full History, Vol I, 1947–1960* (Leiden, Boston: Brill, 2009), 34.
[272] Ibid., 37.

Reasons for Reexamination

On 23 August 1883, the *Echo* published an article stating, "From the moment that the discoveries were declared to the world there was an eagerness in many quarters, quite inconsistent with the true spirit of criticism or scholarship to stigmatize them as forgeries."[273] Notably, evidence of this predetermined verdict emerged as early as 3 August 1883. In a *Times* article we read, "In any case, the *prima facie* presumption must be held to be enormously against the genuineness of the fragment. Such a presumption rests on the improbability of finding manuscripts older by at least sixteen centuries than any extant manuscripts of the same text, on the comparative ease [with] which such fragments can be forged, and on the powerful motives to such forgery attested by the price placed by Mr. Shapira on his property."[274] Aside from these nineteenth-century "improbabilities," other factors led to the declarations of fraud.

First and foremost among the objections was a lingering caution because of the Moabitica affair scandal, which frequently appears in contemporary reports. Even though Shapira was never accused of having participated in the manufacture of those supposed ancient relics, his close association with them fostered suspicion. Any relic from Moab's sands would be viewed with skepticism after the academic world declared the entire Shapira collection a forgery. Hermann Guthe put it this way:

> But if only it [the manuscript] were not from Moab! Thus, will every reader doubtless have said to himself. Indeed, Moab and its treasures of antiquities have had a bad ring among us since 1876, and one is entitled to harbor the greatest disbelief against everything that gets brought to the market under this company. But I repeat, to determine has nothing to do with that. Indeed, everyone will admit to me that one can turn this argument around and say: a forger who demands belief of his product will presently rarely have it appear from Moab if it did not, in fact, originate from there.[275]

The questions before us today are the same ones the nineteenth-century scholars faced. The Shapira case deserves a new hearing based on evidence that

---

[273] Mansoor, "The Case of Shapira's Dead Sea (Deuteronomy) Scrolls of 1883," 225.
[274] Guil, "The Shapira Scroll Was an Authentic Dead Sea Scroll," 14–15.
[275] Guthe, *Fragments of a Leather Manuscript,* 6.

was unavailable in the 1800s. The discovery of ancient scrolls at Khirbet Qumran demands a reassessment. While Shapira's story of the discovery may have been difficult to accept in the nineteenth century, it is far more believable today, given what we know of the twentieth-century discoveries at Khirbet Qumran. The bedouin reportedly discovered Shapira's scroll fragments in a cave near the Dead Sea. The details of that discovery anticipated those of the scrolls in Qumran's Cave 1 by approximately eight decades. Before the discoveries at Qumran in 1947, no one believed that a leather manuscript could survive for thousands of years in that region. Several of the nineteenth-century detractors mentioned this in their assessments of Shapira's scroll. Now, with the benefit of hindsight, those arguments have become moot.

Shapira reported that his leather manuscript was discovered wrapped in linen. The scholars of the day also scoffed at this. *The Times Weekly Edition* from 22 August 1883 observed, "The mention of the linen seems somehow a mistake since even believers in leather can hardly be expected to assign equal staying power to mere flax." According to Shapira's story, the bedouin entered the cave and found a bundle wrapped in cloth. Hoping to find gold or other treasure, they peeled back the layers of crumbling fabric only to find blackened leather strips smelling of asphalt. Again, the similarity of detail between Shapira's story and the reports from the Ta'amireh tribe are striking. Hoping to find treasure, the Ta'amireh bedouin, too, found manuscripts wrapped in linen. Edmund Wilson reported that when the bedouin opened the jar in Cave 1 that contained scrolls, a "very bad smell arose; this turned out to arise from dark, oblong lumps … when they got these lumps out of the cave, they saw they were wrapped up in lengths of linen and coated with a black layer of what seemed to be pitch or wax."[276]

Scholar Joan Taylor records, "One striking thing to note is that Lankester Harding and DeVaux were able to find among the many pieces of linen used to wrap up scrolls and seal jars in Cave 1Q that some of this linen had been impregnated with bitumen. The Bedouin who first discovered the cave also indicated that bitumen had been used as a preservative for the scrolls"[277] The academic discussion of the linen and the black substance frequently found on the linen is extensive and the interpretation thereof varies widely. This was a matter of debate with Shapira's manuscript as well as the manuscripts discovered at Qumran. On 4 August 1883, when Dr. Walter Flight performed various tests on the black substance of Shapira's scroll strips on behalf of the British Museum, he determined that "the black colouring matter, taken from the back and front of the skins, does not appear to be asphaltum but rather wax, like bees-wax, of a very

---

[276] Edmund Wilson, "The Scrolls from the Dead Sea," *New Yorker,* 14 May (1955), 2.

[277] Joan Taylor, *The Essenes, the Scrolls, and the Dead Sea* (Oxford: Oxford University Press, 2012), 281. See her entire discussion in "The Natural Caves," 281–286 where she discusses bitumen, black pitch, bitumen-impregnated linen, and other words and phrases related to the black substance associated with ancient scroll discoveries. In the postscript to her book, Taylor suggests, "The scrolls themselves decomposed into a black gelatinous substance, and this is probably what is seen in linen full of a black substance."

impure dirty kind."[278] Interestingly, G. Lankester Harding also suggested that the black substance sometimes found on the linen covering the scrolls was wax.[279]

Noteworthy are the frequent references to mummies and mummification as a means of interpreting the strange black substance appearing on the backside of Shapira's scroll and other Dead Sea Scrolls. John Trever reported that Ibrahim had told him that the scrolls "had been wrapped like mummies," and this was an indication of their antiquity because "mummification had long since become a lost art."[280] When Shapira wrote to Strack on 9 May 1883 he mentioned that he was familiar with the area where the strips were discovered: "I knew the area well the place the Bedouin spoke of, having been there with Professor Almkvist in the year 1875 and having seen that it is an old burial place, perhaps of some Egyptians settled there, and having found there some small pieces, which seemed to us to be, of embalmed bodies."[281] When Guthe related what Shapira told him of the manuscript's origin and history, he too mentioned the trip with Almkvist and said, "Shapira is supposed to have found mummy remains there."[282]

Mummies and mummification were discussed extensively in Guthe's work as he searched for possible explanations of the "asphalte layer on the backside" of the leather strips. In his first inspection of the fragments he reported, "The backside of the leather strips is painted over with a tough, loosely adhesive asphalt resin, which lays in varying thickness. In some places one can scrape it off with their fingernail. Quite often one perceives the imprint of a woven fabric on the bulk, and in multiple places, small pieces of brownish, weathered, and fragile canvas, the largest of which has about the size of one square centimeter, sticking firmly to the backside."[283]

Guthe then said that according to Shapira, Dr. Paul Schroeder was the first to attempt an explanation of the black backing of the strips. He suggested that "the strips were once wrapped around a mummy." To this Guthe said, "This assumption seems indeed to make the asphalt as well as the cloth pieces clinging to it, which then are thought to be the remains of mummy wrappings, completely comprehensible, and has very easily found acceptance with multiple surveyors. I also for a long time was biased towards this, but now must clarify it as totally inadmissible." In his letter to Ebers of 8 July, Meyer says, "The strips … were clearly used to wrap a corpse. On the back there is mummy balm (that's what it is called)." Guthe also entertained other various possibilities regarding the mummy theory. He ruled out that someone asphalted the strips, folded them, and placed

---

[278] From a report from Dr. Walter Flight addressed to Bond after his assessment. The letter is contained in the British Library *Add. MS. 41294*.

[279] G. Lankester Harding, "The Dead Sea Scrolls," *Palestine Exploration Quarterly*, 81 (1949), 114. See also Joan Taylor, *The Essenes*, 285, where she says, "If this were the case also with the Dead Sea Scrolls manuscripts, then we may expect to find in their chemistry indicators of Dead Sea salts (similar to natron), other minerals, grease or oil, and beeswax."

[280] Trever, *The Untold Story*, 25.

[281] Letter from Shapira to Strack of 9 May 1883, 2.

[282] Guthe, *Fragments of a Leather Manuscript*, 5.

[283] Ibid., 4.

the folded strips between mummy bandages, but then wondered if the asphalt-soaked strips were wrapped around the mummy on top of a corpse that was first wrapped in linen. This might account for the cloth that adhered to the blackened back of the scroll strips, but the front of the strips did not contain the asphalt coating, so this seemed unlikely.

Guthe also considered the length of the strips and the amount of material required to cover a human corpse, but based on his calculations, the length of the leather strips would be more than adequate to accommodate a single mummy. He then considered the possibility that the strips were used on two mummies. This discussion continued for several paragraphs until Guthe finally determined, "Under these circumstances, it appears impossible to interpret the asphalt of the backside of the leather strips as having previously belonged to a mummy. Under the reservation of the results of a microscopic investigation and a chemical analysis, the possibility remains provisionally open, that the leather strips as *such* were furnished backwards with an asphalt layer, either to make them more supple or to better conserve them, or to give them a more antique appearance, and that they only then by accidental means, or deliberately, ended up in contact with mummy canvas, whereon particular pieces clung to the asphalt."

He left the possibility open that somehow the scroll was associated with a buried corpse but then offered reasons why this seemed improbable. He questioned whether Israelite custom would have ever permitted "writings with religious content" to come in contact with the dead since even engaging in the study of laws or prayers in a mortuary chamber was forbidden. "How much less could one then think to enclose a piece of the 'law' with the dead?" Guthe continued:

> Though, already above…, another assumption has been indicated as possible to explain the character of the backside. How should one react towards it? It must be presumed there, that the front side had been written on before the asphalt came to the back. For no one will asphalt a piece of leather, on which is to be written, in advance. Can it be assumed that someone brought asphalt upon it, in order to conserve the leather as a *manuscript?* … There remains only, should one not want to immediately doubt their authenticity due to the asphalt and canvas pieces, the assumption that they have been coated in asphalt in order to make the brittle leather more supple, and that they then accidentally came in contact with yellowed and fragile canvas. This assumption is possible, it cannot be denied, but it can only make claim to likelihood if other substantial grounds for the authenticity of the leather strips yield themselves.

As strange as these references to mummies and mummification are, they provide an interesting link between the scrolls of Qumran and the Shapira scroll. The fact is that the debate about the composition and purpose of the black substance found on these ancient manuscripts is ongoing. Is "the bitumen-impregnated linen wrapping … consistent with a mentality that sought to preserve scrolls in a kind of special burial?"[284] Is it more than a coincidence that there are burial places near the locations of these two scroll discoveries? Scholars will need to consider these questions.

Perhaps approaching a solution to this mystery is the work of Joan Taylor. In *The Essenes, the Scrolls, and the Dead Sea*, in the section "Genizah and Cemetery," she makes some fascinating observations. She points out that "in the Babylonian Talmud, we find a comment that a *sefer*, 'book, scroll' that is worn-out is buried beside a scholar (b.Meg. 26b, cf. Moed Katan 25a, Baba Kamma 17a). It is no longer then in a *genizah*. It is buried."[285] She also notes, "Curiously, worn-out scroll wrappers may be used for making shrouds for corpses that do not have people to bury them (b.Meg. 26B)." She credits this observation to Grace Crowfoot "in her important study of the linen from cave 1Q … Crowfoot in fact was the one to suggest explicitly that scrolls and wrappers were buried and 'it is important to remember that burial in caves was the custom of the country, and so this concealment may only be the equivalent of the correct cemetery burial of the contents of a *Genizah*.'"[286] Taylor observes that the Jewish practice of burying old sacred manuscripts continues to this day, "and is accompanied by ritual."[287]

Perhaps Conder and Clermont-Ganneau's attraction to the cemetery, and Schroeder and Guthe's focus on mummies and mummification, were not so far off after all. If possible, and knowing what we know now, it would be interesting to present these scholars with the Shapira manuscript and the knowledge gained since the Qumran discoveries. One wonders how our present understanding of ancient scrolls might change their verdict. The skepticism of nineteenth-century scholars is understandable, but we now know that many of their doubts were unfounded, especially since the discoveries at Qumran corroborate many of the details of Shapira's earlier cave manuscript discovery.

The story of the discovery of Shapira's scroll does not mention a jar, but not all scrolls discovered at Qumran were in jars either. Based on these accounts, it seems likely that Shapira's scroll was not in a jar when the bedouin found it. This does not mean, however, that it had not been in a jar when it was originally deposited in the cave. Placing documents in jars is an ancient practice attested in Scripture.[288] The leather strips of Shapira's scroll were also folded and not rolled at the time he came to possess them. We don't know what to make of this. We have no way of knowing whether they were discovered in a folded state, or perhaps rolled originally and then folded by the bedouin at some point during the ten years that he owned them and treated them as a talisman. Guthe discussed the folded strips and remarked that the lack of a precedent made rendering judgment

---

[284] Taylor, *The Essenes*, 284.

[285] Ibid., 287.

[286] Ibid., quoting Grace Crowfoot, *Discoveries in the Judean Desert*, I, 25.

[287] Ibid., 288. See also page 292 where she says, "Therefore, it seems possible that manuscripts were buried in the Qumran cemetery."

[288] We know, for instance, that at least as early as the seventh century documents were placed in earthen vessels to ensure their preservation (Jer 32:14).

difficult. He asked, "Does this format teach us that one not only rolled written on leather in Israel, but also folded it? ... and it does not follow from our not knowing any other format, that there absolutely was none."[289]

A nineteenth-century forger would not have known that ancient manuscripts were written on leather, wrapped in linen "impregnated with bitumen," and stashed away in caves near the Dead Sea. Such a forger would have had no way of faking these characteristics of an authentic ancient manuscript—they simply were unknown when Shapira presented his manuscript to the world.

Prior to the discoveries at Qumran, scholars only knew of lapidary examples of ancient Paleo-Hebrew writing,[290] but twentieth-century findings in the Judean Desert revealed twelve examples written on leather.[291] Emanuel Tov has noted that all twelve of these consist of works that are traditionally ascribed to Moses.[292] All of the manuscripts that contain this ancient script were written on strips of leather and in columns. In many of these textual witnesses, vertical and horizontal scoring is evident on the leather.[293] No one who saw Shapira's manuscript in 1883 reported horizontal scoring, but they did confirm vertical marks. Clermont-Ganneau and Ginsburg made much of these vertical score lines, supposing that their presence indicated forgery. They each suggested, whether independently or not we do not know, that the vertical lines were proof that the leather strips were cut from the bottom margin of a "modern" scroll. Their evidence of forgery was that the forger failed to stay within the bounds of those lines, which were presumably made to delineate the boundaries for writing in the original work. Guthe also mentioned those markings but did not conclude that they were an indication of forgery:

> The manner in which the front side of the leather was prepared for writing and the lettering [that] has been applied to it, admittedly does not conform by any means to the rule that the Talmud establishes for Torah rolls, namely that lines for the letters must be drawn between the column borders. Of that alone there is nothing striking. There are indeed, today Torah manuscripts on which the row lines only retroactively have been drawn on the leather or parchment. As a consequence of this, that rule may not be traced to ancient times. The column strokes on both sides of each layer of the leather strips were, as I already emphasized above, without a doubt

---

[289] Guthe, *Fragments of a Leather Manuscript,* 12–13. I am unaware of examples of any Qumran scrolls being folded rather than rolled. Some report that several sheets of the *Hodayot* or Thanksgiving Hymns were folded, but these sheets seem to have become detached from the scroll and later inserted into the larger scroll, whereas Shapira's scroll, at least from the time he came to possess it, seemed to be deliberately folded at every column.

[290] Stone monuments, coins, etc.

[291] Emanuel Tov, *Textual Criticism of the Hebrew Bible,* 3rd ed. (Minneapolis: Fortress Press, 2012), 97. "Fragments of twelve biblical scrolls written in the *paleo-Hebrew* script have been found at Qumran."

[292] Ibid. "The writing in this script must have been preserved for the most ancient books, the Torah and Job—note that the latter is traditionally ascribed to Moses."

[293] Guil, "The Shapira Scroll Was an Authentic Dead Sea Scroll, 17. Guil covers "ruling" in the Dead Sea Scrolls, providing sources from other writers on the subject in section E. Ruling in the Shapira Scroll, beginning on page 17.

drawn before writing, and that the author did not turn at them, apart from the exception mentioned previously, is not inclined to appear suspicious to me, since the lines of the individual rows run straight and sure, and the space covered by writing has a consistently regular form. This makes the impression of a great security and practice of the author, such that he did not require the help of the lines in order to always begin and end the rows evenly. One thinks he wanted to save space by writing left and right over the column strokes.[294]

In Shapira's time, a forger would not have known that some works attributed to Moses were written in Paleo-Hebrew on strips of leather, with vertical score marks bordering both sides of the text.

The Qumran scrolls that were written in Paleo-Hebrew also contain examples of splitting a word at the end of one line and continuing it on the next. Emanuel Tov says that this is customary in texts that are written in this script.[295] The same splitting of words exists in Shapira's manuscript. Additionally, in some places in the Paleo-Hebrew Qumran manuscripts the scribes employed interpuncts or dots to separate words.[296] Shapira's manuscript has interpuncts, and of particular note is how they appear in its version of the Ten Words. The nineteenth-century scholars thought this was a mere mimicking of lapidary examples known at that time. They believed that the forger of Shapira's manuscript had borrowed this feature from a familiarity with the Mesha Stela. In Shapira's time, a forger would not have known that ancient scribal practices included splitting words, nor would he have known to add interpuncts as word separators.

Despite these examples of similarities between Shapira's manuscript and the scrolls found at Qumran, many steadfastly held to the forgery declarations of the nineteenth-century scholars. Based on Trever's photos, W. F. Albright unequivocally declared the Isaiah scroll "the greatest MS discovery of modern times" and "more archaic than the Nash Papyrus." However, he had nothing positive to say about Shapira's manuscript. He is on record as saying, "Since several scholars have compared the new scrolls [those from Qumran] to the so-called archetype of Deuteronomy, offered by the notorious forger Shapira to the British Government for a million pounds, it should be emphasized that there is *nothing whatever in common* between them except the fact that the texts of the Hebrew Bible written in ancient scripts are involved."[297]

---

[294] Guthe, *Fragments of a Leather Manuscript,* 11.

[295] Tov, *Textual Criticism,* 205. "Words are often broken up at the end of a line (split between lines) in the early Hebrew Script, and likewise in biblical scrolls written in the paleo-Hebrew script ... This practice was not used in texts written in the square script and was forbidden by *Sof.* 2.1."

[296] Ibid., 196. "The overwhelming majority of the Judean Desert texts (biblical and non-biblical) use one of two systems for separating words in Hebrew and Aramaic, employing either word-dividers of some kind (mainly dots) in texts written in paleo-Hebrew script." Footnote 8 adds, "Dots or small oblique strokes were used in almost all biblical paleo-Hebrew Qumran scrolls."

[297] Michael Press, "The Lying Pen of the Scribes": A Nineteenth-Century Dead Sea Scroll. http://theappendix.net/issues/2014/7/the-lying-pen-of-the-scribes-a-nineteenth-century-dead-sea-scroll. Emphasis in original.

In 1956, Professor Menahem Mansoor, chairman of the Department of Hebrew and Semitic Studies at the University of Wisconsin, drew criticism from several of his academic colleagues when he called on competent scholars to reexamine the whole Shapira case "for the sake of true scholarship." Mansoor put it this way: "The present writer believes that in light of recent discoveries and of what has been stated above [in his lengthy paper], neither the internal nor the external evidence, so far as yet published, supports the idea of a forgery. Therefore, this writer firmly believes that there is justification in his suggestion for the re-examination of the case."[298] He was not alone. Other scholars and writers stepped forward suggesting the same.[299] John Marco Allegro published the first book in modern times to propose that Shapira and his scroll may have been falsely condemned. In *The Shapira Affair*, published in 1965, he presented "the true story of a nineteenth-century mystery and of the controversy which resulted in discrediting what may have been one of the most important archaeological findings of all time."[300] He, too, was denounced by his academic colleagues. But Mansoor and Allegro were right. Given what we know now, the scroll that claims to present Moses's final words deserves an objective reevaluation.

---

[298] Mansoor, "The Case of Shapira's Dead Sea (Deuteronomy) Scrolls of 1883," 225.
[299] Ibid., 187–188 n 31.
[300] Allegro, *The Shapira Affair*. John Marco Allegro was born in London and educated at Oxford and the University of Manchester. He was an archaeologist, Dead Sea Scroll scholar, and the first British representative on the international team responsible for editing the Qumran scrolls.

O

What Did Moses Write?

On 24 September 1878, within a month of obtaining the leather strips from Selim, Moses Shapira sent a transcription of the fragments to Professor Konstantine Schlottmann at Halle University. Shapira felt his scroll might predate any known version of the Bible, and he hoped for Schlottmann's favorable assessment of it. On 7 October he received Schlottmann's angry reply suggesting that the manuscript was a forgery. The professor seemed to base some of his comments more on theology than critical scholarship. Nonetheless, upon reading Schlottmann's objections, Shapira began to waiver in his opinion, primarily because of the general point that the manuscript contradicted the Bible. He therefore put the manuscript in a bank vault where it would remain for nearly five years.

Around the spring of 1883, Shapira read a book written in 1860 by Friedrich Bleek, *An Introduction to the Old Testament*. Upon reading this work he realized that many eminent scholars questioned whether Deuteronomy was written by Moses or even around the time that Moses lived. Bleek's work identified examples from the canonical text that supported these academic views. Shapira also realized something else—none of the texts that the scholars used to deny Mosaic authorship were present in his manuscript. Moreover, his manuscript, except for its opening and closing lines, used the term *Elohim* rather than the four-lettered name of God. This also suggested that at least the main body of his manuscript may have been written in an earlier period and that a later scribe may have appended the opening and closing lines to bring the manuscript more in line with current usage.

Before reading Bleek, Moses Shapira held to the traditional view, namely that Moses wrote the first five books of the Bible, known as the Torah, Law, or Pentateuch. Fundamentalist Jews and Christians believe that Moses wrote the contents of these books and then placed the completed work into the hands of the Levites, who carefully transmitted them. Of course, Shapira knew of one Jewish source that records the transmission this way: "Moses received the Torah from Sinai and transmitted it to Joshua; Joshua to the Elders; the Elders to the Prophets; and the Prophets transmitted it to the men of the Great Assembly" (Pirkei Avot 1:1).

This classical understanding suggests that the Torah that has come down to modern times can be traced back to Moses's day when Israel received it at Sinai.

He was also familiar with the ritual performed at the close of the synagogue Torah reading service, where the Torah scroll is raised and the congregation recites the following: "This is the Torah that Moses placed before the children of Israel at the LORD'S commandment, by the hand of Moses" (see Num 9:23 and Deut 4:4).

As a fundamentalist, he held that the entire five-volume work was the holy, inspired, authoritative, *inerrant* word of God that He gave through the agency of Moses (Ezra 7:6; Neh 8:1). As a traditionalist, he believed that even the letters, or to borrow a phrase from Jesus of Nazareth, every "jot and tittle" (Matt 5:17–20), were God-given. In short, the traditional view is that Moses wrote the first five books of the Bible as God dictated them to him, and subsequent generations of scribes carefully and accurately produced exact copies from his time to the present. Until reading Bleek, Shapira had not questioned these fundamentalist views.

Nevertheless, by reading the work of eminent Bible scholars he came to see that this traditional view of Mosaic authorship was not unchallenged. The challenges to Mosaic authority were not simply based on Bleek's choosing, or that of other critical scholars, but were evident in the text of the Bible. For instance, nowhere in the five books does it say that Moses wrote them in their entirety. Most of the material contained in the Torah is presented in the third person.[301] More often than not, the Torah tells stories about Moses in a style most naturally understood as being written by someone *other* than Moses. We frequently read, for example, "and the LORD spoke to Moses." If Moses were the writer, it would seem more natural, or at least less awkward, to say something like, "and the LORD spoke to me." Scripture also tells us that Moses was a "very humble man, more so than any man on earth" (Num 12:3), a phrase unlikely penned by the world's most humble man. The book of Deuteronomy informs us, "Never again did there arise in Israel a prophet like Moses" (Deut 34:10).[302] Would the humblest man on earth write such a statement about himself? And in the third person? And how is it that this is recorded after the death of Moses? Who wrote this? We read about Moses' death and burial earlier in the same final chapter of Deuteronomy (Deut 34:5ff). Moses obviously did not write this.

In its present form, the Torah also contains language that is not consistent with the words of a contemporary author. For instance, the writer of Genesis 12:6 informs us that "the Canaanites were then in the land." This implies that the Canaanites were no longer in the land when the passage was written. If Moses wrote the Torah—the five books—before the conquest of Canaan, then this statement seems to be anachronistic. According to information found elsewhere in the Bible, the Canaanites were still in the land until a much later period, certainly until after the conquest of Canaan.

---

[301] The Pentateuch mentions the name of Moses 640 times—Exodus nearly 300, Leviticus 85, Numbers 230, and Deuteronomy 35.

[302] This is not stated as a prophecy ("and never again shall there arise ..."), but as an observation made in retrospect.

These and many more examples led investigators to surmise that someone other than Moses wrote much of the Torah, and Shapira was unable to dispute their logic. He began to wonder what Moses actually wrote. Had traditionalists attributed more to the hand of Moses than the Torah itself claims? The logical place to begin an objective search for answers is in the Torah. What does the Torah say that Moses wrote?

"When Moses had put down in writing the words of this Teaching to the very end, Moses charged the Levites who carried the Ark of the Covenant of the LORD, saying: Take this book of Teaching and place it beside the Ark of the Covenant of the LORD your God, and let it remain there as a witness against you" (Deut 31:24–26; compare Deut 31:9).

These verses inform us that Moses "put down in writing" a particular "Teaching" (*torah* in Hebrew) and gave it to the Levites. At first glance, the reference to Moses writing "this Teaching/Torah," appears to validate the traditional view that he did write the Torah or Pentateuch. However, this understanding becomes problematic when we realize, as we just read, that "this Teaching" was complete—"to the very end"—but there are still three chapters left in *our* Torah! In other words, Deuteronomy 31 records the completion of Moses's writing, while our present book of Deuteronomy, and thus the Torah as we know it today, is *not* complete. Consequently, whatever was completed in Deuteronomy 31 could not have been the traditional Torah (Gen 1:1 through Deut 34:12). So, what did Moses complete and hand over to the Levites, charging them to place it "beside the Ark"?

Within the Torah itself there are seven references to Moses writing something (Exod 17:14; 24:4; 34:27; Num 33:2; Deut 31:9, 22, 24–26). Exodus 17:14 tells us, in the third person: "Then the LORD said to Moses, 'Inscribe this in a document as a reminder.'" The reminder was that God would "blot out the memory of Amalek" (Deut 25:17–19 gives further instruction). Exodus 24:4 tells us that "Moses then wrote down all the commands of the LORD." In verse 7 we learn that the document Moses wrote was called "the record of the covenant"[303]—in other words, and more literally based on the Hebrew, the covenant scroll, a name that best describes a document whose main content was the covenant. Numbers 33:2 informs us in the third person that "Moses recorded the starting points of their various marches," and Deuteronomy begins with a travel record. Based on these third-person statements, we get an idea of what was contained in the scroll that Moses wrote and entrusted to the care of the Levites who carried the ark. Interestingly, all of these references point exclusively to content found in the book of Deuteronomy.

Moses referred to his scroll as the "book of Teaching," literally "scroll of the torah"—*sefer ha-torah* in Hebrew (Deut 31:26). This phrase occurs ten times in the Hebrew Bible, four in Deuteronomy and six outside the Torah (Deut 28:61;

---

[303] Hebrew ספר הברית.

29:20; 30:10; 31:26; Josh 1:8; 8:34; 2 Kgs 22:8, 11; Neh 8:3; 2 Chr 34:15). What clues do these passages provide about what was written in the scroll? They inform us that the scroll of the Torah contained blessings, curses, commandments, and laws. All of these references to the "book of Teaching" point to content found in Deuteronomy.

We also learn that the people were commanded to recite from the book of the Torah day and night, and in Nehemiah we see that the scroll was read before an assembled group. We should note that the reading of the book was accomplished in a morning, "from the first light until midday" (Neh 8:3), and this included "translating it and giving the sense" (v. 8). This implies that the book of the Torah was much shorter than the Pentateuch. To read the entire five books requires more than twenty hours. A morning would allow for reading only a single book, possibly Deuteronomy.[304]

The phrase "Book of Moses," literally "scroll of Moses"—*sefer Moshe* in Hebrew, occurs four times in the Hebrew Bible (Ezra 6:18; Neh 13:1; 2 Chr 25:4; 35:12). Two of these passages reference material exclusive to Deuteronomy. Nehemiah 13:1 refers to Deuteronomy 23:3–5, and 2 Chronicles 25:4 refers to Deuteronomy 24:16.

The "Teaching of Moses," literally "torah of Moses"—*torat Moshe* in Hebrew, is yet another designation for the scroll that Moses wrote. This phrase (with no further qualifiers) occurs eight times in the Hebrew Bible (Josh 8:32; 1 Kgs 2:3; 2 Kgs 23:25; Dan 9:13; Ezra 3:2; 7:6; 2 Chr 23:18; 30:16). The passage in 1 Kings relates King David's charge to Solomon as David's life drew near its end. His parting words were that Solomon should "walk in His [God's] ways" as recorded in the "Teaching of Moses." This phrase is found only in Deuteronomy (8:6; 19:9; 26:17; 30:16). Walking in His ways would guarantee that Solomon would "succeed" or prosper. This phrase, too, only occurs in Deuteronomy (29:8 [v. 9 in English]).

Second Kings 23:25 describes King Josiah. We read that there was no king like him, "who turned back to the LORD with all his heart and soul and might." In the Torah, the phrase "turn back to the LORD," as well as the three-fold "heart and soul and might," are only found in one book—Deuteronomy. Notice, for example, Deuteronomy 6:5: "You shall love the LORD your God with all your heart and with all your soul and with all your might." "Heart and soul" is terminology found in Deuteronomy and nowhere else in the Torah (Deut 4:29; 6:5; 10:12; 11:13; 13:4 [v. 3 in English]; 26:16; 30:2, 6, 10). Also, the phrase "nor did any like him arise after him" (2 Kgs 23:25) bears a striking resemblance to the description of Moses in Deuteronomy 34:10.

Six additional passages mention the "Teaching/Torah of Moses." Two of them (Ezra 3:2; 2 Chr 30:16) refer to Moses as the "man of God." This appellation

---

[304] This was suggested to me by Jono Vandor, founder and host of the popular podcast Truth2U (Truth2U.org), a site with unique and entertaining Tanakh-focused programs. Jono also co-hosts the radio show *Israel on My Mind* and co-leads the *Tanakh Tours* (https://www.tanakhtours.com/) to Israel with the author. He is also a news anchor for Israel News Talk Radio.

is found in the Pentateuch only once, in Deuteronomy 33:1. The remaining passages mention the "Teaching/Torah of Moses" but do not include direct quotations (Dan 9:11, 13; Neh 8:1; 2 Chr 23:18).

Another description of Moses's scroll is the "Book of the Teaching of Moses," literally "book of the torah of Moses"—*sefer torat Moshe* in Hebrew. This designation is used four times in the biblical text (Josh 8:31; 23:6; 2 Kgs 14:6; Neh 8:1). The passage in Joshua 8 relates how Joshua constructed an altar and set up plastered stones on which were inscribed a copy of the "Teaching that Moses had written." The account makes it clear that this is a direct fulfillment of instructions written in the "Book of the Teaching of Moses," and we find the charge to do so in Deuteronomy 27:4–6. The passage in Joshua 23 demands faithful observance to "all that is written in the Book of the Teaching of Moses," and further defines this faithful observance using the phrase "without ever deviating from it to the right or to the left" (23:6). Regarding observance, this phrase is found only in one of the first five books of the Bible—see Deuteronomy 5:29 [v. 32 in English]; 17:11, 20. In 2 Kings 14:6 we read that Judah's King Amaziah followed a specific rule "written in the Book of the Teaching of Moses." The quote comes directly from Deuteronomy 24:16 (the idea may be alluded to in Numbers 27:3 but is found only in Deuteronomy).

Malachi ends with an admonition to be mindful of the "Teaching of My Servant Moses," literally "torah of Moses my servant"—*torat Moshe avdi* in Hebrew (Mal 3:22 [4:4 in English]). We further read that this Teaching originated at Horeb, another name for Mt. Sinai. The name *Sinai* is used twenty-six times in the Torah, but only once in Deuteronomy, which prefers to call the holy mountain Horeb.[305]

In summary, from this survey of the relevant texts it becomes apparent that whenever the biblical writers use the terms "Book of Teaching," "Book of Moses," "Teaching of Moses," "Book of the Teaching of Moses," or "Teaching of My Servant Moses," they are referring to a specific document that Moses himself wrote, the content of which is found in Deuteronomy. Additionally, when mention is made of Moses writing something, the reference is either found in the book of Deuteronomy or refers to something recorded in Deuteronomy.

Based on the biblical evidence, Moses's original scroll would be a shortened form of Deuteronomy, written in the first person and lacking anachronism. It would contain a travel log, commandments, blessings and curses, and would not include Moses's death. Shapira could not help but notice that his scroll was a form of the Bible's book of Deuteronomy, considerably shorter than the version of Deuteronomy found in the Pentateuch. The main body of his scroll was written in the first person. It contained a travel log, but noticeably, the route made better

---

[305] The book of Deuteronomy uses *Horeb* nine times (1:2, 6, 19; 4:10, 15; 5:2; 9:8; 18:16; 28:69). It occurs elsewhere in the Pentateuch only in Exodus (3:1; 17:16; 33:6). *Sinai* occurs only once in Deuteronomy (33:1) and there it appears in a text written in the third person and is therefore obviously the work of another hand. *Sinai* occurs elsewhere in the Pentateuch thirty-four times (Exod 16:1; 19:1, 11, 18, 20, 23; 24:16; 31:18; 34:2, 4, 29, 32; Lev 7:38; 25:1; 26:46; 27:34; Num 1:1, 19; 3:1, 4, 14; 9:1, 5; 10:12; 26:64; 28:6; 33:15, 16).

sense of the geography in his scroll. It also contained commandments, blessings and curses, and did not include Moses's death and burial. It seemed to fit the description of the little scroll written by Moses as described in the Bible, and perhaps most importantly, his scroll contained none of the passages that scholars had identified as later insertions. Based on the texts of the Bible and the judgment of critical scholars, if we imagined an original Moses scroll, it might look very much like Shapira's scroll.

J

The First Great Discovery

The Bible records that in 622 BCE, in the days of Judah's King Josiah, a scroll was discovered in the temple. According to the narrative, this was the very scroll that Moses himself had written. Researchers and Bible students have long maintained that the discovered scroll was a form of Deuteronomy, an association made largely because the details of Josiah's reform closely match content found in Deuteronomy. Eventually, a theory was developed that suggested that the scroll was not the object of a "discovery" at all but that, in reality, it was composed in Josiah's day. In other words, according to some scholars Deuteronomy was not rediscovered in the seventh century BCE but was written at that time to support Josiah's reform. In the words of one such scholar, Deuteronomy was a "pious fraud"![306]

Josiah stands above all the kings mentioned in Scripture. He is the only descendant of David whose birth was prophesied, and according to the writer of Kings, that prediction was made some three hundred years in advance. The prophet even names him! "O altar, altar! Thus said the LORD: A son shall be born to the House of David, Josiah by name; and he shall slaughter upon you the priests of the shrines who bring offerings upon you. And human bones shall be burned upon you" (1 Kgs 13:2).

The story of Josiah's reign is told in 2 Kings 22–23 and 2 Chronicles 34–35. While the two accounts contain significant variations, there are important aspects in which they agree. For instance, we know that Josiah was eight years old when he assumed the throne and that his reign lasted thirty-one years.[307] His father, King Amon, was assassinated.[308] Josiah did what was right, followed the ways of his ancestor David, and did not deviate to the right or to the left.[309] As noted in the previous chapter, the reference to not turning to the right or left points to the book of Deuteronomy.[310] The Chronicler informs us that Josiah began to seek God at the age of sixteen, and when he was twenty he began a "purge" of the land.[311]

---

[306] Richard Elliott Friedman, *Who Wrote the Bible* (New York: HarperCollins, 1987), 102. One cannot help but think of Shapira's comment about "the tendency of showing great scholarship by detecting a forgery."
[307] 2 Kings 22:1; 2 Chronicles 34:1.
[308] 2 Kings 21:23–24; 2 Chronicles 33:24–25.
[309] 2 Kings 22:2; 2 Chronicles 34:2.
[310] Deuteronomy 5:32; 17:11, 20.
[311] 2 Chronicles 34:3ff.

In 622 BCE, the eighteenth year of his reign, King Josiah, then twenty-six years old, commissioned a group of officials to undertake a major restoration of the temple.[312] During the work, the high priest at the time reported a discovery to the scribe Shaphan: "As they took out the silver that had been brought to the House of the LORD, the priest Hilkiah found a scroll of the LORD's Teaching given by Moses. Hilkiah spoke up and said to the scribe Shaphan, 'I have found a scroll of the Teaching in the House of the LORD'; and Hilkiah gave the scroll to Shaphan" (2 Chr 34:14–15).

The language used to describe the discovery is worthy of note. First, the scroll is called the "LORD's Teaching."[313] The phrase "given by Moses" is more accurately rendered as "given by the hand of Moses."[314] In other words, this passage indicates that Hilkiah believed that the newly-discovered scroll was not just *any* scroll, but rather that it was none other than the very scroll that Moses had written—*the* scroll of the teaching! The discovery took place in the temple, where we would expect to find this scroll written by Moses since it was to be kept near the ark.[315]

Hilkiah gave the scroll to Shaphan, who took it to Josiah. Shaphan updated the king on the progress of the work and then told him about the newfound scroll. Shaphan read the scroll to Josiah, and according to both of our sources, "When the king heard the words of the scroll of the Teaching, he rent his clothes."[316]

The king then sent an entourage, including Shaphan and Hilkiah, to a prophetess named Huldah. Although the prophetess predicted the demise of the kingdom,[317] she assured the emissaries that Josiah, due to his heartfelt repentance, had earned himself a peaceful death in that his eyes would "not see all the disaster which I [Jehovah] will bring upon this place."[318] They brought Huldah's message back to Josiah, who immediately initiated a sweeping reform throughout his realm.[319] The detailed description of the reform strongly suggests that it was based

---

[312] The Hebrew Bible mentions that the temple had undergone a previous repair during the reign of Jehoash (2 Kgs 12:1–16). Since that previous work, 218 years had elapsed (Seder Olam 24). Dan Bruce, *Sacred Chronology of the Hebrew Kings,* 90.

[313] תורת יהוה—Torah of Jehovah. See Exodus 13:9; 2 Kings 10:31; Isaiah 5:24; 30:9; Jeremiah 8:8; Amos 2:4; Psalms 1:2; 19:8; 119:1; Ezra 7:10; Nehemiah 9:3; 1 Chronicles 16:40; 22:12; 2 Chronicles 12:1; 17:9; 31:3; 34:14; 35:26.

[314] The Hebrew phrase ביד משה occurs thirty-one times in Scripture, sixteen of which are in the Torah. Interestingly, it never occurs in Deuteronomy. This is to be expected given the cumulative evidence presented in this book.

[315] Deuteronomy 31:26.

[316] 2 Kings 22:11; 2 Chronicles 34:19. The passage in 2 Chronicles omits "the scroll," but otherwise the sources agree verbatim.

[317] 1 Kings 22:14–17; 2 Chronicles 34:22–25. The language is especially interesting. The Chronicler says that the curses mentioned in the book read before the king would come "upon this place and its inhabitants." See Deuteronomy 29:20 for the reference to the curses.

[318] 2 Kings 22:20; 2 Chronicles 34:28.

[319] An interesting archaeological discovery was made in excavations of biblical Tamar, located in the Aravah about thirty miles southwest of the Dead Sea. In biblical times, Tamar was on the extreme southern boundary of Israel (see Ezekiel 47:19 and 48:28 where the future borders list Tamar as the southern boundary). This can be verified from several factors. It is situated very near Ma'ale Akkrabim (Scorpion's Ascent). See the references to Ma'ale Akkrabim in Numbers 34:4; Joshua 15:3; and Judges 1:36. During two major archaeological excavations (1987–1996 and 2005–2009) eight strata were exposed. Stratum 6 dates to the

on material from the book of Deuteronomy. In other words, the actions taken by King Josiah would lead one to believe that he was seeking to apply Deuteronomic law in his kingdom.

Josiah began by reading the contents of the scroll in the hearing of all the people. Deuteronomy is the only book of the Torah that calls for reading the Torah aloud in the presence of all Israel. Even though the public reading is specified to take place "every seventh year, the year set for remission, at the Feast of Booths," there is a striking similarity of language between the text of Deuteronomy and Josiah's actions.[320]

> When all Israel comes to appear before the LORD your God in the place that He will choose, you shall read this Teaching aloud in the presence of all Israel. Gather the people—men, women, children, and the strangers in your communities—that they may hear and so learn to revere the LORD your God and to observe faithfully every word of this Teaching. Their children, too, who have not had the experience, shall hear and learn to revere the LORD your God as long as they live in the land that you are about to cross the Jordan to possess. (Deut 31:11–13)

After reading the teaching to the assembled people, Josiah led them in pledging fidelity to the ancient covenant outlined in the scroll: "The king stood by the pillar and solemnized the covenant before the LORD: that they would follow the LORD and observe His commandments, His injunctions, and His laws with all their heart and soul; that they would fulfill all the terms of this covenant as inscribed upon the scroll. And all the people entered into the covenant" (2 Kgs 23:3).

Here, too, the language is Deuteronomic. Commenting on this verse, the *Jewish Study Bible* makes the following point: "Idioms in this verse echo those in Deuteronomy: *follow the LORD* (Deut. 13:5); *observe His commandments, His injunctions, and His laws* (Deut. 4:45 and 40 other verses); *all their heart and soul* (Deut. 4:29; 6:5); *entered into a covenant* (Deut. 29:11)."[321]

In addition to the references noted in the *Jewish Study Bible* on "all their heart and soul," one should also note the other occurrences of that Deuteronomic phrase.[322]

The reform, as presented in our narratives, continues to show Deuteronomy's influence. In accordance with Deuteronomy 12:2, Josiah demolished the idolatrous sites. More specifically, he burned them, a directive that is found only

---

seventh century BCE, the time of Josiah. One remarkable find, located a few meters east of a Judean fortress, has been proposed to be an Edomite cultic site. When the altar was unearthed, there were numerous cultic items that obviously had been purposely smashed. It is believed that this destruction of the cultic items took place in the time of Josiah's reform. The items include censers, bowls, and other incense burners. These have been restored and are presently on display in the Israel Museum. See, Rudolph Cohen and Yigal Yisrael, *On the Road to Edom, Discoveries from 'En Hazeva*, (Jerusalem: The Israel Museum, 1995).

[320] Deuteronomy 31:10; compare the report in 2 Kings 23:1–2.

[321] Berlin et al., *The Jewish Study Bible*, 772.

[322] The expression "heart and soul" is found in the book of Deuteronomy and nowhere else in the Pentateuch. See Deuteronomy 4:29; 6:5; 10:12; 11:13; 13:4; 26:16; 30:2, 6, 10.

in Deuteronomy.[323] In 2 Kings 23:6, 12, and 15 we find that Josiah beat to dust and scattered the objects associated with unlawful worship.[324] It is also worth pointing out that in destroying the shrines outside of Jerusalem during his reform, he essentially centralized all worship in Jerusalem; this accords with Deuteronomy 12:4–7. Finally, we read the following statement about Josiah's reform: "Josiah also did away with the necromancers and the mediums, the idols and the fetishes—all the detestable things that were to be seen in the land of Judah and Jerusalem. Thus he fulfilled the terms of the Teaching recorded in the scroll that the priest Hilkiah had found in the House of the LORD" (2 Kgs 23:24).[325]

Clues discerned from the details of Josiah's reform indicate that the scroll Hilkiah discovered was Deuteronomy—or a text more similar to it than any other book of the Pentateuch. Due in part to the indications we have been covering, others have also advanced this view. Richard Elliott Friedman, known for his work on the Documentary Hypothesis, summed it up this way:

> Josiah's reforms are connected to instructions that are found in D; the narrative of Josiah's making those reforms is told in terms and phrases that are typically found in D; and Josiah's reforms are traced to the promulgation of a particular scroll, which is identified by the same words as the scroll that Moses writes in D. This interlocking chain of connections led to the extremely widely held view in scholarship that the scroll that was read in Josiah's day was D.[326]

In a note on 2 Kings 22:1–20 ("The discovery of a scroll"), the editors of the *Jewish Study Bible* include the following: "Most, but not all, modern scholars consider this account to be largely historical, reflecting the '(re)discovery' of Deuteronomy in this period."[327]

Commenting on 2 Kings 22:8, the *Jewish Study Bible* has one more note that is instructive for our present quest:

> The *scroll of the Teaching* is referred to simply as *a scroll* in v. 10, but in 23:2 as "the covenant scroll" and in 2 Chron. 34:14 as "a scroll of the LORD's teaching given by Moses." *Scroll,* Heb "sefer," indicates that it was a longish document; *Teaching,* Heb "torah," that it contained instruction; "covenant," Heb "berit," that it contained a contract/agreement. Hilkiah's description suggests that what is novel about the find is that *the Teaching*— marked by the definite article as something already known—was found written in a scroll. The contents of this *scroll* and Josiah's and the people's reaction to it suggest that it was some form of the book of Deuteronomy.

---

[323] See Deuteronomy 7:5, 25; 12:3.

[324] Compare Deuteronomy 9:21, the only reference to such language in the Torah in regard to unlawful worship. I learned this from the work of Richard Elliott Friedman. See, for instance, the introduction to his *The Bible with Sources Revealed* (New York: HarperCollins, 2003).

[325] Compare Deuteronomy 18:9–14.

[326] Richard Elliott Friedman, *The Bible with Sources Revealed,* 26. "D" stands for the supposed Deuteronomic source in the Torah, the "D" of JEPD in the Documentary Hypothesis.

[327] Berlin, et al., *The Jewish Study Bible,* 771.

Often, we can only connect with the ancient world through written materials. However, when we have the opportunity to go beyond such connections we bolster our confidence in the veracity of our literary sources. In that vein, as research for this book was underway, a discovery was made in Jerusalem. Dr. Yiftah Shalev of the Israel Antiquities Authority and Professor Yuval Gadot were leading an excavation of the Givati parking lot located in the City of David National Park. While working in the remains of a large public building that showed evidence of destruction, likely demolished during the Babylonian siege of Jerusalem in 586 BCE, they discovered an ancient seal. Dr. Anat Mendel-Geberovich of the Hebrew University of Jerusalem and the Center for the Study of Ancient Jerusalem deciphered the seal. Her assessment of the one-centimeter seal turned up some interesting points. Dr. Mendel-Geberovich suggested that the seal belonged to a well-known person. She made this determination because it only contained a first name. In her opinion, this was all that was needed to identify the seal's owner, as he must have been known to all. The words on the seal, written in a script from the First Temple period, read, *LeNathan Melekh Eved haMelekh*— (belonging) to Nathan Melekh Servant of the King. One named Nathan Melekh is mentioned in the Bible, and only in a single verse: "He [Josiah] did away with the horses that the kings of Judah had dedicated to the sun, at the entrance of the House of the LORD, near the chamber of the eunuch Nathan-melech, which was in the precincts" (2 Kgs 23:11).

The Nathan Melekh of 2 Kings 23:11 was a servant of King Josiah and likely took part in the king's religious reform. While the academic world stops just short of claiming that the seal discovered in the Givati parking lot belonged to the Nathan Melekh mentioned in 2 Kings 23:11, it does not seem unreasonable to make that association. Could it be possible that the archaeological team unearthed a seal with the name of someone who actually witnessed Josiah's reform? Quite fortuitously, the seal of another person who figures in our story was discovered earlier. To be more precise, two seals of this person with identical inscriptions have surfaced.[328] The name of the owner was Baruch ben Neriah. The seals indicate that Baruch was a scribe. We know of a man by this name from the Bible. Baruch ben Neriah was the scribe for a very significant person in the biblical world—Jeremiah, a prophet at the time of the first great discovery.

---

[328] The first seal with an unknown provenance came to light in 1975. Some suggest that it was originally discovered during excavations of the so-called "burnt house," directed by Yigal Shiloh, though this has not been confirmed. The second seal, identically inscribed, surfaced in 1996. This one, in addition to the name, contained a fingerprint.

The Prophet Jeremiah

Jeremiah was "the son of Hilkiah, one of the priests at Anathoth in the territory of Benjamin."[329] Anathoth is first mentioned in the book of Joshua among the towns assigned to the Levites. Specifically, it was one of four Levitical communities in the tribal territory of Benjamin.[330] It was also to Anathoth that Solomon banished Abiathar after the death of his father, David, because Abiathar had supported Adonijah as king.[331]

We know from Jeremiah's opening verses that he was a prophet and the son of a priest named Hilkiah, which was also the name of the high priest who discovered the "scroll of the LORD's Teaching given by Moses."[332] Several authorities propose that the priest Hilkiah who found the scroll was Jeremiah's father. An article entitled "The Prophet Jeremiah," posted by the Chabad-Lubavitch organization, says, "Jeremiah was born in a priestly family, in the town of Anatoth belonging to the Tribe of Benjamin. His father was the prophet and Kohen-Gadol (High Priest) Hilkiah."[333]

The entry "Hilkiah" in the *Jewish Encyclopedia* identifies eight people from the Bible with that name.[334] According to that article, medieval commentators Abravanel and Kimchi proposed that Jeremiah's father was the high priest who discovered the scroll. While it is tempting to give credence to that view, we cannot say for sure. Richard Elliott Friedman puts it this way: "Jeremiah … was a priest from Anathoth. And his father was a priest named Hilkiah. (Not to overstate the case, we do not know if Jeremiah's father was the same priest Hilkiah who found the book.)"[335] Nonetheless, the idea is worthy of consideration.

Biblical chronology tells us that the scroll was discovered in the eighteenth year of Josiah's reign. By that time, Jeremiah had been receiving the word of the LORD for five years.[336] However, when the king wanted to "inquire of the LORD,"

[329] Jeremiah 1:1.
[330] Joshua 21:17–18.
[331] 1 Kings 2:26–27.
[332] 2 Chronicles 34:14; cf. 2 Kings 22:8.
[333] https://www.chabad.org/library/article_cdo/aid/112327/jewish/The-Prophet-Jeremiah.htm/.
[334] http://jewishencyclopedia.com/articles/7696-hilkiah.
[335] Friedman, *Who Wrote the Bible,* 126.
[336] From the opening words of Jeremiah we learn that the word of the LORD first came to Jeremiah in the thirteenth year of Josiah's reign and the scroll was discovered in the eighteenth year of his reign (1 Kgs 22:3; 2 Chr 34:8).

it was to the prophetess Huldah that he sent his delegation, not to Jeremiah.[337] The texts are silent as to why he chose Huldah.[338] Some speculate that Jeremiah may have been too young, but we simply do not know the reason.

Information gleaned from the book of Jeremiah suggests that his preaching began *after* the discovery of the scroll. Jack R. Lundbom says it this way: "No prophetic preaching, in any event, should be dated before the year 622."[339] Jeremiah says that when the words of the LORD were found, he devoured them.[340] The reference to *finding* the words of the LORD seems to allude to the discovery of the scroll that was *found* in 622 BCE. One thing is clear: Jeremiah's preaching features Deuteronomic language, and the discovered scroll was a form of the book of Deuteronomy.

If Hilkiah the priest who discovered the scroll and Hilkiah the father of Jeremiah were the same person, Jeremiah certainly would have had access to the scroll. If he read a scroll that he believed to be the authentic Moses scroll and that did not agree with the Torah of his day, we can understand how he could suggest that the scribes' lying pen had made the Torah a lie.[341] Further, if the discovered scroll lacked any reference to elaborate sacrificial ritual, his words in chapter 7:21–26 would make more sense.

It should not be surprising that it was in the temple that Hilkiah found the "scroll of the LORD's Teaching given by Moses." Moses entrusted the completed scroll to the care of the Levites and charged them to place it "beside the ark."[342] An interesting point about the discovery during Josiah's reign, however, is that the ark is not mentioned. One would think that if the ark had been in the temple at the time of the refurbishment, it would be mentioned, at least in passing. According to Hilkiah's report of the discovery we learn only that he found the scroll in "the house of the LORD."[343] Jewish commentator Rashi reported from an otherwise unknown source that the scroll was discovered "under a layer of stones where they had concealed it when Ahaz burned the Torah."[344] Abravanel said that Hilkiah "discovered it in its hiding place, between two rows of stones."[345]

Where was the ark? It seems odd that if it were in "the house of the LORD," it would not be mentioned. The most logical conclusion is that the ark was not present in the temple when Hilkiah discovered the scroll, and the biblical writers confirm this.

Kings and Chronicles report that in the same year in which the scroll was discovered, Josiah commanded all the people to "keep the Passover to the

---

[337] 2 Kings 22:13ff; 2 Chronicles 34:21ff.
[338] Zephaniah was also a prophet "during the reign of King Josiah son of Amon of Judah" (Zeph 1:1).
[339] Jack R. Lundbom, "Jeremiah (Prophet)," in *Anchor Bible Dictionary.*
[340] Jeremiah 15:16.
[341] Jeremiah 8:8.
[342] Deuteronomy 31:25–26.
[343] 2 Kings 22:8; 2 Chronicles 34:14.
[344] Rabbi A. J. Rosenberg, ed., *The Book of Kings 2, A New English Translation of the Text, Rashi and a Commentary Digest* (New York: The Judaica Press Inc., 1989), 409.
[345] Ibid.

LORD."[346] According to both accounts, there had not been such a Passover in a very long time.[347] At the time of that Passover, the ark suddenly appeared again: "[Josiah] said to the Levites, consecrated to the LORD, who taught all Israel, 'Put the Holy Ark in the House that Solomon son of David, king of Israel, built; as you no longer carry it on your shoulders, see now to the service of the LORD your God and His people Israel'" (2 Chr 35: 3).

The king's instructions prove that the ark was not in the temple prior to that time. According to the Chronicler, Josiah was responsible for returning it in preparation for the Passover of 622 BCE. We have no record that it was seen in public after that time.

Twenty-three years after the death of King Josiah, the Babylonian ruler Nebuchadnezzar destroyed Jerusalem. We have two records of Jerusalem's fall and neither mentions the ark (2 Kgs 25:13–17; Jer 52:17–23). Where did it go?[348] Richard Elliott Friedman sums up the mystery this way:

> For some reason, the biblical sources do not tell us what happened to the Ark containing the tablets of the Ten Commandments. Archeology, too, has shed no light on this at all. The disappearance of the Ark is the first great mystery of the period, and it remains one of the great mysteries of the Bible. There is no report that the ark was carried away or destroyed or hidden. There is not even any comment such as "And then the ark disappeared, and we do not know what happened to it," or "And no one knows where it is to this day." The most important object in the world, in the biblical view, simply ceases to be in the story.[349]

The ark of the covenant was the center of everything and had been with the children of Israel since the wilderness days. It was last mentioned during Josiah's Passover of 622 BCE but was absent by the time of the fall of Jerusalem. This means that sometime during a period of thirty-six years the ark went missing.[350] The last word on the ark, at least as far as the Bible is concerned, comes to us in the form of a prophecy of Jeremiah during Josiah's reign: "And when you increase and are fertile in the land, in those days—declares the LORD—men shall no longer speak of the Ark of the Covenant of the LORD, nor shall it come to mind. They shall not mention it, or miss it, or make another" (Jer 3:16).[351]

What would lead Jeremiah to say such a thing? It is possible that at the time of his pronouncement the ark was already out of sight, but not yet out of mind. If

---

[346] 2 Kings 22:3, 8; 23:21–23; 2 Chronicles 34:8, 14–15; 35:1, 19.

[347] 1 Kings 23:22; 2 Chronicles 35:18.

[348] There are numerous legends about the disappearance of the ark. Sources agree that it was never in the Second Temple. Josephus in his *Jewish Wars* 5.5 and the Roman Tacitus in his *Histories* V.9 say as much. Josephus also informs us that in 64 BCE, when Pompey entered the temple he saw the sacred articles, but when Josephus relates what was seen, the ark is not listed (*Jewish War* 1.152–153; *Antiquities* 14:71–72). When Ezekiel describes the future temple (chapters 40–48) he does not mention the ark.

[349] Friedman, *Who Wrote the Bible*, 156.

[350] From the Passover of 622 BCE to 586 BCE is thirty-six years.

[351] Jeremiah 3:6 indicates that these prophetic words date to the "days of King Josiah."

so, where did it go? Rabbinic tradition holds that Josiah hid the ark.[352] If this is true, he had to hide it between 622 BCE and 609 BCE, the thirteen years between his famous Passover and his death. If Josiah did hide the ark, it is also possible that Jeremiah did not know its whereabouts since we have no record of the two men ever directly interacting. Unfortunately, the Bible offers no help in substantiating this view.

Another possibility is that Jeremiah was responsible for the disappearance of the ark. But if he were involved, why would he mention it at all? Both Jeremiah and his father were priests, and it may have been his father who discovered the scroll. Even if the discoverer was not his father, we know that Jeremiah had close connections to an inner circle of people who would have been able to effect the ark's removal from the temple. We also know that Jeremiah was actively hearing from the LORD during the last eighteen years of Josiah's life. So he was in Jerusalem when the ark disappeared, whether or not he was involved in its disappearance.

According to an account in 2 Maccabees, Jeremiah was personally involved in hiding the ark. While the document is late, dated by most scholars no earlier than 110 BCE, it is presented as a work containing historical records. The relevant story reads as follows:

> One finds in the records[353] that the prophet Jeremiah ordered those who were being deported to take some of the fire, as has been mentioned, and that the prophet, after giving them the law, instructed those who were being deported not to forget the commandments of the Lord, or to be led astray in their thoughts on seeing the gold and silver statues and their adornment. And with other similar words he exhorted them that the law should not depart from their hearts. It was also in the same document that the prophet, having received an oracle, ordered that the tent and the ark should follow with him, and that he went out to the mountain where Moses had gone up and had seen the inheritance of God. Jeremiah came and found a cave-dwelling, and he brought there the tent and the ark and the altar of incense; then he sealed up the entrance. Some of those who followed him came up intending to mark the way but could not find it. When Jeremiah learned of it, he rebuked them and declared: "The place shall remain unknown until God gathers his people together again and shows his mercy. Then the Lord will disclose these things, and the glory of the Lord and the cloud will appear, as they were shown in the case of Moses, and as Solomon asked that the place should be specially consecrated." (2 Macc 2:1–8 NRSV)

---

[352] B. Yoma 53b–54a; y. Shek. 6:1–2; 49C.

[353] The Greek word used here for "records" (*apographēs*) is used four other times in the LXX or Septuagint (Greek translation of the Old Testament), always for an official register. It is even used in Daniel 10:21 for an official "book of truth" revealed to Daniel. It might indicate that the author of 2 Maccabees does indeed have in his possession some kind of written source.

The Babylonian destruction in 586 BCE seemingly marked the end of the kingdom of Judah. Its last king witnessed the execution of all the nobles of Judah, as well as his own sons, and then his eyes were put out.[354] The Davidic throne, which was supposed to last forever, was cast to the ground. The temple, that chosen and consecrated house where the name of God was to be forever—the place to which His eyes would look and His ears would be attentive to the prayers of His people—was burned to the ground.[355] This had been the hope and confidence of the people of the kingdom of Judah after the short-lived revival under Josiah. Now, everything was in ruins. The towns of Judah and the streets of Jerusalem were desolate. Neither the sound of mirth and gladness nor the voices of bridegroom and bride were any more heard.[356] The ark, which had been "the most important object in the world, in the biblical view,"[357] simply vanished from the story. Like the Urim and Thummim, it was gone, and Jeremiah said it didn't matter. He didn't use those exact words, but his pronouncement indicated that everyone would agree with him one day.

One is left to wonder if Jeremiah—prophet, priest, and possibly even the son of a high priest—was told by God to hide the most precious objects until a time prepared for their disclosure. Perhaps there is something behind the legend in Maccabees, but short of finding those items in a cave in modern-day Jordan, there simply is no way of knowing.

What about the scroll discovered in the days of Josiah? What if it wasn't a pious fraud after all? What became of the scroll that was written by the hand of Moses?

---

[354] Jeremiah 39:4–7.
[355] See, for example, 2 Chronicles 7:16 and Solomon's dedicatory prayer in 2 Kings 8, as well as God's response in 2 Kings 9:1–5.
[356] Jeremiah 7:34; 16:9; 25:10.
[357] Friedman, *Who Wrote the Bible,* 156.

Searching for the Hand of Moses

The biblical writers state unequivocally that Moses wrote a scroll, but do their references to Moses's original work point to a long-lost document? Has it joined the ranks of other ancient texts referred to in Scripture that have not survived to our day? The Hebrew Bible mentions several. There is a "Book of the Wars of the LORD," but all we know of its contents is a fragmentary quote preserved in Numbers 21:14. Joshua 10:13 and 2 Samuel 1:18 mention a "Book of Jasher," but those two brief passages are all we have of this work. Other works that have not come down to us include the "Annals of the Kings," sometimes followed by "of Judah" and other times by "of Israel."[358] Scripture also contains various references to books of or about specific people. For instance, three sources are mentioned as containing "the other events of Solomon's reign, early and late,"[359] and additional works related to the life of Manasseh.[360] And there are others. Is the scroll written by the hand of Moses yet another of these lost books?

Over a period of several generations, biblical scholars concluded that Moses did not write the five books traditionally ascribed to him. Today, most biblical scholars would be hesitant to recognize any of the Pentateuch as reflecting Moses's hand. Their investigations led them to theorize that the Pentateuch was developed by combining various independent hypothetical sources into a final edited work. One proposed source recorded a version of ancient Israel's stories and used the divine name *Jehovah* from the beginning. This source was designated as "J" for Jehovah. Another source recorded a version of the stories but referred to the Deity by the generic term *Elohim,* until in its version, *Jehovah* became known in Israel (Exod 3:13–15; 6:2–3). This source was designated as "E" for Elohim. A third source, comprising the largest collection, covered mainly legal and priestly matters. This source was designated as "P" for Priests.

Early in the nineteenth century a German scholar named W. M. L. De Wette, while working on his dissertation, suggested that the book of Deuteronomy—with its unique language and differences from the other three sources—represented a fourth source of the Pentateuch. This fourth source was designated "D" for

---

[358] 1 Kings 14:19, 29; 15:7, 23, 31; 16:5, 14, 20, 27; 22:39, 46; 2 Kings 1:18; 8:23; 10:34; 12:20; 13:8, 12; 14:15, 18, 28; 15:6, 11, 15, 21, 26, 31, 36; 16:19; 20:20; 21:17, 25; 23:28; 24:5; Esther 10:2; 2 Chronicles 16:11.
[359] 2 Chronicles 9:29.
[360] 2 Chronicles 33:18–19.

Deuteronomy. Based on these four hypothetical sources, scholars developed "the theory known as the 'Documentary Hypothesis,' which postulates that the Pentateuch was composed by the amalgamation of sections and subsections derived from four independent source-documents, J, E, P, D."[361]

De Wette denied the Mosaic authorship of Deuteronomy, and nearly every scholar since has followed his lead. Shapira expressed in his 9 May 1883 letter to Strack that he was familiar with the notion that Deuteronomy was written neither by Moses nor during his time. Directly or indirectly, this view can be traced to De Wette's work. While respecting the efforts and advances achieved by earlier scholars, it is not necessary to deny Mosaic authorship altogether. Building on their observations and considering the same texts on which they based their theories, we can submit several observations.

In chapter sixteen we demonstrated that biblical clues about the scroll that Moses wrote point to content in the book of Deuteronomy. In chapter seventeen we covered the biblical account of the discovery of the scroll written by the hand of Moses. All of this indicates that the scroll discovered in Josiah's day was a form of Deuteronomy. Richard Elliott Friedman says plainly, "The book that the priest Hilkiah said he found in the Temple in 622 B.C. was Deuteronomy."[362] He goes on to relate that this view is not new. As early as the church fathers, others had said the same. In 1808, De Wette also recognized that Deuteronomy was the discovered scroll, though he denied its Mosaic authorship. Instead, notes Friedman, he suggested, "Deuteronomy was written not long before it was 'found' in the Temple, and the 'finding' was just a charade. The book was written to provide grounds for Josiah's religious reform ... De Wette referred to it as 'pious fraud.'"[363]

Perhaps this biblical evidence and its dependence on Deuteronomic language point to a primitive core within our present book of Deuteronomy as the original material written by Moses. Clearly, as De Wette and subsequent scholars noted, Deuteronomy is different from the other books of the Pentateuch. It is the only one of the five that contains sections written in the first person. There are more than one hundred laws that appear only in Deuteronomy. There are narrative differences too, such as the story of the so-called spies and whose idea it was to send them into Canaan. In Numbers 13:2 it is the LORD who says to Moses, "Send men to scout the land of Canaan," whereas in Deuteronomy 1:22 Moses reports, "Then all of you came to me and said, 'Let us send men ahead to reconnoiter the land.'" Also, according to Numbers 20:10–13 and 27:12–23, Moses was not allowed to enter the promised land as punishment for his disbelief, but Deuteronomy attributes the cause to the people.[364] There are even differences in

---

[361] Umberto Cassuto, *The Documentary Hypothesis and the Composition of the Pentateuch,* trans. Israel Abrahams (Jerusalem: Shalem Press, 2006), 18.
[362] Friedman, *Who Wrote the Bible,* 101.
[363] Ibid., 102.
[364] See Deuteronomy 1:37, 3:24–28.

the Ten Words as listed in Exodus 20 and Deuteronomy 5, although both texts claim to report God's words spoken from the mount on the day of assembly.[365]

One of the significant differences between Deuteronomy and the rest of the Pentateuch involves the treatment of the sacrificial cult. Deuteronomy does not mention the elaborate details that are known in the other books. The *mishkan,* or tabernacle, plays no part in Deuteronomy. Nor does Deuteronomy single out Aaron's sons as a select group, but rather is satisfied with "the Levitical priests, the whole tribe of Levi" officiating.[366] Sacrifices are restricted to a centralized place in Deuteronomy, a stipulation with which no one in the biblical period seems to be familiar. Patriarchs, priests, and prophets reportedly sacrificed at altars in many locations, with no suggestion that this was prohibited. Since Josiah was the first to advance this centralization of worship, De Wette suggested that this requirement was not known prior to his reform. He said this was evidence of fraud and an indication that the text was composed in the seventh century BCE.

The ark of the covenant, described in detail and given such importance elsewhere in biblical literature, is hardly mentioned in Deuteronomy. There, it is a box that Moses built to hold the two stone tablets, whereas in Exodus we read of an ark of the testimony made by the spirit-filled artisans Bezalel and Oholiab.[367] In Exodus, Leviticus, and Numbers the two stone tablets are known as the testimony, but never in Deuteronomy.[368]

Deuteronomy allows for the establishment of a monarchy (Deut 17:14–20). However, anyone who reads the account of the people's request to Samuel for a "king like the nations" should notice that nothing in the narrative indicates a familiarity with divine permission to establish a human monarchy. On the contrary, at no time was this "torah of the king" cited in support of the request. Everyone in the story seemed surprised by the request, which supposedly was to be expected when "you come into the land" (Deut 17:14). Samuel did not appear to be aware of a predicted request for a "king like the nations." Instead, he saw the request as a rejection of his leadership. Neither does the account mention that God acknowledged that such a request had been predicted long before. He told Samuel that the people's request was a rejection of Him.[369]

Samuel was told to warn the people "solemnly, and tell them about the practices of any king who will rule over them."[370] Samuel obliged and then recorded them in a document, which he deposited "before the LORD." The Hebrew text says that "he wrote them [the rules of the monarchy] in THE scroll" and put it before the LORD.[371] According to this passage, Samuel wrote the "torah of the

---

[365] See Ross K. Nichols, "A Comparison of the Ten Words," https://www.academia.edu/43772655/A_Comparison_of_the_Ten_Words_in_English_with_Explanatory_Notes.
[366] Deuteronomy 18:1ff.
[367] Compare Deuteronomy 10:3 with Exodus 36:1–2; 37:1.
[368] See, for example, Exodus 25:16, 21–22; 31:18; 32:15; Leviticus 16:13; Numbers 4:5; 7:89.
[369] 1 Samuel 8:7.
[370] 1 Samuel 8:9b.
[371] 1 Samuel 10:25.

king." We have no record in the Bible of any king having "a copy of this Teaching written for him on a scroll by the Levitical priests" as required by the torah of the king.[372] One of the stipulations in the "torah of the king" was that the monarch must not have many wives, but even King David had multiple wives.[373] The Damascus Document, one of the Dead Sea Scrolls, mentions this in its discussion about taking a second wife while the first is alive:

> The principle of creation is, male and female he created them. Also, those who entered the ark went in two by two. And concerning the prince it is written, he shall not multiply wives to himself; but David had not read the sealed book of the Law which was in the ark (of the covenant), for it was not opened in Israel from the death of Eleazar and Joshua, and the elders who worshipped Ashtoreth. It was hidden and (was not) revealed until the coming of Zadok.[374]

This is an interesting observation. The writer said that David multiplied wives because he had not read the sealed book of the law. Also of note is the statement that this sealed book was "not opened in Israel from the death of Eleazar and Joshua." Joshua 24:29–33 records the deaths of Eleazar and Joshua. Note that verse 26 mentions Joshua writing in a "book of divine instruction." The Hebrew there is *sefer torat Elohim,* literally "a scroll of the Torah of God."

Within the Hebrew Bible, then, we have hints that portions of Deuteronomy were added after Moses's time. Does Joshua 24:26 suggest that Joshua added to a document called the scroll of the Torah of God? Is it possible that Moses did not include the torah of the king in his scroll, but that Samuel added it after the people's surprising request when they rejected God and chose to be ruled by a king like the nations? The author of the Damascus Document attempted to explain why the celebrated King David was unfamiliar with a specific rule for the monarchy—one that he was supposed to write for himself, keep with him, and read from all the days of his life. Evidently, David did not know about this torah of the king. It seems clear that Moses did not write it, and it could have been written after David's time.

According to texts from the Hebrew Bible, Moses wrote a scroll. It was known by several names—the Book of the Teaching, the Book of Moses, the Teaching of Moses, the Book of the Teaching of Moses, and the Teaching of My Servant Moses. When Moses completed his Torah scroll, he entrusted it to the Levites, specifically those who carried the ark.[375] They kept it beside the ark that Moses made. As the name implies, this covenant scroll had the ten-word covenant as its focus. It also contained a travel itinerary of sorts, commandments and laws, blessings and curses. Beyond these component parts indicated in Scripture, Moses likely penned little else. Over time, despite Moses's warning to "not add anything

---

[372] Deuteronomy 17:18.
[373] Deuteronomy 17:17; 1 Samuel 25:43; 2 Samuel 5:13.
[374] Geza Vermes, *The Complete Dead Sea Scrolls in English* (London: The Penguin Press, 1997), 130.
[375] Deuteronomy 31:24–26.

to what I command you or take anything away from it," this appears to be precisely what occurred.[376]

The authentic scroll of Moses likely would have been written in the first person; it would have addressed a contemporary audience and therefore would have lacked anachronistic language. A copy of the entire document could have been written on a few stones or read aloud to an assembly in a morning's time.[377] Moses's scroll was sealed away, perhaps in or near the ark that contained the tablets of the covenant. The biblical record indicates that Moses's message either was ignored or was unknown to most. The people of Israel relied on the religious authorities to instruct them, but both the leaders and the people failed to follow the teaching. Eventually its words, and even its location, were forgotten.

The account of the Moses scroll's rediscovery in the days of Josiah makes it clear that the people had not been following its precepts. The Passover, for example, had not been correctly observed in hundreds of years. The nation needed a great reform and a re-covenanting, and the Torah was read to a people who no longer knew its contents. It is likely that during the reform, perhaps Josiah, Jeremiah, or his faithful scribe Baruch ben Neriah made a copy of Moses's scroll. Jeremiah boldly claimed that the scribes had subverted the Torah and indicated that sacrifices were not part of the covenant when God freed their fathers from the land of Egypt.[378]

A form of the authentic Moses scroll became incorporated into a consolidated document containing other sacred histories so that our present Torah reflects a composite work. As Israelite religion developed, many of those other works were attributed to Moses, and later practices were projected back to Moses's time. Tradition attributes to Ezra the final editing of our present Torah.

Perhaps the most expansive view of such post-Mosaic addenda is raised by Rabbi Elazar ben Rabbi Matitya Hasid (France/Byzantium/Israel, thirteenth century). He wrote the following:

> As is known when Jeshurun was in the Babylonian Exile, the Torah was forgotten until the arrival of Ezra the kohen, sofer mahir[379] in the Torah of the Lord. He returned the Torah to them, and did not change anything from all of the commandments which God commanded Moses. Regarding the narrative portions, however, in which there is no harm in expanding and embellishing in the spirit of the words already there, this prophet (i.e., Ezra) did not desist. And it may be that by the word of God he added what he added.[380]

---

[376] Deuteronomy 4:2.
[377] Joshua 8:32; Nehemiah 8:3.
[378] Jeremiah 7:21–22. See also Amos 5:25.
[379] Ezra was a priest (*kohen*) and a skilled scribe (*sofer mahir*). See Ezra 7:6, 11.
[380] Joshua Berman, *Ani Maamin: Biblical Criticism, Historical Truth, and the Thirteen Principles of Faith* (Maggid, 2020), 207.

This brings us back to the question of what became of the scroll that was discovered in the days of King Josiah. We know that Jeremiah was a prophet during that time. At least one ancient source reports that in the days leading up to the Babylonian destruction he secreted away holy items in a cave east of the Jordan Rift in the ancient territory of Moab. The account in 2 Maccabees also mentions Jeremiah giving them the law. One wonders how literally to understand this. We also have a text that says Jeremiah put certain scrolls "into an earthen jar, so that they may last a long time."[381]

Perhaps the scroll discovered in the days of Josiah by a high priest named Hilkiah, possibly the father of the prophet-priest Jeremiah, really was the original document that Moses himself penned. When the words of the original Torah were found, Jeremiah "devoured"[382] them and proclaimed them to the people of his day, but they refused to heed the message. Jeremiah knew that ultimately, in days to come, God would make a new covenant with Israel and Judah. In that covenant, true to the ideal expressed by Moses, He would place the Torah in their inmost being and inscribe it upon their hearts.[383]

One possible scenario is that at the time the Moses scroll was discovered, the torah of the king either was instituted, or if it already existed, was finally followed, and two copies of the scroll were made. Knowing that the decreed destruction was coming,[384] Jeremiah went to work. He gave the copies of the Torah to those who were being deported and urged them not to forget the commandments of the LORD, further exhorting them not to let the Torah depart from their hearts. Perhaps with the aid of trusted friends, he clandestinely had the scrolls moved to a cave east of the Jordan Rift Valley. Whether they were originally placed in an earthen jar, we may never know, but his intention would have been to preserve them for an undisclosed moment in the future. There, in a Transjordanian cave, the strips of leather would remain, hidden away undetected awaiting another great discovery. Or maybe Jeremiah had the scrolls buried in a cave because, like the ark, he felt that the scroll written on leather strips would no longer be necessary in the days of the new covenant when God would inscribe the Torah on the hearts of the people. We have no way of proving this scenario, but one wonders.

Biblical clues about the scroll that Moses wrote point us to a form of Deuteronomy. Scholars recognize that the scroll discovered by Hilkiah was a form of Deuteronomy. Following De Wette, scholars have declared the discovered scroll a pious fraud. Interestingly, Shapira's scroll was discovered in a cave east of the Jordan. It represents a form of Deuteronomy but with significant variations. It contains what the Bible said Moses wrote. When leading nineteenth-century scholars examined the scroll they deemed it a forgery, and this has been the majority opinion in the academic community ever since. It is certainly intriguing

---

[381] Jeremiah 32:14.
[382] Jeremiah 15:16.
[383] Jeremiah 31:31–34.
[384] 2 Kings 22:16.

that Shapira's scroll contains what the Bible says Moses wrote. Perhaps detecting forgeries will always be a way of showing great scholarship, but given what we know today, we must reconsider all the evidence of its authenticity.

ᚱ

The Evidence of Authenticity

In the foreword to his 31 August 1883 publication on the Shapira fragments, Hermann Guthe said, "Whoever publishes 'fragments' of an unattested manuscript must necessarily, when it comes to the question of authentic or inauthentic, refrain from leading to the proof of the former, such that he does not understand the total scope of that which applies to that question. He is faced with two alternatives, either to leave the matter undecided, or to prove the inauthenticity of the whole from the fragments themselves."[385]

There are several criteria for assessing the authenticity of Shapira's manuscript: the details of the discovery, external evidence, and internal evidence. Guthe said that the story of the discovery of the scroll fragments, as related by Shapira, "means absolutely nothing for our knowledge surrounding the origin of the manuscript, one will be able to determine nothing for and nothing against its authenticity itself." He also said, "a possibility to verify our story is thus in my view completely nonexistent. Who will track down that bedouin? Or the original owner? Or the cave in which the strips were supposedly found during the time of Moab's subjugation under the Turks."[386] One can see his point, but this is not totally true. There are, in fact, elements of the story that can help us test the veracity of Shapira's account.

Shapira claimed that bedouin fleeing from their enemies found refuge in a cave and there discovered the leather strips. Initially, they had hoped that the blackened bundles contained treasure. It is uncanny that decades later, when Ta'amireh bedouin discovered the Qumran scrolls in a cave, they too had hoped for treasure. It is a known fact that in the mid-1860s, the time of the reported discovery of the fragments, the wali of Damascus was persecuting the bedouin tribes. So this element of the story checks out. Shapira reported that he acquired the leather strips in 1878. Guthe confirmed this when he reported, "It is thus to be regarded as doubtless, that the leather strips have been in the possession of Shapira since the year 1878." Shapira related that he learned of the fragments in the home of Sheik Erekat of Abu Dis, and that the sheik had arranged the meetings that resulted in his acquisition of the manuscript. We have verified that Sheik Erekat was known at the time as one who had intimate connections with the East.

---

[385] Guthe, *Fragments of a Leather Manuscript,* 1.
[386] Ibid., 6.

Therefore, he would have been in a position—and was the most likely person—to make such arrangements with the bedouin east of the Jordan.

Guthe questioned "whether the alleged place of discovery appears conceivable" and initially considered this as a probable cause for doubt of its authenticity. He wrote, "Moab and its treasures of antiquities have had a bad ring among us since 1876, and one is entitled to harbor the greatest disbelief against everything that gets brought to the market under this company."[387] He then added, "One can turn this argument around and say: a forger who demands belief for his product will presently rarely have it appear from Moab, if it did not in fact originate from there."[388] His clarification makes sense. Given the stain of the Moabitica affair, Shapira certainly would have avoided any reference to Moab unless he felt there was good reason to believe the manuscript really was discovered there.

In weighing possible reasons that the manuscript would have been found in Moab, Guthe included among his assumptions that "the manuscript was brought over [to Moab] by exiles from west Jordan," concluding that this "possibility cannot be precluded." We have shown that at least one ancient source relates that Jeremiah gave the Torah to some who were going into exile, and in the same passage we read that certain other holy relics were hidden in a Transjordanian cave.[389] There are other explanations for finding a scroll hidden in a cave east of the Jordan, but the narrative of 2 Maccabees is a textual witness that bears consideration.

As far as the authenticity of the manuscript itself is concerned, Menahem Mansoor stated, "Neither the internal nor the external evidence, so far as yet published, supports the idea of forgery."[390] In chapter fifteen, Reasons for Reexamination, we covered some of the external evidence originally used to disqualify the scroll. As shown in that chapter, the Qumran discoveries provide us with some compelling reasons to reconsider the genuineness of the leather strips. When Shapira presented his manuscript to the scholars of his day, they simply had nothing with which to compare it.

Despite the consistently expressed doubts of nineteenth-century experts, we now know that leather manuscripts can survive more than 2,000 years in a cave in the region of earth's lowest point. Thanks to the discovery of the Dead Sea Scrolls in the Judean Desert, we not only have leather documents more than 2,000 years old, but we also know that some of them, particularly those whose content is traditionally attributed to Moses, were written in Paleo-Hebrew script. In these Paleo-Hebrew manuscripts, words were often divided at the end of one line and continued on the next. This also occurs in Shapira's Paleo-Hebrew manuscript.

---

[387] Guthe, *Fragments of a Leather Manuscript,* 13.
[388] Ibid.
[389] 2 Maccabees 2:1–8.
[390] Mansoor, "The Case of Shapira's Dead Sea (Deuteronomy) Scrolls of 1883," 225.

These leather Paleo-Hebrew manuscripts also include interpuncts as word dividers, and most have vertical score lines to mark the boundaries of writing, as is the case in the Shapira fragments. Like Shapira's manuscript, these ancient scrolls also were wrapped in linen with traces of a black residue. Even the column height, believed at the time to be proof against its authenticity, is no longer a plausible reason for disqualification. We now know of other uncontestably genuine ancient documents whose dimensions are remarkably similar to those of Shapira's leather strips.[391]

Early critics also seized on another supposed proof of forgery. Initial claims were that Shapira's manuscript showed more wear along one edge than on the other, suggesting that the smoother side was evidence of its being cut from a larger scroll. When Clermont-Ganneau was finally allowed to examine the manuscript in January of 1884, he observed that the upper and lower edges showed similar signs of wear. Rather than admit that his former conclusion was in error, he said that both the upper and lower edges had been cut. Sketches of Shapira's manuscript, as well as photographs of the leather strips in the British Library dossier Add. 41294, show similar wear on the upper and lower edges. Based on these drawings and photos of the Shapira manuscript, one observes a similarity with many of the ancient scrolls discovered in the Judean Desert.

At least one expert sent by *The Daily News* on 22 August 1883 to investigate the conclusions of Clermont-Ganneau and Ginsburg reported, "The portion of the Deuteronomy manuscript examined by the present writer was written on leather of a thicker character, differing considerably from that usually employed in synagogue rolls." Additionally, Shlomo Guil notes that "when unrolled, the Leviticus scroll, 11QpaleoLev, demonstrates an arc-like shape." And based on the drawings of Christian David Ginsburg, "the shape of the Shapira scroll was also in an arc-like form."[392] This, too, is confirmed by the drawings and photographs of Shapira's leather strips. Since there was no precedent in the nineteenth century for these now well-established characteristics of ancient scrolls, Shapira could not have faked them.

In Mansoor's assessment of the Shapira case, he notes, "It is most significant that both Neubauer and Ginsburg became convinced that the manuscripts were a forgery, not on the basis of external evidence but mainly on internal evidence."[393]

From the outset of the Shapira saga, his manuscript was identified as an early form of Deuteronomy. The possibility was even entertained that the sixteen leather

---

[391] Mansoor reports, "Frank M. Cross, (BASOR, no. 141, 1950, p. 111) referring to the single copy of the Book of Chronicles found in Cave IV, points out that this manuscript is found on a three-inch strip of leather." See Mansoor, "The Case of Shapira's Dead Sea (Deuteronomy) Scrolls of 1883," 185 n 14. Also, Shlomo Guil writes that the "height [of 11QpaleoLev] at its present state is 7.5 centimetres" and that according to Guthe, the height of Shapira's leather strips "varied between 7.5 and 9.7 centimetres." He concludes, "It is therefore obvious that the dimensions of the fragments of 11QpaleoLev and those of the Shapira scroll, in the state which they were discovered, are quite similar." Guil, "The Shapira Scroll was an Authentic Dead Sea Scroll," 24.
[392] Ibid.
[393] Mansoor, "The Case of Shapira's Dead Sea (Deuteronomy) Scrolls of 1883," 205.

strips might represent the earliest version of the Torah's final book. According to Shapira's daughter Maria, her father told her, "I verily believe that these parchments are the original book of Deuteronomy!"[394] She also recalled him saying, "If we can establish their authenticity, which I am pretty sure we can, they will turn out to be the very oldest manuscript in the whole world, actually the original, Mosaic Deuteronomy."[395] Sir Walter Besant recounted the day he first laid eyes on the manuscript. He said that when Shapira arrived at the offices of the Palestine Exploration Fund he claimed to have a "document which would simply make students of the Bible and Hebrew scholars reconsider their ways; it would throw a flood of light upon the Pentateuch ... What was the discovery? ... So he told me ... it was nothing less than a contemporary copy of the book of Deuteronomy written on parchments. A contemporary copy!"[396] The Quaritch sales catalogue originally listed the Shapira fragments with the following description: "BIBLE. The most original MS of Deuteronomy, from the hand of Moses (? ben Amram)."[397] It also listed a possible date for the manuscript as "Ante-Christum 1500."

While Shapira entertained the possibility that his manuscript was the original book of Deuteronomy, at times his estimates were more cautious. Writing to Hermann Strack, he suggested, based on the forms of the characters, that the document could date to "an early time, as between the date of the Mesha Stone and the Siloam inscription, or about the sixth century B.C." He continued, "But one must be very cautious ... the date may be very late. The question will be for scholars to decide."[398] On 14 August 1883, the *London Standard* reported: "Among those who hold that the manuscript is genuine, the divergency of opinion as to the date is great. Some 8th century, some to the time of the captivity, while a third party places it to be the Maccabean period."[399] The form of the letters was a primary reason for the proposed early dating of the manuscript. Ginsburg had stated that the alphabet was "in favour of the genuineness of the document," and further that the writing suggested a date as early as 800 BC.[400] Based on his careful examination of the script, as well as the orthography, Guthe said, "Our Hebrew manuscript wants to be old, very old."[401]

Critical biblical studies also provide support for the authenticity of Shapira's manuscript. After his first look at the manuscript, Claude Conder remarked to Walter Besant, "I observe that all the points objected to by German critics have vanished in this new epoch-making *trouvaille*. The geography is not confused,

---

[394] Harry, *"The Little Daughter of Jerusalem,"* 213.
[395] Ibid., 214.
[396] Besant, *Autobiography,* 162.
[397] Allegro, *"The Shapira Affair,"* 73.
[398] Ibid.
[399] *The London Standard,* 14 August 1883.
[400] "Literary Gossip," *The Athenæum,* no. 2910, 4 August 1883, 147.
[401] Guthe, *Fragments of a Leather Manuscript,* 27.

and Moses does not record his own death."[402] At least as far back as the Middle Ages, Ibn Ezra had recognized that the passages in Deuteronomy that mention Moses's death were written by someone other than Moses.[403] Scholars also believed that language referring to the exile, particularly that found in the book of Deuteronomy, was inserted later, "when the terror of foreign rule and deportation befell Israel."[404] Since none of these "exilic" passages were present in Shapira's manuscript, Guthe said that the "form of the speech will have arisen earlier," adding that such passages "stem from the middle of the eighth century B.C. So old will the text be—it would be a precious gift for science! A noncanonical piece of writing, but older than that piece of the canon which corresponds to its contents—perhaps the original copy thereof? It is truly compelling, to paint for oneself the tremendous consequences that this find—if it really were a find—would precipitate for Old Testament science. I leave that for the enjoyment of the reader."[405] Eduard Meyer wrote to Georg Ebers, "The content is glorious, an endorsement of criticism that couldn't be grander. All glosses are missing, the narrative and afterwards the admonition follow their calm, simple, clear course, much shorter than our text, which is full of contradictions and confusions."[406]

In Shapira's 9 May 1883 letter to Strack, he said, "I see now that most of the variations between our MS and the Bible are of such a character, as are already used by many eminent scholars, as a proof that our Deuteronomy was not written by Moses or about his time. All such passages are not to be found in our MS."[407] In the same letter, Shapira informed Strack that in the intervening years between Professor Schlottmann's rejection of the scroll and the time he retrieved it from the bank vault, he became familiar with biblical criticism through Friedrich Bleek's *Introduction to the Old Testament*. He went on to relate to Strack, "What a change came over my mind after studying the above book."[408]

One of the scholars' hypothetical sources, the one they deemed to represent the earliest biblical stratum, was designated with the letter E, standing for Elohim. In this proposed source text, the Hebrew Deity is referred to as Elohim until Moses's time, when the name Jehovah was revealed.[409] Shapira undoubtedly found it especially interesting that in his manuscript, with the exception of its opening and closing lines, the name Jehovah did not appear. Instead, the Deity was referred to as Elohim. He noted to Strack, "Could we suppose that the first

---

[402] Besant, *Autobiography*, 163–164.

[403] Abraham ben Meir Ibn Ezra (1089–1164) was one of the most distinguished Jewish biblical commentators and philosophers of the Middle Ages.

[404] Guthe, *Fragments of a Leather Manuscript*, 35. For example, see Deuteronomy 4:25ff; 8:19; 28:36–37, 45–68; 29:21–27; 31:16–22.

[405] Guthe, *Fragments of a Leather Manuscript*, 35.

[406] Letter from Eduard Meyer to Georg Ebers, 8 July 1883, "Der Briefwechsel zwischen Georg Ebers und Eduard Meyer (187–898)," Vorbemerkung von G. Audring. https://www.geschichte.hu-berlin.de /de/bereiche-und-lehrstuehle/alte-geschichte/forschung/briefe-meyer/ebers.

[407] Shapira letter to Strack, 9 May 1883, British Library *Add. MS. 41294.*

[408] Ibid.

[409] Exodus 3:13–15; 6:2–3.

and last verse were added by a Jehovistic scribe who copied an Elohistic MS?"[410] Guthe considered the same, stating, "Perhaps the Yahwists have written the latter, but the Elohist the text."[411] In Adolf Neubauer's critique of Shapira's manuscript, despite his overall negative appraisal, he said that this feature "is certainly the cleverest thing in the new Deuteronomy, as it turns the fragments into an Elohistic text."[412] Throughout the text of the Shapira manuscript we find *Elohim eloheikha* (God your God), where the authorized texts read *YHVH eloheikha* (Jehovah your God). Originally, Ginsburg had stated that the phrase as found in the manuscript was evidence of forgery since it was unattested in the Hebrew Bible, but later corrected his earlier statement saying, "I should have said, 'in the Pentateuch.'"[413] Others were quick to point out Ginsburg's oversight anyway. The phrase appears in this precise form in Psalms 45:8 and 50:7.[414]

It is fascinating that Shapira's manuscript not only "lacks all the points objected to" by scholars who hold to the discipline of source criticism, but that it also includes so much of what the Pentateuch indicates that Moses wrote. As explained in previous chapters, Moses's scroll is reported to contain a travel itinerary of sorts, commandments and laws, blessings and curses. Of all that the Pentateuch says that Moses wrote, the only thing missing in the Shapira manuscript is a reminder to blot out the name of Amalek (Exod 17:14–16). In our canonical text, this command is fulfilled in Deuteronomy 25:17–19. Given the fragmentary nature of some sections of the manuscript, it is not beyond the realm of possibility that these two verses originally were part of the document. These words about Amalek are presently part of a section known to scholars as the law code of Deuteronomy (chaps. 12–26), none of which appears in Shapira's document.

This law code also contains approximately 100 laws that are not included in the other books of the Pentateuch. It is noteworthy that if one reads the last verse in Deuteronomy 11 and then skips forward to the first verse of chapter 27, there is no apparent break in the narrative. This suggests that the law code may have been inserted later, during the final composition of the Pentateuch. Scholars have noted that this section emphasizes a centralization of the cult that was apparently unknown from the time of the patriarchs and well into the biblical period. The torah of the king mentioned previously in our study is also in this section.[415] This passage, too, seems to have been unknown; the biblical narrative describes the request in Samuel's day as a surprise even to Samuel.[416] The Deuteronomy law

---

[410] Shapira letter to Strack, 9 May 1883, British Library *Add. MS. 41294*.

[411] Guthe, *Fragments of a Leather Manuscript*, 38.

[412] "The Shapira Manuscripts," *Palestine Exploration Fund Quarterly Statement* (Oct. 1883), 200.

[413] "The Shapira MS. of Deuteronomy," *The Athenæum*, no. 2912, 18 August 1883, 206.

[414] Neubauer corrected Ginsburg, saying, "Dr. Ginsburg, by the way, states from memory that the expression אלהים אלהיך, 'God thy God,' does not occur in the Old Testament. It does however, occur in the Elohistic Psalms, xlv, 8 and l, 7." See "The Shapira Manuscripts," *Palestine Exploration Fund Quarterly Statement* (Oct. 1883), 200.

[415] Deuteronomy 17:14–20.

[416] See 1 Samuel 8:6.

code also includes a version of the festivals, but a careful reading of biblical history indicates at least an unfamiliarity with the details of how they are to be kept. At times, it suggests that they were not kept for extended periods.[417]

Shapira's manuscript includes a version of the ten-word covenant. This was central to the entire document. It is different from the Decalogue that appears in the canonical Hebrew Bible, which itself contains at least two slightly different versions of the so-called Ten Commandments.[418] The enumeration of the ten commands has proven to be a source of disagreement since Scripture tells us that there are "ten words" or "ten matters" but offers no help in how to number them. [419] When Shapira's manuscript was revealed, it was widely reported that it contained an additional commandment: "You shall not hate your brother in your heart," but upon close examination one will see that there are still only the requisite ten precepts. The wording of the commands is different, but the Shapira Decalogue contains all that is present in the canonical version, arranged in nine succinct statements plus the commandment mentioned above for a total of ten. Each "word" or "matter" in the Shapira manuscript begins on a separate line and concludes with the phrase "I am *Elohim eloheikha*" (God your God).

One intriguing feature of the covenant in Shapira's manuscript is that a dot or interpunct separates each word in the text of the ten words. Interpuncts appear elsewhere in the manuscript, but only in the Decalogue do they occur between each word. There is one interesting exception to this pattern, which Guthe noted: "In the text of the Decalogue, however, the individual words are separated by points [interpuncts], admittedly with two notable exceptions: between the negative particle לא and the verb, the point regularly is missing, as well as between the particle את and the following noun. The negation and its verb, the emphatic particle את and its noun, then, are to be viewed as an especially close phrase, equal to one word. This writing confronts the reader as an original feature, it surprised me not a little. For it coincides with the Hebrew language usage, which does not tolerate the separation of the negation from the verb, and connects the particle so closely with the following noun that its own meaning has been completely lost."[420] Guthe further noted that prior to Shapira's scroll, "we know the usage of the interpuncts for Hebrew and the related languages only from inscriptions."[421]

The use of interpuncts was initially believed to be the result of a forger mimicking known lapidary examples, namely the Mesha Stela and the Siloam

---

[417] Consider the case of Passover. According to Exodus 12:14, "you shall celebrate it as a festival to the LORD throughout the ages … for all time." The wilderness tradition relates a 40-year period in which only one Passover is mentioned (Num 9). Joshua 5:10 records a Passover "in the steppes of Jericho" when they enter the land. Second Kings 23:22 informs us that Passover was not kept, at least not properly, since the "days of the chieftains who ruled Israel," or as the Chronicler puts it, since the "time of the prophet Samuel" (2 Chr 35:18).

[418] Nichols, "A Comparison of the Ten Words," https://www.academia.edu/43772655/A_Comparison_of_ the_Ten_Words_in_English_with_Explanatory_Notes.

[419] Differences in numbering exist between Catholic and Protestant Christians as well as Jews.

[420] Guthe, *Fragments of a Leather Manuscript,* 24.

[421] Ibid.

Inscription. However, Guthe showed that this could not be the case since he observed that Shapira's manuscript employed these interpuncts in a unique way. Concerning the Mesha Stela, Guthe said that except for one occurrence in line 11, "the negation לא does not altogether occur there." He continued:

The Siloam inscription has a point after every word; though unfortunately את and לא do not occur in it … I find, thus no model for the way in which, in our manuscript, the words of the Decalogue are separated. It should apparently serve to allow this part of Moses' speech to especially stand out, and by distinguishing every individual word, to ensure the survival of it against any changes. Or—do we have a copy of the original, "written" by God Himself on the stone tablets, before our eyes?? Unfortunately, we must now recognize our complete ignorance as to whether, in ancient times, a difference in the setting of interpuncts while writing on leather or on stone was customary, and entirely as to whether the Ten Commandments were ever in Jerusalem in this form on stone tablets. Thus, this peculiarity of the manuscript does not suit a fruitful examination. But it is interesting![422]

Guthe was impressed with this feature of the manuscript and remarked again later that "the peculiar use of the interpuncts in the rendering of the Decalogue" appeared to be an attempt to "depict a copy of the original engraved in stone."[423]

One other section of Shapira's manuscript deserves special attention. It contains blessings and curses that were to be proclaimed on Mounts Gerizim and Ebal when Israel entered the promised land. This is even more interesting since the corresponding account in the canonical Deuteronomy lacks the blessings altogether. Deuteronomy 27:12 says, "these shall stand on Mount Gerizim to bless the people … And these shall stand on Mount Ebal for the curse." However, the narrative of our canonical Deuteronomy records only the curses (Deut 27:15–26). In Shapira's Torah we have both blessings and curses, and even more interesting is the fact that each blessing and each curse corresponds to one of the commands in the ten-word covenant.

The Shapira manuscript presents Moses's first-person account of the Israelite journey from Egypt to the Transjordanian Plains of Moab. The account bears a resemblance to our canonical version. According to the manuscript, Israel is a chosen people whose fathers enter Egypt as seventy souls, and there grow into a large and powerful nation. They are delivered from Pharaoh, and signs and wonders accompany them to Horeb, where in a fearsome display they hear the voice of Elohim declaring His ten-word covenant to them from the midst of fire. Elohim writes the ten-word covenant on two tablets of stone, which Moses shatters when he witnesses the people worshipping a molten calf. Moses makes new tablets "like the first ones," and Elohim writes the covenant on this set as well. Moses places the tablets in an ark that he has made for them.

---

[422] Ibid., 24–25.
[423] Ibid., 30.

The children of Israel remain at Horeb for about a year and then journey to Kadesh-barnea, where they also stay for an extended period. The manuscript describes the people as stiff-necked and relates their rebellious episodes at Massah, Kibroth-hattaavah, and Kadesh-barnea. As a result of their rebellion and refusal to enter the promised land, the possession of that good land is delayed and ultimately denied to an entire generation, except for Joshua, Caleb, and the "little ones." After the rebels die off, the people resume the journey, traveling from Kadesh-barnea eastward through the big and fearful wilderness.

Along the way, they pass the borders of Esau, Moab, and Ammon and defeat the Amorite king Sihon and Og, king of Bashan. In Beth-peor, the people of Israel anger Elohim when they whore with the women of Moab and Midian, join in their sacrifices, and bow to their gods. Their illicit behavior brings a plague that is only stayed after a fierce battle.

Moses declares that Elohim will fulfill His sworn oath to give the good land to Israel, not because of their righteousness but because of His love for their fathers. Moses further instructs the people, promising blessings for obedience and curses for disobedience. He tells the Israelites that when Elohim takes them into the land, they are to recite the blessings and curses from Mount Gerizim and Mount Ebal. The manuscript lists both the blessings and the curses.

In Moses's last words to Israel he says that Elohim has informed him that he will not cross the Jordan River. Joshua will succeed him and lead the nation into the good land. With a final exhortation to be strong and courageous and a promise that Elohim will go before them, the manuscript ends.

When some of the points presented in this book are considered separately, they may appear speculative. Nonetheless, the convergence of so much evidence presents a compelling case for the authenticity of Shapira's sixteen leather strips. The details of the manuscript's discovery bear an uncanny similarity with the reports of what later was deemed "the greatest manuscript discovery of modern times." The physical characteristics of Shapira's manuscript resemble those of other scrolls discovered in the Judean Desert caves. Shapira's scroll lacks what critical scholarship identified as later interpolations and contains material consonant with what the Bible says Moses wrote.

Taken together, all of this evidence makes Shapira's manuscript a promising candidate for a text that resembles the scroll that Moses wrote. According to the Bible, during the days of Josiah the Torah written by Moses was discovered in the temple. We are not told what happened to this precious scroll after it was discovered, but we know that the temple where it was presumably kept was destroyed less than forty years later. One account reports that when Judeans were carried into exile, Jeremiah entrusted the Torah to some of them and then led a group east of the Jordan where they hid some of the holiest items in a cave. One can only speculate whether this report reflects historical reality, but it is within the realm of possibility.

Unfortunately, no one knows the present whereabouts of the leather strips. Only if they are recovered will it be possible to assess their authenticity scientifically. The capabilities are obviously greater today than they were in the nineteenth century. We can now detect writing not visible to the naked eye and even produce photographs of the hidden texts. If the scroll fragments were found, we could perform scientific tests on them, including radiocarbon dating. Fortunately, we can read and study Shapira's manuscript even though we do not presently possess the leather fragments. We have transcriptions of the bulk of the manuscript as seen through the eyes of some of the nineteenth century's greatest Hebraists. Building on their efforts, we have included in this book a new Hebrew transcription of the fragments and an English translation.

The decision about the authenticity of the Shapira Torah we now leave to the reader. Was Shapira able to produce a forged manuscript that contained all of what the Bible says Moses wrote, while at the same time containing no traces of what scholars identified as later interpolations? If so, how could he produce a forgery that just happened to closely resemble the scrolls that would not be discovered for more than six decades after his death? Not even the most skilled of forgers could have fabricated—decades in advance—a scroll that conformed to the physical and linguistic characteristics that we now know were common in the Dead Sea Scrolls. Viewed objectively, it appears unlikely that Shapira's leather strips could have been forged. This would mean that Shapira was no forger and that since 1883 he has been wrongly accused and his name and reputation unfairly maligned. Perhaps the reader may suppose that I am wrong and that Shapira's manuscript was truly fake. But what if it wasn't? Which is the greater sin? Believing in a false document, or disbelieving the truth?

May this work serve as a call for a long-overdue and well-deserved reassessment of what very well might be the greatest manuscript discovery of modern times. As Moses Shapira told Strack, "The question will be for scholars to decide." Especially important in this regard is the advice of Georg Ebers to Eduard Meyer. He told his protégé, "It is no art to declare suspicious things wrong, but it takes courage and certain knowledge to publicly declare that what is tainted with the smell of the fake is still genuine. Good luck!"[424]

As for this writer, I have come to believe that Moses Wilhelm Shapira presented an authentic ancient Torah scroll to the world, and the world rejected his treasure and wrongly labeled him a forger. Should the evidence presented in this book vindicate Shapira in your mind, I invite you to join me in helping to restore honor and blessing to his name and his memory. May they henceforth always be for a blessing.

And now, I present to you the reader—the Moses scroll.

---

[424] Letter from George Ebers to Eduard Meyer, 10 July 1883, "Der Briefwechsel zwischen Georg Ebers und Eduard Meyer (187–898)," Vorbemerkung von G. Audring. https://www.geschichte.hu-berlin.de /de/bereiche-und-lehrstuehle/alte-geschichte/forschung/briefe-meyer/ebers.

W

The Moses Scroll:
An English Translation

Translated and Annotated by Ross K. Nichols

In this translation we have retained most personal and place names familiar to English readers. Words in brackets [ ] indicate hypothetical but likely reconstructions where portions of Hebrew text are missing, and occasional *italics* help make the English more readable. The translation follows the transcription contained in chapter twenty-two and follows the Hebrew verse designations as closely as English grammar and syntax permit.

Editorial Headnote[425]

A1[426] These are the words that Moses spoke,[427] according to the mouth[428] of Jehovah,[429] to all of the children of Israel[430] in the wilderness, across **A2** the Jordan in the Aravah.[431] •[432]

---

[425] The scroll begins with an editorial headnote, written in the third person. The remainder of the document is written as a first-person account attributed to the hand of Moses. Like many biblical writings from antiquity, this editorial headnote was clearly added sometime after the composition of the original scroll. It informs the reader by providing a setting for the contents that follow. Based on the words, the document was written or edited west of the Jordan. The scroll also ends with a short editorial endnote. See footnote 498.

[426] Verses are based on fragment and line designations in Shapira's manuscript. A1 is fragment A, line 1. DA3 is fragment D, column A, line 3.

[427] The Hebrew phrase אלה הדברם אשר דבר משה matches the opening words of the Bible's book of Deuteronomy. Compare Deuteronomy 1:1.

[428] The phrase "according to the mouth of Jehovah," על פי יהוה in Hebrew, does not appear in Deuteronomy 1:1, but it does occur one other time in our scroll, its closing line. The phrase occurs in the Masoretic Text in twenty-one verses, including one in Deuteronomy (34:5). Of the twenty occurrences of the phrase in the Torah, Richard Elliott Friedman attributes nine to P, six to the Redactor, one to J, and one to *other* (Richard Elliott Friedman, *The Bible with Sources Revealed*, HarperOne, 2003).

[429] The four-lettered name of the Hebrew Deity (יהוה) is known as the Tetragrammaton. In the Hebrew Bible it appears nearly 7,000 times. In the Moses scroll it appears only in its opening and closing lines. The opening and closing lines, both clearly added sometime after the original composition, suggest that the scroll was originally written by an Elohist scribe, before the Tetragrammaton was known to the Hebrews. Exodus 3:13–15 and Exodus 6:2–3 have long been noted by scholars as evidence that the name *Jehovah* was introduced at a later time, but was added into earlier texts anachronistically when it had become known as God's "name forever" and His "appellation for all eternity" (Exod 3:15).

[430] The audience here is "all *of the children of* Israel," whereas the canonical Deuteronomy is addressed to "all Israel."

[431] The geographic references in the Moses scroll are the same as those that appear in Deuteronomy, but the order is different. Deuteronomy lists בעבר הירדן במדבר בערבה, while the Moses scroll has them listed as במדבר בעבר הירדן בערבה. I have retained the geographical term *Aravah,* which refers generally to the Great Rift Valley.

[432] Interpuncts appear throughout the scroll and were recorded in the transcriptions of Guthe/Meyer and Ginsburg. At times, they seem to represent an early form of punctuation or a way to emphasize a word or

Elohim our Elohim[433] spoke to us in Horeb,[434] saying, • "You have dwelt long enough[435] at this ^{A3} mountain. Turn and set out[436] for yourselves, and go to the hill country[437] of the Amorites, and to all the inhabited places in the ^{A4} Aravah, in the mountains, and in the foothills, and at the coast of the sea." •

And we set out from Horeb, and we walked ^{A5} all that great and fearful wilderness that you saw, and we came ^{A6} to Kadesh-barnea. And I said unto you, "You have come today to the hill country of ^{A7} the Amorites. Go up and possess the land as He spoke unto you." ^{A8} [But] you were [un]willing[438] to go up, and you murmured, and you said, "In hatred of [us], to exterminate us ..."[439] And Elohim was angered,[440] ^{A9} and He swore, saying, "As I live, [^{B1}][441] ^{B2}[442] surely all the people who have seen my signs and my wonders that I did ^{B3} these ten times, since they have not listened to my voice, they will not see the good land ^{B4} that I

---

phrase; at other times, they appear to indicate a shift in the narrative content. In some ways, they seem to serve a similar function as the "white spaces," known as *petucha* and *setumah,* the opened and closed sections of the Masoretic Text.

[433] Throughout the scroll the Deity is referred to as *Elohim,* with the exceptions mentioned in note 429 above. I have transliterated the Hebrew rather than translate *Elohim.* Whenever *Elohim* is followed by אלהנו or אלהך, I rendered it as "Elohim our Elohim," and "Elohim your Elohim," respectively. The Hebrew אלהים אלהיך occurs frequently in the scroll, and this precise phrase is found in the Hebrew Bible in two places (Pss 45:8; 50:7).

[434] The scroll always uses *Horeb* and never *Sinai.* It is therefore more akin to our Deuteronomy, which uses *Horeb* nine times (1:2, 6, 19; 4:10, 15; 5:2; 9:18; 18:16; 28:69). *Horeb* is used outside of Deuteronomy only in Exodus (3:1; 17:6; 33:6). *Sinai* is preferred outside of Deuteronomy, being used thirty-four times in Exodus, Leviticus, and Numbers. *Sinai* occurs only once in Deuteronomy (33:1), where it appears in a third-person text.

[435] Literally, "Much is to you dwelling."

[436] The Hebrew ויסע literally means to "pull out," i.e. pulling out tent stakes in preparation for travel.

[437] The Hebrew rendered "hill country" is הר, which literally means "mountain." I have followed the traditional reading in this translation.

[438] Here Ginsburg's transcription indicates a gap. One can, with a high degree of certainty, supply the missing negation as I have indicated in the text. The people had been commanded to "go up," and they were criticized for their disobedience. Obviously, they did not do as they were commanded. This is also supported by the narratives contained in the canonical texts, so I have translated accordingly.

[439] The transcription is incomplete in this passage. Compare Deuteronomy 1:27.

[440] This line of text is fragmentary. Its contents are only supplied in Ginsburg's transcription. He transcribed the Hebrew as וינאף, which means "and He [Elohim] committed adultery." His report of this reading created a stir at the time. Based on the canonical text, we read that God was "angered," which in Hebrew is ויקצף. Both of these Hebrew words contain five letters, the first two letters and the final letter are the same. One has to wonder, given that only Ginsburg recorded the reading, if he perhaps misrepresented the Hebrew word in his transcription. I have followed the latter in this translation, though it is possible that the people made this charge against Elohim, namely that in their view He was in a sense unfaithful, and thus the resulting anger of Elohim and His harsh sentence of forty years wandering in the wilderness.

[441] Meyer recorded a line but indicated that this first line of fragment of B was illegible.

[442] Guthe and Meyer recorded line breaks in their transcription, though Ginsburg did not. Thanks to their careful and detailed work, we also know which fragments were assigned to Guthe and which to Meyer. This leather strip was assigned to Meyer. He only provided a full transcription for the words of one line, and two words of the next line from the entire strip. It seems logical, even though Ginsburg did not indicate which fragment he was transcribing, that he was more successful in deciphering this fragment. We know this because his transcription matches the narrative flow without a break, indicating that he was working from fragment B. Ginsburg's success in deciphering this fragment could be due to the fact that he had the fragments for nearly a month; Guthe and Meyer worked on them for only a few days. Since only Guthe and Meyer precisely indicated the breaks in the lines of text, I had to assign them for fragment B by creating a hypothetical reconstruction. Elsewhere in the document I follow the "verse" divisions provided by Guthe and Meyer; therefore they represent, as faithfully as possible, the work of the scribe who created the scroll. In my reconstruction, fragment B has thirteen lines of text. Fragment G in the manuscript has five columns of text. Three of these columns contain twelve lines, and two of the columns contain thirteen.

swore to give to their fathers, • except their little ones, and Caleb the son of Jephunneh, and Joshua the son of Nun who stands ^{B5} before you. They will go there, and I will give it to them. • But you, turn for yourselves and set out toward the wilderness in the direction of the Sea of Reeds,[443] ^{B6} until the entire generation of the men of the rebellion have completely died off from the midst of the camp." And you dwelled in Kadesh-barnea until the men of ^{B7} the rebellion had completely died from the midst of the camp...

"You are crossing today a border of the children of Esau, who dwell ^{B8} in Seir. Do not harass them, and do not strive against them in battle, because I did not give a possession to you from their land, • ^{B9} because it was given as possession to the sons of Esau." •

The Horites[444] dwelled in it from antiquity,[445] but the children of Esau dispossessed them and they dwelled in their stead. •

^{B10} And we turned and we passed the wilderness of Moab, • and Elohim said to me, "You are passing today a border of Moab. Do not ^{B11} harass them and do not strive against them in battle because I did not give to you a possession from their land, because I gave ^{B12} to the children of Lot the possession of Ar." •

Rephaim dwelled in it from antiquity, and the Moabites call them Emim, and ^{B13} Elohim destroyed them, and they dwelled in their stead. •

And we turned, and we crossed the Wadi Zered,[446] and Elohim spoke unto me, saying, "Arise ^{DA1} and cross the Wadi Arnon. Today I have begun to give before you Sihon ^{DA2} the Amorite, king of Heshbon, and his land." • And we went out to meet Sihon toward Jahaz, ^{DA3} and we smote him until no survivor remained to him. And we captured all of his cities from Aroer, ^{DA4} which is on the rim of the Wadi Arnon, unto the Gilead, and unto the Wadi Jabbok—the entirety ^{DA5} Elohim gave before us. •

And we turned and we crossed in the direction of the Wadi Jabbok, and Elohim, our Elohim spoke ^{DA6} unto me, saying, "You are crossing today a border of the land of the children of Ammon. ^{DA7} Do not harass them and do not strive against them in battle, because I gave the land of the children of Ammon to the children of Lot as a possession."

---

[443] The Hebrew *Yam Suf* is traditionally translated as "Red Sea," but this can be misleading. This name refers to three bodies of water. One is in the region east of the Nile Delta, one is the body of water known as the Gulf of Suez, and one is the body of water known as the Gulf of Aqaba.

[444] Horites, חרם in Hebrew, are believed to be the Hurrians, known from other ancient Near Eastern texts. In the Bible we encounter them in patriarchal times (Gen 14:6), and in Genesis 36:20–30 we learn that the ancestor of the Horites was Seir, from whom the region acquired its name.

[445] Hebrew לעלם. The word refers to an indeterminate *age.*

[446] *Wadi* is used in place of the Hebrew *nachal,* despite its Arabic origin, since *wadi* is an accepted word that specifically refers to a watercourse that is dry except during seasonal rainy periods.

DA8 ⁘ Rephaim dwelled in it from antiquity, and the Ammonites call them Azamzumim,[447] and Elohim destroyed them **DA9** from before their faces, and they dwelled in their stead. •

And Elohim said to me, "Send men **DA10** to scout out[448] Jazer." And we captured Jazer and we dwelled in the Amorite cities. •

DB1 And Og, the king of Bashan, went forth to meet us for battle, and we smote him until no survivor remained to him. **DB2** And we captured sixty cities from them—the entire region of the Argob, fortified with walls, doors, **DB3** and bars, • besides the very many unwalled cities and all of the cities of the tableland, **DB4** and all of the Gilead, and all of the Bashan unto Salecah and Edrei. • It also was Rephaim land **DB5** because Og, king of the Bashan, remained as a remnant of the Rephaim. •

And we turned **DB6** and we set out toward the Negev, and we dwelled in front of Beth-peor. • And the daughters of Moab went forth at that time, **DB7** and the women of Midian to meet you, and they called to you to eat from their sacrifices, **DB8** and you ate from their sacrifices, and you drank from their libations, and you bowed to their gods, **DB9** and you whored with the Midianite women, • and you were joined to Baal-peor in that day. **DB10** And the anger of Elohim burned upon you, and He plagued a great plague against you at that time. ⁘ **DC1** And I sent men from you to battle the Midianites, **DC2** and you smote them with the edge of the sword, and you captured from them very many captives, **DC3** and the plague was restrained. •

And Elohim commanded me at that time to teach you statutes and **DC4** judgments to do them in the land that you are crossing there to possess it. • Guard yourselves. **DC5** You shall not add to His command and you shall not diminish from it. • Guard yourselves, lest you forget and **DC6** you make a carved thing for yourselves, or a formed thing, a shape of any figurine, which is in the heavens above, or which is on the earth **DC7** below, or which is in the waters under the earth, • and His anger burn against you and He destroy **DC8** you quickly from that good land. •

And you shall know today, **DC9** and you shall guard His statutes and His commandments for the sake of your good and **DC10** for lengthening days upon the land which Elohim your Elohim **EA1** gives to you. •

Hear, O Israel,[449] Elohim our Elohim, Elohim is one, **EA2** and you shall love Elohim your Elohim with all of your heart and with all of your soul[450]—very **EA3**

---

[447] Compare Deuteronomy 2:20, where they are called Zamzummim.

[448] The Hebrew לרגל means literally to "pace by foot." It implies a sense of surveying the land, in this case scouting in preparation for a military attack based on the information gained through reconnaissance.

[449] I have retained the classical rendering "Hear, O Israel" as a translation of the Hebrew שמע ישראל. In contrast to the canonical text, the *Shema* here precedes the Ten Words.

[450] I have translated the Hebrew root word נפש according to the traditional "soul," despite the fact that it reflects an understanding much different from what the Hebrew means. The main idea of the Hebrew word is the "essence of life" rather than a separate component of a person. When man was created and the breath of life was breathed into his lifeless body, only then did man become a "living soul." In the Hebrew Bible, a "soul" can die and therefore the idea of an immortal soul is foreign to the Hebrew Scriptures. Here, the

exceedingly.[451] • And these words, which I am commanding you today, [EA4] shall be upon your heart and taught incisively[452] to your children. And you shall speak of them when you sit [EA5] in your house, and as you walk along the way, • and when you lie down, and when you rise. And you shall bind [EA6] them for a sign upon your hand, and they will be as bands[453] between your eyes[454], and [EA7] you shall write them on the doorframes[455] of your house and your gates, because Elohim made[456] [EA8] a covenant with you in Horeb on the day of the assembly. And I, I stood between Elohim [EA9] and you at that time because you were awestruck by the face of the fire and [you did] not [go up], [EA10] to declare the word of your Elohim to you, saying,[457]

[EB1] I am • Elohim • your Elohim • who • liberated[458] you • from the land of • [EB2] Egypt, • from a house of • servitude. • [EB3] There shall not be • to you • [EB4] other • Elohim. • You shall not make • for yourselves • a carved thing,[459] • or any • [EB5] formed thing[460] • that is • in the heavens • above, • or that is • on the earth • [EB6] below. • or that is • in the waters • under • the earth. • You shall not bow down •

---

command is to "love Elohim with all of your heart, and with all of your lifeforce." In other words, with all of your being.

[451] The Hebrew reads למאד מאד, reflecting a doubling of the word which means "very." It is a way to present the superlative in Hebrew. The translation of the phrase as "very exceedingly" attempts to convey this in English.

[452] The rendering "taught incisively" is an attempt to get close to the Hebrew ושננתם. The wording here matches the canonical text of Deuteronomy 6:7. Most English Bibles say something like "teach them diligently." The Hebrew root word שנן carries the connotation of "whet" or "sharpen;" the idea seems to be to cut or to prick—*incise*. The point is to instill the words in, or teach them to, one's children. Thus, my rendering to teach them "incisively."

[453] The scroll has an unprecedented reading here. The passage in Deuteronomy 6:8 has לטטפת where our scroll reads לתתוהת (per Ginsburg) or לתתוכת (per Guthe). Both indicate uncertainty about the word in the scroll, but both of them noted the substitution of the expected ט in Deuteronomy with the ת in the scroll. Some English translations render the Hebrew as "frontlets."

[454] From an early time, this passage was interpreted in a literal sense, which led to the practice of binding *tefillin* or *phylacteries* on the arm and head. Ancient examples of these were discovered at Qumran.

[455] The Hebrew מזזת is known even today in the custom of placing a *mezuzah,* a small decorative box, on the doorframe. It contains Scripture passages (Deut 6:4–9; 11:13–21).

[456] The Hebrew word translated "made" is כרת, literally "cut."

[457] What follows is a unique version of the famous ten-word covenant. In our scroll, each word in the Hebrew, is separated by an interpunct (•). This feature was unprecedented in a leather document until the discovery of the Qumran scrolls. Prior to these discoveries, the practice was known only through lapidary examples. The ten-word covenant of the Moses scroll is unique, however, since its scribe placed an interpunct between every word. The only exceptions are also noteworthy. Whenever the negation לא is followed by a verb, or the particle את is followed by a noun, these were treated as a single word and even written as such. Hebrew grammar treats these as a single grammatical unit and our scroll's example proposes an early way of presenting this in ancient writing. The ten words have come to be known as the Ten Commandments, largely due to mistranslations of the Hebrew that have been perpetuated in popular culture. In the Bible, these are referred to as the ten words. The canonical Bible contains two renditions of these words (Exod 20; Deut 5). The two versions in our Bible contain many variations between them. See Ross K. Nichols, *A Comparison of the Ten Words in English with Explanatory Notes,* https://www.academia.edu/43772655/A_Comparison_of_the_Ten_Words_in_English_with_Explanatory_Notes.

[458] The scroll reads החרתך where both Exodus 20:2 and Deuteronomy 5:6 read הצאתיך.

[459] Hebrew פסל.

[460] Hebrew תמנה.

EB7 to them, • and you shall not serve them.[461] • I am • Elohim • **EB8** your Elohim.[462] •

EB9 Sanctify[463] • [the seventh day].[464] • **EC1** Six • days • I made[465] • the heavens • and the earth • **EC2** and all • that is • in them, • and I ceased[466] • on the seventh • day. • **EC3** Therefore, • you shall cease • also, • you, • and your animal, • and all • that • is yours. • **EC4** I am • Elohim • your Elohim. •

EC5 Honor[467] • your father • and your mother.[468] • I am • Elohim • your Elohim. •

EC6 You shall not kill[469] • the soul[470] of • your brother. • I am • Elohim • your Elohim. •

---

[461] Compare Exodus 20:2–6 and Deuteronomy 5:6–10.

[462] The order and counting of the "ten words" have been a source of disagreement among members of different biblical faith traditions. This is due in part to the fact that the texts do not associate a number with the individual "words." Our manuscript, however, clearly demonstrates how its version of the ten words are to be counted in that each "word" ends with the phrase "I am Elohim your Elohim." It should also be noted that the scribe began each of the ten words on a new line, regardless of how many words were on the line on which the previous word ended.

[463] I have used the English "sanctify" for the Hebrew קדשׁ. In its basic form, the word means "to be separate" or "set apart." The idea is to set the seventh day apart from the other days of the week. Our English word *holy* is based on this Hebrew word. Consequently, something that is "holy" is "set apart" and treated in a special way. The seventh day is the first *thing* designated as *holy* in the Bible (Gen 2:3). The version of the ten words in our scroll follows the version in Exodus, rather than Deuteronomy's version, concerning the reason for the seventh day's sanctity. Note also that the order of the words in our scroll does not correspond with that found in either Exodus or Deuteronomy. Here, the word concerning the seventh day is listed second. Compare Exodus 20:8–11 and Deuteronomy 5:12–15.

[464] Neither Ginsburg nor Guthe transcribed anything here, but rather indicated that the text was not discernable. I propose that the original reading is as I have it, "Sanctify [the seventh day]." The proposed and supplied reading is based on the readings contained in the blessings and curses found later in the manuscript. Each "word" in our ten words has a corresponding blessing and curse. It is these which inform us that this was the reading.

[465] Throughout the scroll the ten words are presented as a record of the words spoken by Elohim. This is indicated by their presentation in the first person. Compare the canonical versions, which are both presented in the third person.

[466] Here we have the Hebrew שׁבת, from which we get the English *Sabbath* and the Hebraized *Shabbat*. It also occurs in verse EC3.

[467] The Hebrew here, as well as in our canonical texts, is based on the root כבד. The meaning of the word is associated with the idea of giving weight. When we give weight to something, or in this case some*one,* the idea is that we do not take them lightly. This is confirmed later in this document in the corresponding blessing and curse.

[468] Compare Exodus 20:12 and Deuteronomy 5:16. Our manuscript consisted of two distinct copies of the same text, which were reported to be, for the most part, identical. In Ginsburg's transcription as he published it in August of 1883, he included the phrase למען יארכן ימך, "thereby lengthening your days." Both Exodus 20:15 and Deuteronomy 5:16 contain this phrase as a promise associated with honoring one's parents. Ginsburg reported, though, that only one of the two copies of the Moses scroll contained this phrase. "Dr. Ginsburg says that the words 'that thy days may be long' are omitted in one duplicate." During his assessment of the fragments, he commissioned a drawing of four columns of the Moses scroll; these included the columns that contained the ten words. In the drawing, the phrase is absent. Given this, and the fact that Guthe and Meyer did not include it in their transcription, I have not included it here. See "Shapira's MSS," *The Old Testament Student,* Vol. 3, No. 1 (Sep. 1883), 23–25. See also, "The Shapira MS. of Deuteronomy," *The Athenæum,* no. 2911, 11 August 1883, 178.

[469] Commentators have debated the meaning of the Hebrew used in this "word." It is often said that biblical literature clearly distinguishes between murder and killing. A careful study of all of the examples of both words will show, however, that the difference between the terms is not so vast. I have translated as "kill" knowing the arguments against the use of this term. My point is to emphasize that taking human life, regardless of the reason, is to be avoided if at all possible, also realizing that there are times when it may be necessary and other times when it is even commanded.

[470] The Hebrew here is נפשׁ. See note 450.

EC7 You shall not commit adultery[471] • with the woman • of your neighbor. • I am • Elohim • your Elohim. •

EC8 You shall not steal • the property[472] of • your brother. • I am • Elohim • your Elohim. •

ED1 You shall not swear • by My name • to deceive,[473] • because • I am • passionate.[474] • **ED2** The iniquity of • fathers • will be upon • children • unto a third • and unto a fourth *generation* • **ED3** for lifting • My name • to deceive.[475] • I am • Elohim • your Elohim. •

ED4 You shall not respond • against your brother • *with* a testimony of • deceit.[476] • I am • Elohim • **ED5** your Elohim. •

ED6 You shall not desire[477] • [your neighbor's] woman, • his servant, • his maidservant, • **ED7** or anything • that is • his. • I am • Elohim • your Elohim. •

ED8 You shall not hate • your brother • in your heart.[478] • I am • Elohim • your Elohim. •

---

[471] In the Bible, a man can have more than one woman. This is evident throughout the patriarchal narratives, for example, where it is not condemned. What is not allowed is for a man to take a woman that belongs to another man. I have used the commonly employed English word *adultery* for the Hebrew נאף.

[472] This is more specific than the versions found in Deuteronomy 5:19 and Exodus 20:15. The Hebrew word הן in our manuscript means "goods" or "property." Additionally, the word in our scroll specifies theft from one's brother, whereas the canonical versions prohibit theft in general: "You shall not steal."

[473] This word prohibits swearing by the name of Elohim to deceive. The corresponding versions in our canonical texts prohibit the "lifting of the name for falsehood," which appears to have conveyed the same meaning in antiquity. To *lift the name* meant to use the name in an oath. Many have come to know this "commandment" through faulty English translations that often present the Hebrew as a prohibition against "taking the name of the LORD in vain." This is an unfortunate translation and has led to a misunderstanding of the original intent. Anciently, one could "swear by the name" (Deut 6:13; 10:20). However, one must never bring the name of Elohim into an oath in an attempt to deceive. This version clarifies the original intent of this word. Compare Exodus 20:7 and Deuteronomy 5:11. See Ross K. Nichols, *Swearing by the Name of YHVH*, https://www.academia.edu/41521919/Swearing_by_the_Name_of_YHVH.

[474] The Hebrew קנה is often translated as "jealous" or "zealous." The root meaning evokes the idea of passion; I have rendered it here accordingly.

[475] In the canonical versions, the transgenerational transfer of a father's iniquity to his descendants is associated with the worship of "other Elohim" (Deut 5:9; Exod 20:5). There, we see a differentiation between those "who hate Me" and those "who love Me and keep my commandments." Here, a transfer of the iniquity from fathers to children unto the third and fourth generation is stated as a fact with no further qualification. If one swears by the name of Elohim with the intention to deceive, the result is a transfer of iniquity from fathers to children. This, according to our text, is because Elohim is passionate.

[476] Compare Exodus 20:16 and Deuteronomy 5:19 (v. 17 in Hebrew). The canonical versions read "your neighbor," where here it says, "your brother." People have come to know this as the commandment against "bearing false witness." The phrase in Exodus 20 is עד שוא and the corresponding verse in Deuteronomy reads עד שקר. In our scroll, the Hebrew is עדת שקר. This reading connects the previous word with this one through a linguistic association. A person is prohibited from swearing by the name of Elohim to *deceive,* and from responding with a *deceitful* testimony against one's brother. Both employ the Hebrew שקר.

[477] Compare Exodus 20:17 and Deuteronomy 5:21 (v. 17 in Hebrew). In the Moses scroll, one is prohibited from desiring (חמד) a neighbor's woman, servant, maidservant, or anything that is his. Similarly, in Exodus 20:17 one is not to desire (חמד) a neighbor's house, wife, male or female servant, ox, donkey, or anything that is his neighbor's. Deuteronomy 5, however, only associates the Hebrew חמד with the woman of one's neighbor. Everything else belonging to one's neighbor is associated with a different Hebrew word—אוה. Our scroll, in this instance, is closer to the reading of Exodus. This is generally known as the prohibition against *coveting.*

[478] This verse is not part of the ten-word covenant in the canonical versions. The exact wording, however, occurs in Leviticus 19:17. In 1883 it was widely reported that this manuscript contained an eleventh commandment. This was not accurate. As it turns out, this version contains only ten words. Despite the

ED9 Elohim spoke these ten words.[479]

[Fragmentary column F][480]

FA1 [… "Y]ou [speak] with u[s and we will hea]r, [but let n]ot [Elohim] speak with **FA2** [us lest] we die. And Elohim heard [your] word[s. And Elohim said to me, "I have heard the words that this people have spoken to you. They are good, **FA3** all that] they have spoken. • Oh tha[t they had such a heart in them as this, to fear Me and to **FA4** guard all of My commandments all the] days, in order that [it might go well with them and their sons after them.]

GA1 [   ][481] "upon the land which I swore to give to them and to their children after them." • Hear, O Israel! **GA2** You are crossing the Jordan today to enter to dispossess strong and mighty nations, big and fortified cities **GA3** with walls. Do not say in your hearts, "These are many nations, we are unable to dispossess them." Do not be afraid of them. **GA4** Remember what Elohim did to Pharaoh and to all of Egypt—so will Elohim do to all of your enemies. • **GA5** Because Elohim, He is crossing before you. He is a consuming fire. • He will destroy them, and He will consume them quickly before you. • **GA6** Moreover, Elohim will send leprosy[482] among them • until those hiding and those remaining utterly perish from before **GA7** you. • If you will only guard His commandments, and His judgments, and His statutes, which I am commanding you today.

GA8 And you shall know today that it is not because of your righteousness that Elohim your Elohim is giving before you this land to possess. **GA9** Because you have been a stiff-necked people[483] from the day that He brought you out of Egypt until today you have been rebellious **GA10** [against] Elohim your Elohim. • At Horeb, on the day that I went up the mountain to receive the two stone tablets—

---

differences in wording and arrangement, the Moses scroll contains all of the canonical versions' words. This prohibition of hating one's brother in your heart is the tenth.

[479] Compare Exodus 20:1 and Deuteronomy 5:22. The Moses scroll and the version of the ten words in Deuteronomy agree in that this phrase occurs at the close of the covenant's words.

[480] Dr. Eduard Meyer transcribed four fragmentary lines of a piece designated "layer F." Guthe reported that Fragment F, columns A and B issued from Meyer. Meyer commented, "Fragment F of 4 layers; layer A." He further added, "Line 3 belongs to the second copy of the text." Only a few words are discernable, but from the letters and few words recorded, this column of text seems to relate the request of the people to not hear the voice again "lest they die" and of Elohim's response. This determination is based on the following: Line 2 has the phrases "lest we die," as well as "and Elohim heard [your] word[s]." Line 3 may read "they have spoken"?, but also the Hebrew ...מי, which seems to be the beginning of the Hebrew phrase in our canonical text, (מי יתן) "Oh tha[t they had such a heart in them as this,]" see Deuteronomy 5:26 (v. 29 in English). Line 4 of fragment F has "days," and "that it might." See transcription. Interestingly, the language of line 1 and the first half of line 2 more closely follow Exodus 20:16, but from the second half of line 2 through line 4, our manuscript fragment more closely resembles Deuteronomy 5:25–26.

[481] The beginning of this line is only recorded in Meyer's transcription. It is lacking in Ginsburg's, which begins with the final two words *Shema Israel*—שמע ישראל.

[482] The canonical version reads "hornets" (Deut 7:20—צרעה), where Ginsburg proposed a reading of "leprosy"—צרעת in the Moses scroll. However, it should be noted that neither Ginsburg nor Meyer was certain of the reading. Both recorded the first letter as ה and final two letters as עת. Based on the certainty of the final two letters, the word is not "hornets." If the text did read "leprosy," it should be noted that leprosy in the Bible, צרעת, is not what is known as Hansen's disease today.

[483] The Hebrew עם קשה ערף is more literally translated as "a people of hard neck." This phrase gave way to the popular phrase "stiff-necked people." The image conveyed by the Hebrew is one of obstinance. I have retained the traditional reading.

and upon them ^{GA11} was written all of the words that Elohim spoke with you in the mount, from the midst of fire, in the day of assembly— ^{GA12} you made a molten calf[484] for yourselves and angered Elohim. And I fell down before Elohim in the mountain burning with fire … ^{GB1} And the two tablets were in my hands and I saw your sin, and I shattered the two tablets before your eyes. ^{GB2} And I interceded on your account at that time, forty days and forty nights. • And at Taberah, ^{GB3} and at Massah, and at Kibroth-hataavah you were rebellious against your Elohim. •

At that time, Elohim ^{GB4} said to me, "Carve two stone tablets for yourself like the first ones and ^{GB5} ascend the mount to Me." And I ascended the mount, and the two ^{GB6} tablets were in my hands. • And Elohim wrote on the tablets the ten words which He spoke to you in the mount on the day ^{GB7} of the assembly, and He gave them to me, • and behold them—they are in the chest that I made.[485]

And at Kadesh-barnea, when Elohim said to me, ^{GB8} "Go up and possess the land," you were rebellious against your Elohim and you did not go up, and you did not hearken to His voice. ^{GB9} And Elohim said *to me that He intended*[486] to destroy you, but I interceded, standing on your behalf in the mount forty days ^{GB10} and forty nights, on your behalf. And Elohim hearkened also that time and did not destroy you in a moment.[487]

^{GB11} It is not because of your righteousness that your Elohim is giving to you power to do mightily. Rather, Elohim attached with your ^{GB12} fathers to love them, and He chose their seed after them from all of the peoples. • Because Elohim ^{GB13} your Elohim, He is Elohim of elohim,[488] and Master of masters,[489] the mighty and awesome El. He is your boasting,[490] ^{GC1} and it is He who does the great and awesome things ^{GC2} with you. • Your fathers went down to Egypt with seventy souls, ^{GC3} and now you are a people, mighty and many. •

If you will only guard all of the commandments that I am commanding you ^{GC4} today, to do them—to love your Elohim, to walk in all of His ways and in all of His statutes, • then Elohim will dispossess all of ^{GC5} the men of the place upon

---

[484] The Hebrew עגל מסכה is commonly translated as "golden calf," but the Hebrew מסכה means "molten." The Moses scroll uses the same phrase as that found in four passages of the Hebrew Bible (Exod 32:4, 8; Deut 9:16; Neh 9:18).

[485] The Moses scroll, like the canonical Deuteronomy 10:1–5, knows only of an "ark" made by Moses. There is no mention of the elaborate golden ark described elsewhere in Scripture. *That* ark was made by two spirit-filled artisans named Betzalel and Oholiab. Here and in Deuteronomy 10, the ארן is a "chest" made by Moses. I have used the English word *chest* to distinguish it from the "other" ark. See James D. Tabor, *That "Other" Ark of the Covenant,* https://jamestabor.com/that-other-ark-of-the-covenant/.

[486] The *italicized* phrase is added in the English for clarity.

[487] The destruction of Israel in "a moment"— רגע is threatened elsewhere in the Bible (see Exod 33:5; Num 16:21, 45).

[488] *Elohim* is plural in the Hebrew. Most English versions translate this "God of gods," and so to make a similar distinction, the first Elohim is capitalized and the second is not – thus "Elohim of elohim."

[489] The Hebrew in this passage is אדני האדנם. *Adon* means "lord" or "master." Due to the confusion over the often misused "lord" in English translations, I have elected to render it as "master."

[490] The Hebrew root word הלל (*hallel*) is often translated into English as "praise." A more literal meaning is "boast" or "brag," and so that is how I have translated it. The popular *hallelujah* is often translated as "praise God," but a more accurate translation would be "boast ye *of* Yah."

which the sole of your feet tread. • No man shall stand before you because a fear of you, ^{GC6} and a dread of you will be upon the face of all of the land upon which you tread. •

See, I am putting before you today a blessing ^{GC7} and a curse. The blessing if you will listen to the commandments and statutes, and a curse if you will not listen but turn ^{GC8} from the way which I am commanding you today. And it will be that when Elohim brings you into the land which you are ^{GC9} going there to possess, you will give the blessing on Mount [Gerizim] and the curse on Mount Ebal.[491] • Are they not across ^{GC10} the Jordan in the direction of the going down of the sun, in the land of the Canaanites, opposite Gilgal, beside the oaks of Moreh? •

And these will stand on ^{GC11} Mount [Ebal]: Reuben, Zebulon, and Gad, Asher, Dan, and Naphtali. • And these will stand on Mount Gerizim: ^{GC12} Simeon, and Judah, and Issachar, Manasseh, and Ephraim, and Benjamin. • And the Levites will stand opposite of Mount Gerizim and ^{GC13} they will respond, and they will say in an exalted voice:

"Blessed is the man who loves Elohim his Elohim and worships Him alone, and ^{GD1} serves Him alone." And all of the people, they will respond and they will say, "Amen." •

"Blessed is the man who sanctifies the seventh day ^{GD2} and ceases thereon." And all of the people, they will respond and they will say, "Amen." •

"Blessed is the man who honors his father and his mother." And all ^{GD3} of the people, they will respond and they will say, "Amen." •

"Blessed is the man who does not take vengeance and does not hold a grudge against his brother's soul." And they will respond,[492] "Amen." •

^{GD4} "Blessed is the man who does not defile his neighbor's woman." And all of the people, they will respond and they will say, "Amen." •

^{GD5} "Blessed is the man who does not wrong his neighbor." And all of the people, they will respond and they will say, "Amen." •

"Blessed is the man ^{GD6} who does not swear in My name to deceive." And all of the people, they will respond and they will say, "Amen." •

"Blessed is the man who does not ^{GD7} deal falsely, and does not practice deceit with his neighbor." And all of the people, they will respond and they will say, "Amen." •

"Blessed is the man who does not lift ^{GD8} his eyes toward the property of his neighbor." And all of the people, they will respond and they will say, "Amen." •

---

[491] A similar narrative occurs in Deuteronomy 27, but there, surprisingly, only the curses are recorded. In the Moses scroll we have both, and the blessings and the curses correlate to its version of the ten-word covenant.
[492] Here, the expected refrain "and they will respond and they will say" is shortened to "and they will respond." It is likely that the scribe inadvertently left out the Hebrew phrase כל העם ואמרו. This is a fairly common scribal mistake referred to as haplography. It typically occurs when a scribe is writing several lines with similar wording. He loses his place and fails to notice it due to the repetition.

"Blessed is the man who loves **GD9** his neighbor." And all of the people, they will respond and they will say, "Amen." •

"Blessed is the man who establishes all of the words **GD10** of this Teaching[493] to do them." And all of the people, they will respond and they will say, "Amen." •

And the Levites, they will continue, **GD11** and they will respond, and they will say in an exalted voice, "See, if you will diligently listen to your Elohim's voice, to guard to do **GD12** all of His commandments, then all of these blessings will come upon you. You will be blessed in the city. You will be blessed **GE1** in the field. Your basket and your kneading trough will be blessed. • The fruit of your womb and the fruit of your ground, the offspring of your **GE2** herds and the young of your flock will be blessed. You will be blessed when you come in, and you will be blessed when you go out. Your Elohim will give you **GE3** your enemies, smiting them before you. • Elohim will command the blessing in all that your hands do. • **GE4** Elohim will establish you as a sanctified people for Himself, and all of the people of the earth will see it and they will be in awe of you. • And Elohim will open **GE5** the heavens for you to give your land rain in its time, and you will lend to many nations but you will not borrow. **GE6** You will be above, but you will not be beneath."… **GE7** … •

And the Levites will continue, with their faces opposite Mount Ebal, **GE8** and they will respond and they will say in an exalted voice:

"Cursed is the man who makes **GE9** a carved thing or a molten thing, the work of a sculptor's hand." And all of the people, they will respond and they will say, **GE10** "Amen." •

"Cursed is the man who does work on the seventh day to profane it." And all of the people, they will respond and they will say, "Amen." •

"Cursed is the man who esteems his father and his mother lightly."[494] And **GE11** all of the people, they will respond and they will say, "Amen." •

"Cursed is the one who strikes his neighbor in secret." And all of the people, they will respond and they will say, **GE12** "Amen." •

"Cursed is the man who draws near to any close relative, or who commits adultery **GE13** with his neighbor's woman, or who lies with any animal." And all of the people, they will respond and they will say, "Amen." •

"Cursed is the **HA1** one who moves his neighbor's land boundary." And all of the people, they will respond and they will say, "Amen." •

"Cursed is the man who swears **HA2** by My name to deceive." And all of the people, they will respond and they will say, "Amen." •

---

[493] Teaching—Torah in Hebrew—תרה.

[494] The Hebrew מקלה translated "esteem lightly" represents the opposite meaning of the Hebrew כבד, "to give weight or honor."

"Cursed is the one who takes a bribe to testify deceitfully against **HA3** his associate."[495] And all of the people, they will respond and they will say, "Amen." •

"Cursed is the man who lifts his eyes toward his neighbor's **HA4** woman, or toward his house, or toward his maidservant, or toward all that is his." And all of the people, they will respond and they will say, "Amen." •

"Cursed is the man **HA5** who hates his brother in his heart." And all of the people, they will respond and they will say, "Amen." •

"Cursed is the man who **HA6** does not establish all of the words of this Teaching[496] to do them." And all of the people, they will respond and they will say, "Amen." •

HA7 And the Levites will continue to read[497] in an exalted voice, and they will say, "And it will be, if you do not listen to your Elohim's voice, to guard **HA8** to do all of His commandments and His statutes, then all of these curses will come upon you. You will be cursed in the city, **HA9** and you will be cursed in the field. Your basket and your kneading trough will be cursed. The fruit of your womb and the fruit of your ground, **HA10** the offspring of your herds, and the young of your flock will be cursed. • You will be cursed when you come in, and you will be cursed when you go out. • **HA11** Your Elohim will give you to be smitten before your enemies. Elohim will send the curses against all of the work of your hands. • **HA12** Elohim will make you for a horror, a proverb, and an insult among all of the people of the earth. Elohim will restrain the heavens. **HB1** The stranger in your midst will ascend higher above, and you will descend lower beneath. He will lend to you, **HB2** but you will not lend to him. Elohim will cause you to perish, and He will destroy you from upon the face of the ground that you are **HB3** to enter there to posses it." •

I am 120 years old today. I am unable to go out or to **HB4** come in before you, and Elohim has said to me, "You shall not cross the Jordan." Joshua, who stands before you, he, he will **HB5** cross the Jordan, and he will go with you into the good land that **HB6** [you are to enter] there to possess it. • Be strong and courageous. Do not fear and do not be dismayed because Elohim your Elohim, **HB7** He will go before you. **HB8** [   ]

Editorial Endnote[498]

HB9 These are the words that Moses commanded to all of the children of Israel **HB10** according to the mouth of Jehovah in the plains of Moab before his death. •

---

[495] The word translated as "associate" is the Hebrew עמית. It occurs in ten passages in the Hebrew Bible. Nine of these are in Leviticus (5:21 [twice]; 18:20; 19:11, 15, 17; 24:19; 25:14 [twice], 15, 17), and one in Zechariah 13:7. The word means "associate," "fellow," or "relations."

[496] Teaching—Torah in Hebrew—תרה.

[497] לקרא can mean "to call" or "to read." I have elected to use *read*, as it is likely that the Levites would be *reading* these blessings and curses from the scroll that Moses wrote.

[498] It appears that this editorial note, like the one with which the scroll begins, was appended to the original Moses scroll by a later scribe. It stands out because (a) it is an informational conclusion to the contents of the scroll, (b) it is written in the third person, (c) like the opening editorial headnote, it uses the name *Jehovah*, whereas the rest of the manuscript uses *Elohim*, and (d) it refers to the death of Moses.

The Moses Scroll:
A Hebrew Transcription

Transcribed and Arranged by Ross K. Nichols

In the summer of 1883, three Hebrew scholars produced transcriptions of a manuscript belonging to Moses Wilhelm Shapira, antiquarian and agent for the British Museum. The text was written on strips of leather in ancient Paleo-Hebrew script. It consisted of two nearly identical copies of a previously unknown version of what many believed to be a shortened form of Deuteronomy, but with notable variations.

The following text combines for the first time the transcription of Christian David Ginsburg with that of a team consisting of Hermann Guthe and Eduard Meyer. Combining these transcriptions enables us to reliably recreate the text of Shapira's manuscript as seen by those nineteenth-century Hebraists.

Ginsburg's transcription is the more complete and serves as the base text for our composite edition. For Ginsburg's text we used photocopies of the transcription as it appeared in three installments in *The Athenæum*, as well as Shlomo Guil's, *The Text of the Shapira Dead Sea Deuteronomy*.[499] Additionally, we checked these Hebrew versions against the drawing of four columns of the Paleo-Hebrew text that Ginsburg commissioned. Ginsburg did not specify which manuscript strips he used in his transcription. We have relied on Guthe and Meyer's work to correlate the transcriptions and their respective leather strips.

Guthe and Meyer divided the sixteen strips into two groups, separating the two nearly identical bodies of text. They then gave letter designations to seven strips that contained one copy of the text. Some of those strips consisted of multiple columns of text, while others had only single columns. The two scholars divided the work of deciphering and transcribing the text between them. They identified not only the letter designation of the fragment on which the transcription was based, but also noted the end of each line of text by inserting a vertical line.

---

[499] "The Shapira MS. of Deuteronomy," *The Athenæum*, no. 2911, 11 August 1883, 17–; no. 2912, 18 August 1883, 206; no. 2913, 25 August 1883, 242–4, and Shlomo Guil, "The Text of the Shapira Dead Sea Deuteronomy," 2018. https://www.academia.edu/36489543/The_Text_of_the_Shapira_Dead_Sea_Deuteronomy_Scroll.

We have overlaid Guthe and Meyer's transcription onto the base text produced and published by Ginsburg. This has made it possible to recreate the content of the manuscript according to each leather fragment, column, and line and to indicate where the transcriptions differ.

Our transcription contains the following features:

- Letters, words, or interpuncts appearing in gray indicate that one, but not both, of the transcriptions contain this material.
- **Black** text indicates that Ginsburg's transcription matches Guthe's or Meyer's exactly.
- Where Guthe or Meyer expressed uncertainty about a letter or series of letters, those characters are underlined.
- Footnotes point out divergent readings between the transcriptions, including single-letter differences.
- Guthe and Meyer used an asterisk when they could discern the presence of a character but were unable to identify it with certainty. Those instances are footnoted.
- Thanks to the work of Guthe and Meyer, we know where most of the lines begin and end. The exceptions are when (1) it was not possible to find either the end of one line or the beginning of the next due to words missing in one or both of these places where Ginsburg supplied text but Guthe or Meyer expressed uncertainty, or (2) when as in the case of the fragment identified as Fragment B, Ginsburg recorded text that was not recorded by Guthe and Meyer. In these instances we have estimated the length of the line(s) and reconstructed them accordingly.
- Throughout this document we have designated the lines as follows: Line 1 of fragment A is designated as A1; line 1 of fragment D, column B, is designated as DB1; and so forth.
- When Guthe or Meyer recorded a word that Ginsburg did not record, we have inserted a footnote but have not altered Ginsburg's text.

Although we have made every effort to avoid transcription errors, feedback is welcomed and encouraged.

	Fragment A – Individual Piece
A1	אלה הדברם אשר דבר משה על פי יהוה אל כל בני ישראל במדבר בעבר
A2	הירדן בערבה • אלהם אלהנו דבר אלנו בחרב לאמר • רב לכם שבת בהר
A3	הזה פנו וסעו לכם ובאו הר האמרי ואל כל שכנו בע
A4	רבה בהר ובשפלה[500] ובחף הים • ונסע מחרב[501] ונלך א

---

[500] Guthe records וב**לה.
[501] Guthe records כל חת.

תַ502 כל המדבר הַגדל503 והנרא504 הזה אשר505 ראתם ונבא	A5
עד קדש ברנע ואמר אלכם באתם היום עד הר	A6
האמרי עלו ורשו את הארץ כאשר דבר....	A7
.. אבתם לעלת ותרגנו ותאמרו בשנא ... לאבדנו וינאף	A8
אלהם וישבע לאמר חי אני	A9

Fragment B – Individual Piece

506	B1
כי כל העם הראם את אתתי ואת מפתי507 אשר עשתי	B2
זה עשר508 פעמם...לא . [ ] . לא • שמעו בקלי אם יראו את הארץ הטבה	B3
אשר נשבעתי לתת לאבתהם • בלתי טפכם וכלב בן יפנה ויהשע בן העמד	B4
לפנך המה יבאו שמה ולהם אתננה • ואתם פנו לכם וסעו המדברה דרך ים סף	B5
עד תם כל הדר אנשי המרבה מקרב המחנה ותשבו בקדש ברנע עד תמו אנשי	B6
המרבה למת מקרב המחנה...[א]תם עברם היום את גבל בני עשו הישבם	B7
[בש]עיר לא [תצר]ם ולא תתגר בם מלחמה כי לא אתן מארצם לכם ירשה •	B8
כי לבני עשו נתתה ירשה • החרם מעלם ישבה בה ובני עשו ירשם וישבו תחתם •	B9
ונפן ונעבר את מדבר מאב • ויאמר אלהם אלי אתם עברם היום את גבל מאב לא	B10
תצרם ולא תתגר בם מלחמה כי לא אתן מארצם לכם ירשה כי לבני לט נתתי	B11
ער ירשה • רפאם מעלם ישבו בה והמאבם יקראו להם אמם וישמדם	B12
אלהם וישבו תחתם • ונפן ונעבר את נחל זרד ויאמר אלהם אלי לאמר קמו	B13

---

502 Guthe records *א.

503 Guthe records ה....ל.

504 Guthe records הנרא.

505 Guthe records הַאשר, apparently associating the ה of הזה in the preceding word recorded by Ginsburg.

506 Guthe indicates the presence of a line 1 of fragment B but makes no attempt to transcribe any of its contents. We have therefore retained an empty line. The continuity, however, of Ginsburg's text indicates that he was able to read it and therefore, our hypothetical A9 is likely B1.

507 Guthe records וּמַכתי.

508 Guthe records עטן. He also says, "The rest of piece B is missing in my copy, as is piece C, which is also detached." The narrative supplied by Ginsburg suggests that his copy is readable, although he does not indicate which fragment he is transcribing. Ginsburg's transcription records the words of Guthe's (B2) as following חי אני in the previous line. The transcriptions of both Ginsburg and Guthe have this line of text followed by זה ע**, which is the beginning of the next line in Guthe's fragment B. Ginsburg supplies an uninterrupted narrative from this point forward. I have therefore speculated that he is working from fragment B. The line breaks beyond B3 are a hypothetical reconstruction based on estimated line lengths. My reconstructed fragment B contains 13 lines of text. Fragment G consists of five columns—three with 12 lines of text, and two with 13 lines of text.

Fragment D – Column A	
ועברו את נחל ארנן היום החלתי לתת לפנך את סיחן מ	DA1
לך חשבן האמרי ואת ארצו • ונצא לקראת סיחן יהצה	DA2
ונכה עד לא השאר לו שרד ונלכד את כל ערו מערער א	DA3
שר על שפת נחל ארנן עד הגלעד ועד נחל יבק הכל נתן אלה	DA4
ם אלהנו לפננו • ונפן ונעבר דרך נחל יבק ויאמר אלהם	DA5
אלי[509] לאמר אתם עברם היום את גבל ארץ בני עמן לא תצ	DA6
רם ולא תתגר בם מלחמה כי לבני לט נתתי ארץ בני עמן ירשה •	DA7
רפאם[510] מעלם ישבו בה והעמנם יקראו להם עזמזם וישמ	DA8
[ד]ם אלהם מפנהם וישבו תחתם • ויאמר אלהם אלי שלח אנ	DA9
שם[511] לרגל את יעזר ונלכד [את] יעזר ונשב בערי האמרי • ויצא	DA10
Fragment D – Column B	
עג מלך הבשן לקראתנו למלחמה ונכהו עד לא השאר לו ש	DB1
רד ונלכד מאתם ששם ער כל כבל הארגב בצרת חמה דלת	DB2
ם וברחם[512] • לבד מערי הפרזם הרבה מאד וכל ערי המשר	DB3
וכל הגלעד וכל הבשן עד סלכה ואדרעי[513]• ..... ארץ רפאם	DB4
גם הוא כי עג מלך הבשן מיתר הרפאם נשאר • ונפן	DB5
ונסע נגבה ונשב מול בת פער • ויצאו בעת ההוא בנת	DB6
מאב ונשי מדין לקראתכם ותקראן [ל]כם לאכל מזבח[514]	DB7
הן ותאכל[515] מזבחהן ותשתו מנסההן[516] ותשתחו לאלה[517]	DB8
הן ותזנו את נשי המדינם • ותצמדו לבעל פער ביום	DB9
ההוא וחרה אף אלהם עלכם ויגף בכם בעת ההוא	DB10
Fragment D – Column C	
מגפה גדלה • ושלחתי מכם אנשם ללחם את המדינם ו	DC1
הכתם אתם לפי חרב ושבתם מאתם שבי הרבה[518] למאד ות	DC2
עצר המגפה • ואתי צוה אלהם בעת ההוא ללמד אתכם חקם ומש[519]	DC3
פטם לעשתם בארץ אשר עברם שמה לרשתה • השמרו לכם	DC4

---

509 Guthe records י**.

510 Guthe records the letters אם......

511 The difficulty for Guthe in recording שם at the beginning of this line suggests that the right edge of this fragment was difficult to read, possibly due to the condition of the fragment. This makes the third consecutive line of text on the right hand (leading edge), and the fourth out of the final five lines of text on fragment D, column A, where Guthe cannot discern the letters.

512 Guthe records וברחם.

513 Ginsburg records a series of dots .... where Guthe records an interpunct.

514 Guthe records מהג*יהן.

515 Guthe records ותא*לו.

516 Guthe records מנת*הן.

517 Guthe records *לה.

518 Guthe records שביה רבה.

519 Guthe records ומ*.

לא תספו אל[520] מצותו[521] ולא תגרעו ממנו • השמרו לכם פן תשכחו ו	DC5
עשתם לכם[522] פסל ותמנה תבנת כל סמל אשר בשמם ממעל ואֶ[שר בארֶ	DC6
ץ מ]תֶחֶת[523] ואשר במים מתחת לארץ • וחרה אפיֶ[524] בכם וֱהֱשֱמֶדְתּי[525]	DC7
את[כם[526] מהרה מן[527] הארץ הטבה הֱזאת • ויֱדֱע ..[528] היום ו	DC8
[שמֶ]רת[529] את חקתו[530] ומצותו למען יטב לכם [ו	DC9
למען] תארכו[531] ימם על האדמה אשר אלהם אלהך	DC10
Fragment E – Column A	
נתֶן[532] לכם[533] • שמע ישראל אלהם אלהנו אלהם אחד	EA1
ואהבת את אלהם אלהך בכל לבבֶ[ך[534] ובכל נפשך למ	EA2
אד מאד[535] • וֱהֱיֶוֱ[536] הדברם האלה אשר אנכ מצוך היו	EA3
ם על לבבך ושננתם[537] לבנך ודברת אתם בֶשֶב	EA4
תך בבתך ובלכתך בדרך • וֱבֶשֱכֱבֱך[538] ובקמֶך וקשרת	EA5
ם אתם לאות על ידך והיו לתֶתֶוֶתֶת[539] בין עינֶך[540] וכת	EA6
בֶ[תֶם][541] עֱלֶ[542] מזזת בתך ושערך כי אלהֶם כרת	EA7
עמֶך ברֶת[543] בחרב ביֶום הקהל וֱאֱנֶכ עמדתי בין אלהם	EA8
ובֶי[נֶכם][544] ... בעת הזאת כי פחדתם[545] מפני האש ולא	EA9
ההד להגד לכם דבר אלהכם לאמר[546]	EA10

---

[520] Guthe records עֶל.
[521] Guthe records מצוֶתֶי.
[522] Guthe records כֶל **ועשת.
[523] Guthe records ת**מֶ.
[524] Guthe records אֶפֶו.
[525] Guthe records וֱהֱשֱמֶ*.
[526] Guthe records ****.
[527] Guthe records מֶעֶל.
[528] Guthe records וֱידֶעֶת.
[529] Guthe records רֶת**.
[530] Guthe records חקו ואת.
[531] Guthe records תֶאֱרֱכֶן.
[532] Guthe records תֶן*.
[533] Guthe records ךֶ*.
[534] Guthe records לֶבֶ**.
[535] Guthe records מֶת.....
[536] Guthe records וֱהֱ**.
[537] Guthe records לֶךֶ between ושננתם and לבנך.
[538] Guthe records בֶשֱכֱבֶך.
[539] Guthe records לֶתֶתֶוֶכֶת.
[540] Guthe records עֶנֶך.
[541] Guthe records בת אתֶם.
[542] Guthe records *עֶ.
[543] Guthe records עֶם ... ת.
[544] Guthe records בֶנֶכם....
[545] Guthe records פֶחֶדת.
[546] Guthe records a fragmentary transcription of this line that shows no obvious association with Ginsburg's transcription. Guthe records ....ת.... הֱקֶל *גֶדֶל.....

	Fragment E – Column B
EB1	אנכ • אלהם • אלהך • אשר • החרתך • מא
EB2	רץ • מצרם • מבת • עבדם •
EB3	לא יה [hole יה] [547] • לכם •
EB4	אלהם • אחרם • לא תעש [ה hole] [548] • לַכם • פֶסֶל • וכל • תמ
EB5	נה • אשר • בשמם [549] • ממעל • ואשר • בארץ • מ
EB6	תחת • ואשר • במים • מתחת • לָארֶץ • לא תש [550]
EB7	תחו • להם • ולא תעבדם • אנכ • אלהם •
EB8	אלהך •
EB9	קדש ......
	Fragment E – Column C
EC1	שת • ימם • עשתי • את השמם • ואת הא
EC2	רץ • וכל • אשר • בם • ושבתי • ביום • השבעי •
EC3	על • כן • תשבת • גם • אתה • ובהמתך • וכל • אשר
EC4	לך • אנכ • אלהם • אלהך •
EC5	כבד • את אבך • ואת אמך • למען • יארכן • ימך [551] • אנכ • אלהם • אלהך •
EC6	לא תר[צ]ח • את נ[פ]שי • אחך • אנכ • אלהם • אלהך •
EC7	לא תנאף • את אשת • רעך [552] • אנכ • אלהם • אלהך •
EC8	לא תגנב [553] • את הן • אחך [554] • אנכ • אלהם • אלהך •
	Fragment E – Column D
ED1	לא תשבע • בשמי • לשקר • כי • אנכ • אקנא • את
ED2	עון • אבֹת [555] • על • בנם • על • שלשם • ועל • רבעם • לנ
ED3	שא [556] • שמי • לשקר • אנכ • אלהם • אלהך •
ED4	לא תענו • באחך • עדת • שקר • אנכ • אלהם • אל
ED5	הך •
ED6	לא תחמד • אשת •.... • עבדו • ואמתו • וכל • אש

---

[547] Guthe records יה where Ginsburg records יהיה but also notes a hole in the fragment where these letters likely appeared.

[548] Guthe records תעש but also notes a hole in the fragment where ה likely appeared.

[549] Guthe records four asterisks where Ginsburg records בשמם.

[550] Guthe records ת*.

[551] "Shapira's MSS," *The Old Testament Student,* Vol. 3, No. 1 (Sep. 1883), 23–25: "Dr. Ginsburg says that the words 'that thy days may be long' are omitted in one duplicate." See Ginsburg, "The Shapira MS. of Deuteronomy," *The Athenæum,* no. 2911, 11 August 1883, 178. The "copy" from which Guthe transcribed did not contain this phrase as is evidenced in his published work, and the drawing of four columns of the Paleo-Hebrew text, commissioned by Ginsburg, also lack this phrase. It is included here with Ginsburg's note.

[552] Guthe records ש.......ע....ך.

[553] Guthe records תג**ב*.

[554] Guthe records ר*ך.

[555] Guthe records אבֹך.

[556] Guthe records a י at the end of the word.

ר • לו • אנכ • אלהם • אלהך •	ED7
לא תשנא • את אחך • בל[בבך][557] • אנכ • אלהם • אלהך •	ED8
את עשרת הדברם הא[ל]ה דבר אלהם	ED9

Fragment F – Column A[558]

......תה עמנ.......ע וא ידבר עם...	FA1
כם ולא נמת • ושמע אלהם את דבר...	FA2
ם .... דֵבֵר*רו • מֵי • י	FA3
.... ימם .. מען ל	FA4

Fragment G – Column A

*ם על הֵאֵדֵמה אשר נשבעתי לתת להם ולבנהם אחרהם[559] • שמע ישראל[560]	GA1
אתם עברם היום את הירדן לבא לרשת גוים רבם ועצמם ערם גֵדֵלֵת ובֵצ	GA2
רת חֵמה לא[561] תאֵמרו בלבבכם רֵבם המה הגוים האלה לא נכל להרשם לא תראֵ[562] מה	GA3
ם זכר אֵת אשר עֵשֵה אלהם לפרעה ולכל מצרם כן יעשה אלהם לכל איבך •	GA4
כי אלהם הוא העבר לֵפֵנך אש אֵכֵלֵה הוא • הוא ישמדם ויכנעם מחרה[563] לֵפֵ	GA5
נך • גם את ה..צֵרעֵת[564] ישלח אלהם[565] בם • עד אבֵד יאבד הנֵסֵתרם הנשארם מלֵפֵ	GA6
נך רֵק אם[566] תשמרו[567] את מצותו[568] ומשפטו וחקתו אשר אנכ מצוך היום ו	GA7
ידעת[569] היום כי לא בצדקתך[570] אלהם אלהך נתן לפנך את הארץ הזאת לרשתה	GA8
כי עם קשה ערף הית מן היום אשר יֵצאת ממצרם עד היום ממרם הית	GA9

---

557 Guthe records בל*בֵבֵך.

558 This fragment appears only in Meyer. Guthe reported that Fragment F, columns A and B issue from Meyer. Meyer only recorded four fragmentary lines from column A. He commented, "fragment F of four layers; layer A, Line 3." In a footnote he added, "belongs to the second copy of the text," seemingly suggesting that line 3 comes from the second copy.

559 The opening of this line appears only in Meyer.

560 Meyer records יש***.

561 Meyer records כמ.

562 Meyer records תירא.

563 Meyer records מהרה.

564 Meyer records ה**עת.

565 Meyer records **הם.

566 Meyer records *ם.

567 Meyer records תשמר.

568 Meyer records מצ***.

569 Meyer records *דעת*.

570 Meyer records בצדקת*.

ם את אלהם אלהך • בַחרב בַיום עלתי[571] ההר לקחת את שני לחת האבנם[572] ועלהם[573]	GA10
כתבם כל הדברם אשר דבר אלהם עמכם בהר מתך האש ביום הקהל	GA11
קצפתם את אלהם ועשתם לכם עגל מסכה ואתנפל לפני אלהם בהר הבער כאש[574] ...	GA12

ושַנַי לחת[575] בידי וארַא חטאתכם[576] ואשבר את שני לחת[577] לע	GB1
ינכם וָאתפַלל בעדכם בעת ההוא ארבעם יום וארבעם ללה • וַבתבערה[578]	GB2
ובמסַה ובקברת התאוה ממרם היתם את אלהכם[579] • בעת ההוא אמר אל	GB3
הם אלי פסל לך שני[580] לחת אבנם כראשנם ו	GB4
עלה אלי ההרה ואעל ההרה ושני	GB5
[ה]לחת בידַי • ויכתב[581] אלהם על הלחת את עשרת[582] הדברם אשר דבר אלכם בהר בי[583]	GB6
ום הקהל ויתנם[584] אלי • והנם בארן אשר עשתי ברנע באמר אלי	GB7
אלהם[585] עלו ורשו[586] את הארץ ממרם[587] היתם את אלהכם ולא עלתם ולא שמעתם[588] בק	GB8
לו ויאמר אלהם להשמדכם[589] ואתפלל[590] בעדכם בעמד בהר ארבעם יום	GB9
וארבעם ללה בעדכם[591] ? וישמע[592] אלהם גם בפעם ההוא ולא השחת אתכם כרגע	GB10

---

[571] Guthe records עַל**.

[572] Meyer records לח**בנם.

[573] Meyer records an asterisk at the end of line 10 and the beginning of line 11.

[574] Meyer records כאש.

[575] Meyer records וְשַנַי * לח.

[576] Meyer records the word (ואקצף) between חטאתכם and ואשבר.

[577] Meyer records הלחַת.

[578] Meyer records ובתב***.

[579] Meyer records ה**ם א*****כם.

[580] Meyer records ש*י.

[581] Ginsburg's transcription records the obvious mistake of ויכתב. Meyer records ויכתב here. I have corrected to the reading of Meyer.

[582] Meyer records הדברם א***.

[583] Meyer records וביום.

[584] Meyer records ויתנ*.

[585] Between ובקדש and עלו, Meyer records, with obvious uncertainty, ה....בא..בראהם.

[586] Meyer records ו**ו.

[587] Meyer records ממ**.

[588] Meyer records ש*עתם.

[589] Meyer records להשמד א***ם.

[590] Meyer records ואת*פל.

[591] Meyer records באכַם. The question mark is in the text of Ginsburg's transcription and has been retained here.

[592] Meyer records וישע.

לֹא בצדקתך אלהך נתן לך כח לעשת חיל ... [רק חשק אלהם] באב[593]	GB11
תכם לאהבה אתם ויבחר בזרעם[594] אחרהם מכל העם • [כי אלהם]	GB12
אלהכם הוא אלה [?] אלהם[595] ואדׁנׁי האדנם הׁאֵל הגבר והנרא [הוא הׁלתך[596]ת]	GB13

Fragment G – Column C

והוא אשר עשה אתך	GC1
את הגדלת ואת הנראת • בשבעם נפש ירדו אבתכם למצר	GC2
ם [וׁ]עׁתה הית[597] לעם עצם ורב • כי אך [אם] תשמר[ו[598] את[599]] כל המצוה[600] אשר אנכ מצוה[601] ה	GC3
יום לעשת[602] לאהבה את אלהכם ללכת בכל דרכו ובכל חקתו • והרש אלהם את כ	GC4
ל אנׁשׁי המקם כל אשר תׁדׁרֹך[603] כׁף רגלכם בו • לא יתיצב אׁיׁ[שׁ] לׁפׁנׁכׁם[604] כׁ[י פׁ]חׁדׁכׁ	GC5
ם ומראכם יהיה על פני כל הארץ אׁשׁ[ר תׁ]דׁרׁכׁו בו • ראה אנכ נתן לׁפׁנׁכׁם היום בר	GC6
כה וקללה את הברכה אם תשמעו אל מצות[ׁי וׁחׁקׁתׁי[605]] והקללה אם לא תשמעו וסרתם	GC7
מהדרך אשר אנכ מצוה אתכם היום [וׁהׁיׁה כׁי יׁ]בׁאך אלהם אל הארץ אשר את	GC8
ה בא שמה לרשתה ונתת את הברכה על הר [גׁרׁזׁם[606]] והקללה על הר עבל • הׁלׁא [המה] בעבר	GC9
הירדן[607] דרך מבא השמש בארץ הכנעני [נׁגׁ]דׁ[608] גׁלׁגׁל[609] אצל אלׁנׁי מׁרׁא[610] • ואלה יֵעׁמׁדׁו עׁל הׁ	GC10

---

[593] Meyer records this line with obvious uncertainty: רק.........אבשמר......

[594] Meyer records ב**עם*.

[595] Meyer records אל האלהם. The question mark is in the text of Ginsburg's transcription and has been retained here.

[596] Meyer records part B of this line with obvious uncertainty: וא*ן .. אדנם אׁ.....והנרא הו* *הלתך.

[597] Guthe records היתׁם.

[598] Guthe records תשמ*ן.

[599] Guthe records *א.

[600] Guthe records ה*צוה.

[601] Guthe records צותך.

[602] Guthe records לעשתה.

[603] Guthe records תׁקׁם.

[604] Guthe records בׁפׁנכם.

[605] Guthe records מצות אלהם.

[606] Guthe records [hole!].

[607] Guthe records ה***ן.

[608] Guthe records בׁעׁ.....

[609] Guthe records הגלגל.

[610] Guthe records אלן *רא.

[ר עבל] ראובן[611] זבולן [ו]גד אשר דן[612] ונפתלי • ואלה יעמדו על הר גרזם	GC11
שמען ויהודה ויששכר[613] מנשה ואפרם ובנימן • ועמדו[614] הלוים נגד הר גרזם ו	GC12
[ענ]ו ואמרו בקל רם [ב]רך האיש אשר יאהב[615] אלהם אלהנו[616] ולו לבדו ישתחו ואתו	GC13
Fragment G – Column D	
לבדו יעבד וענו כל ה<u>ע</u>[ם] ואמרו אמן • ברך הא[י]ש אשר יקדש את י[ו]ם[617] השבעי	GD1
וי<u>שבת</u>[618] בו וי<u>ענ</u>ו[619] כל העם ואמרו אמן • [ברך האיש] מכבד אבו ואמו וענו כל	GD2
העם ואמרו אמן • ברך [ה]א[י]ש אשר לא יקם ולא יטר את נפש אחו וענו א	GD3
מן • ברך האיש אשר לא יטמה את אשת רעהו וענו כל העם ואמרו א[620]	GD4
מן • ברך האיש אשר לא [ין]ה[621] את רעהו וענו [כל העם ואמרו אמן • ב]רך האיש	GD5
אשר לא ישבע ב[ש]מי לשקר וענו כל העם ואמרו אמן • ברך האיש אשר לא	GD6
יכחש ול[א י]<u>שקר</u>[622] ברעהו וענו כל העם ואמרו אמן • ברך [האיש] אשר לא נשא	GD7
עינו אל ה[ר]כש רעהו וענו כל העם ואמרו אמן • ברך האיש אשר יאה	GD8
ב את ר[ע]הו [וענו] כל העם ואמרו[623] אמן • ברך האיש אשר יקם את כל דב	GD9
רי התרה ה[ז]ות ל[ע]שת [א]תם וענו כל העם ואמרו אמן • ויספו הלוי	GD10
ם וענו [ויאמרו ב]קל רם[624] ראה אם[625] שמע תשמע בקל אלהך לשמר לעש	GD11

---

[611] Guthe records ראובן. Ginsburg records ראוכן. It is hard to imagine a misreading of ב and כ in this ancient script, as they do not look anything alike. Perhaps this was a mistake in the transcription. I have retained Guthe's version.

[612] Guthe records ד*.

[613] Guthe records ...<u>שכ</u>*.

[614] Guthe records <u>ועדו</u>.

[615] Guthe records יה**.

[616] Guthe records אלהו.

[617] Guthe records היום.

[618] Guthe records וישבת. Ginsburg has the same, though the י is hardly discernable in his transcription.

[619] Guthe records וענו.

[620] Guthe indicates that he is missing two and a half lines.

[621] Guthe records ***.

[622] Guthe records <u>שקר</u>*.

[623] Guthe records ואמ*ו.

[624] Guthe records בקל **.

[625] Guthe records א*.

[ת א]ת כל מצותו ובאו עלך כל הברכת האלה ברך אתה בער ברך אתה	GD12

Fragment G – Column E

בשדה ברך טנאך ושארתך[626] • ברך פרי בטנך ופרי אדמתך שגר [א][627]	GE1
לפך ועשתרת צאנך ברך אתה בבאך וברך אתה בצאתך יתן אלה[628]	GE2
את אביך נגפם לפנך • יצו אלהם[629] את הברכה בכל מעשה יד[630] • יק	GE3
מך אלהם לו לעם קדש וראו כל עמי הארץ ויראו[631] ממך • יפתח אלהם[632]	GE4
לך את השמם לתת[633] מ[טר] ארצך בע[ת]ו ו[ה][ל]ו[ת גוים [רב]ם ו[אתה ל[א [ת]לו	GE5
ה והית[634] [למעלה] ול[א תהיה [ל]מטה ... מה ...[635]	GE6
[א]בתכם ...[636] • [ו]יסבו הל[ו][י]ים את פ[נה]ם [נ]גד הר עב	GE7
ל ויענו ו[יאמ]רו [ב]קל ר[ם] ארר ה[אי]ש אשר [יעש]ה	GE8
פ[ס]ל ומסכה מעש[ה] י[ד]י חרש וענו כל העם ו[אמרו	GE9
א[מ]ן • אר[ר האיש א[שר יעשה מלאכה ביום השביעי לחללו וענו כל העם ואמרו אמן • א]רר מקלה[637] אבו ואמו ו	GE10
ענו כל העם ואמרו אמן • ארר מכה רעהו בסתר וענו כל העם ואם	GE11
רו אמן • ארר האיש אשר יקרב אל כל שאר בשרו ואשר ינאף	GE12
את אשת רעהו ואשר יבעל עם כל בהמה וענו כל העם ואמרו אמן • ארר	GE13

Fragment H – Column A

מ[ס]ג גבל רעהו וענו כל העם ואמרו אמן • ארר האיש אשר ישבע	HA1
בשמי לשקר וענו כל העם ואמרו[638] אמן • ארר לקח שחד[639] לה[עד עד[640] שקר בעם	HA2
תו וענו כל העם[641] ואמרו אמן • ארר האיש אשר[642] י[שא עינ]ו[643] אל אשת ר	HA3

---

[626] Guthe records שארתך*.

[627] Guthe records * *שג*.

[628] Guthe records *אלה.

[629] Guthe records *אלה.

[630] Guthe records *יד.

[631] Guthe records ויראו*.

[632] Guthe records *אלה.

[633] Guthe records תת*.

[634] Guthe records רק between והית and למעלה.

[635] For part B of this line, Guthe records ...ויתרך אלהם רק לטבה על האדמה.

[636] Guthe records part A of this line נתן לכם.....

[637] Guthe records *מקל.

[638] Meyer records ה*** ו***ו.

[639] Meyer records ש**.

[640] Meyer records עדת.

[641] Meyer records ם.........*ת*.

[642] Meyer records ויחמד between אשר and וישא.

[643] Meyer records ענו.

עהו ואל בתו ואל אמ[תו]644 ולכל אשר לו וענו כל העם ואמרו אמן • ארר הא י	HA4
ש אשר ישנא את645 אחו בלבו וענו כל העם646 ואמרו אמן • ארר האיש ש	HA5
ר לא ינ[ק]ם את כל דברי התו[ר]ה הז[א]ת647 לעשת אתם וענו כל העם ואמרו אמן •	HA6
וי[ס]פו הלוים לקרא בקל רם ויאמרו והיה648 אם לא תשמע בקל אלהך649 [לש]	HA7
מר לעשת את כל מצותו ו[ח]קתו650 ובאו עלך כל הקללת האלה ארר אתה בע	HA8
ר ואר[ר]651 אתה בשדה ארר [ט]נאך ושארתך ארר פרי בטנך ופרי אדמת	HA9
ך שגר אלפך ועשתרת [צאנך]652 • ארר אתה בבאך653 וארר אתה בצאתך ית •	HA10
נך אלהם נ[גף לפ]ני איב[ך] ישלח654 אלהם את המארה בכל מעשה ידך655 יתנך •	HA11
אלהם לשמה [ל]משל656 ולשננה בכל עמי הארץ יעצר אלהם את השמם	HA12
Fragment H – Column B	
הגר657 אש[ר]658 בקר]בך יעלה מעלה מעלה659 וא[תה]660 תרד מטה מטה ילוך	HB1
ואת[ה]662 לא תלו[נו] יאבד וי[שמ]ך661 אלהם את[ך] מעל פני הא[א]דמה662 אשר אתה בא	HB2

---

644 Meyer records ואמת*.

645 Meyer records ת*.

646 Meyer records ם**.

647 Meyer records ה*את.

648 Meyer records ו***ה.

649 Meyer records אלהם.

650 Meyer records חקתו*.

651 Meyer records וא**.

652 Meyer records וע**** ***ך.

653 Meyer records בב*ך.

654 Meyer records ישל*ך.

655 Meyer records ך*י.

656 Meyer records משל*.

657 Meyer records גר*.

658 Meyer records ישב between אשר and בקרבך.

659 Meyer records מאלה.

660 Meyer records הוא between מטה and ילוך.

661 Meyer records ו*שמ*.

662 Meyer records אדמ*ך מן אתכם.

ש[מ]ה [לרשתה] • בן[663] מַאֶה ועש[ר]ם [שנה אנכ[664] ה]יום לא אכל[665] [666] לצאת ול	HB3
בא לפנכם ואלהם אמר אלי לא תעבר את[667] הירדן[668] יהשע[669] העמד[670] לפנך [הוא] יע	HB4
בר את הירדן והוא יבא אתכם אל הארץ הטבה אש	HB5
ר .. שמה לרשתה • חזקו ואמצו אל תראו[671] ואל תחַפדו[672] כי אלהם אלהכם הוא הה	HB6
לך .... הזאת ... לפנכם ...... כי .... [673]	HB7
.... [674]	HB8
.... אלה הדברם אשר צוה משה לכל[675] בני ישראל[676]	HB9
על פי יהוה בערבת מאב לפני מתו •	HB10

---

[663] Ginsburg's transcription reads כן.

[664] Meyer records נכ*.

[665] Meyer records כל*.

[666] Meyer records ע** between כל* and ל*את.

[667] Meyer records **.

[668] Meyer records היר*ן.

[669] Meyer records יהש*.

[670] Meyer records ה**.

[671] Meyer records תר**.

[672] Meyer records תח**.

[673] Meyer records עמך after לך, but Ginsburg's version also indicates that the line is fragmentary.

[674] Meyer records that this line of text was not discernable by transcribing a series of dots.

[675] Meyer records את כל.

[676] Meyer records ב** ***אל.

The Ten Words
with Blessings and Curses
According to the Shapira Scroll

Number	Ten Words	Blessings	Curses
I	I am • Elohim • your Elohim • who • liberated you • from the land of • Egypt, • from a house of • servitude. • There shall not be • to you • other • Elohim. • You shall not make • for yourselves • a carved thing, • or any • formed thing • that is • in the heavens • above, • or that is • on the earth • below. • or that is • in the waters • under • the earth • You shall not bow down • to them, • and you shall not serve them. • I am • Elohim • your Elohim. •	"Blessed is the man who loves Elohim his Elohim and worships Him alone and serves Him alone." And all of the people, they will respond and they will say, "Amen." •	"Cursed is the man who makes a carved thing or a molten thing, the work of a sculptor's hand." And all of the people, they will respond and they will say, "Amen." •
II	Sanctify • [the seventh day]. • Six • days • I made • the heavens • and the earth • and all • that is • in them, • and I ceased • on the seventh • day. • Therefore, • you shall cease • also, • you, • and your animal, • and all • that • is yours. • I am • Elohim • your Elohim. •	"Blessed is the man who sanctifies the seventh day and ceases thereon." And all of the people, they will respond and they will say, "Amen." •	"Cursed is the man who does work on the seventh day to profane it." And all of the people, they will respond and they will say, "Amen." •
III	Honor • your father • and your mother. • I am • Elohim • your Elohim. •	"Blessed is the man who honors his father and his mother." And all of the people, they will respond and they will say, "Amen." •	"Cursed is the man who esteems his father and his mother lightly." And all of the people, they will respond and they will say, "Amen." •

IV	You shall not kill • the soul of • your brother. • I am • Elohim • your Elohim. •	"Blessed is the man who does not take vengeance and does not hold a grudge against his brother's soul." And they will respond, "Amen." •	"Cursed is the one who strikes his neighbor in secret." And all of the people, they will respond and they will say, "Amen." •
V	You shall not commit adultery • with the woman • of your neighbor. • I am • Elohim • your Elohim. •	"Blessed is the man who does not defile his neighbor's woman." And all of the people, they will respond and they will say, "Amen." •	"Cursed is the man who draws near to any close relative, or who commits adultery with his neighbor's woman, or who lies with any animal." And all of the people, they will respond and they will say, "Amen." •
VI	You shall not steal • the property of • your brother. • I am • Elohim • your Elohim. •	"Blessed is the man who does not wrong his neighbor." And all of the people will respond and say, "Amen." •	"Cursed is the one who moves his neighbor's land boundary." And all of the people will respond and say, "Amen." •
VII	You shall not swear • by My name • to deceive, • because • I am • passionate. • The iniquity of • fathers • will be upon • children • unto a third • and unto a fourth *generation* • for lifting • My name • to deceive. • I am • Elohim • your Elohim. •	"Blessed is the man who does not swear in My name to deceive." And all of the people, they will respond and they will say, "Amen." •	"Cursed is the man who swears by My name to deceive." And all of the people, they will respond and they will say, "Amen." •
VIII	You shall not respond • against your brother • *with* a testimony of • deceit. • I am • Elohim • your Elohim. •	"Blessed is the man who does not deal falsely and does not practice deceit with his neighbor." And all of the people, they will respond and they will say, "Amen." •	"Cursed is the one who takes a bribe to testify deceitfully against his associate." And all of the people, they will respond and they will say, "Amen." •

IX	You shall not desire • [your neighbor's] woman, • his servant, • his maidservant, • or anything • that is • his. • I am • Elohim • your Elohim. •	"Blessed is the man who does not lift his eyes toward the property of his neighbor." And all of the people, they will respond and they will say, "Amen." •	"Cursed is the man who lifts his eyes toward his neighbor's woman, or toward his house, or toward his maidservant, or toward all that is his." And all of the people, they will respond and they will say, "Amen." •
X	You shall not hate • your brother • in your heart. • I am • Elohim • your Elohim. •	"Blessed is the man who loves his neighbor." And all of the people, they will respond and they will say, "Amen." •	"Cursed is the man who hates his brother in his heart." And all of the people, they will respond and they will say, "Amen." •
		"Blessed is the man who establishes all of the words of this Teaching to do them." And all of the people, they will respond and they will say, "Amen." •	"Cursed is the man who does not establish all of the words of this Teaching to do them." And all of the people, they will respond and they will say, "Amen." •

Acknowledgments

This book would not have been possible without the help and encouragement of family and friends. My interest in all things biblical traces back to a childhood filled with stories from the pages of the Bible. I fell in love with the people and places of the Book of books because my mother, Karen Fay Montgomery, did her part to train a child in the way he ought to go.

"He who finds a wife," says Proverbs 18:22, "has found happiness and has won the favor of the LORD." This is certainly the case for me. Bridget has been by my side for nearly four decades. I appreciate that she has always been supportive, although I am not sure that from her perspective my involvement in this writing project looked much different than any other. Either way, I am thankful for her enduring patience in this process and with me in general.

I appreciate the encouragement and expressed interest from our six children (Ty, Callin, Emily, Zachariah, Seth, and Tobias) and our eight grandchildren (Asher, Kalel, Ezekiel, Ainsley, Natalie, Owen, Juliette, and Lincoln) in Saba's latest "Bible project." A special thanks to my youngest grandson, Lincoln, who was in my lap for much of the writing process, and my sincere apologies to Ainsley for missing the birthday trip to the doll store as the final edits for the book were in the works on her special day. May they all live long, happy, and prosperous lives and grow to love the ancient yet timeless words contained in the pages of the Hebrew Bible.

A special thanks to David and Patty Tyler for their loyal friendship and generous support over the years and particularly during the writing of this book. They were part of our small research team, and their interest, input, and many ideas helped me all along the way. The translation of Guthe's *Fragmente einer Lederhandschrift enthaltend Mose's letzte Rede an die Kinder Israel* was for me a significant breakthrough in putting the pieces together. So I especially appreciate and acknowledge their generosity in sponsoring that project. I am also grateful for the careful translation of Guthe's work by Mitchell Golde. Mitchell performed the task with professionalism, and I look forward to sharing that complete work with a larger audience soon.

Don and Carol Walls deserve great credit if compliments are extended for the finished product since they were the editorial team that turned my best efforts at laying out the story into a much more polished work. They worked tirelessly and without complaint through the various iterations of the book, offering at every turn a slightly better way of expressing what I had attempted to say. If there are faults with the presentation, it should be known that it is far better thanks to their work than when I submitted it to them. It must be rare for a writer to find an editorial team that is not only skilled at the editing process but also so versed in biblical literature and history that substantive input is provided to the author by the editors. I cannot thank them enough for their help in bringing this book from draft to its finished state.

Everyone has heard the adage "Don't judge a book by its cover," but in the case of *The Moses Scroll* I hope that people do just that. Daniel Wright applied his immense talents to design the cover and the illustrations within the book. We frequently talked about various aspects of the project, and he somehow turned my rough ideas into something of beauty. I am equally thankful for his external and artistic contributions to the book as I am for his constant internal and conceptual contributions. It has been a joy to work with Daniel. He also assisted in page design and layout, working closely with the editors to produce the elegant pages within the book.

Anna Jakubowski gave generously of her time and talents to build the official website for *The Moses Scroll* (https://themosesscroll.com/). She always responded quickly and ably to my requests. Her help, and the encouragement of her husband, Darek, are much appreciated.

James Tabor's work has inspired and guided me for more than three decades. No one person has had a greater influence on my understanding of the Bible than he. I would not have known about Moses Shapira and his manuscript had he not sent me that 15 December 2019 email. I am especially grateful for his countless insights and suggestions that made this book far better than it would have been had he not been there to advise me. I appreciate that he wrote the foreword. Not only was he the one person who knew the story well enough to do it justice, but for me, it was the highest honor to have my teacher and mentor write it. I look forward to many more adventures with him in the literature and the land of the Bible.

On the specific subject of Moses Shapira, I wish to acknowledge those who belong to a small and special group of Shapiramaniacs or Shapiraologists. I can only hope that they all consider this work a positive contribution to their own research. I stand on the shoulders of giants when it comes to this subject. I am thankful for the research of Yoram Sabo, who has been on the quest since 1979. His contributions have greatly advanced the knowledge of Shapira. From his trove of assembled documents related to Shapira, Matthew Hamilton provided more than we requested and showed himself willing to help at every turn. Chanan Tigay's gifted writing ability pulled me into this intriguing story. While I arrived at different conclusions than he did, I am thankful for his contributions. I benefitted from Shlomo Guil's academic research and especially his work on the text of Shapira's manuscript. I am also appreciative to Professor Shimon Gibson, whose expertise on nineteenth-century Jerusalem and Shapira helped me. I also wish to thank Professor James Charlesworth for his kind and encouraging words when I met him for the first time in Israel in February 2020. The detailed work of Rabbi Fred Reiner was very helpful. I learned some key details from his published articles.

I also want to acknowledge the work of past researchers, particularly Professor Menachem Mansoor and John Marco Allegro. The works of these two scholars were always on my desk. They both suggested that the matter should be reexamined in light of new evidence, so I can only hope that the present work, at least partially, has achieved this result.

I made use of the work of several scholars and authors, past and present, as I conducted research for this book, among them Richard Elliott Friedman, Emanuel Tov, Joan Taylor, Eveline van der Steen, Neil Asher Silberman, John Trever, and others. I appreciate their contributions to my understanding of the subjects contained in this book, though their mention does not mean to suggest that they would endorse the ideas contained herein. Of special note was the work of Shapira's younger daughter, Maria, known by her penname Myriam Harry. Her *The Little Daughter of Jerusalem,* while written in the form of a novel, provided insight into the life and times that formed the backdrop to the story.

I am also thankful that the nineteenth-century scholars, in spite of their decisions on the authenticity of Shapira's manuscript, accurately recorded the details of their work. This enables us to see the scroll through their eyes and reassess it in light of our current knowledge. Particularly helpful were the works of Christian David Ginsburg, Hermann Guthe, and Eduard Meyer. Thanks to the archives of the British Museum, the Palestine Exploration Fund, and the digitized editions of *The Times, The Athenæum, The Jewish Chronicle, The New York Times* and other nineteenth-century publications we were able to accurately relate these events.

Many other faithful friends encouraged me during the writing process. Jono Vandor kindly read several versions of the work and offered his invaluable suggestions and many insights, and then somewhere along the way he got pulled into the fascinating story. Ilan Pomeranc encouraged me and provided assistance, particularly with the research of materials written in modern Hebrew. Ralph Buntyn, an author, respected friend, and counselor, gave me helpful advice from the beginning and checked in on my progress from time to time. A special thanks are in order for the members and friends of United Israel World Union, particularly the officers and board members and local members, David and Sherry Cole, Jon and Linden Langberg, PJ Danner, Mark Loyd, and Michael Perdue. Barry Page, himself an author, read the book and gave his hearty recommendation, for which I am grateful. Todd Young listened intently on several occasions as I filled him in on the details of the research at my office. Ron Vanderham read an early version of the work. Victor Stewart helped me with some of the research, and Don Smith shared encouraging words of wisdom on his private porch at Biblical Tamar Park in the wilderness of Israel.

I would be remiss if I didn't acknowledge my own teachers who have inspired me to search deeper into the biblical texts: Joe Good, Andy Garza, Dr. James Tabor, and Johnny Powell, my Hebrew teacher. Without their guidance at crucial points in my quest, I would not have arrived at my current place.

And finally, thanks to all who have chosen to read this book. An unread book is hardly worth the paper on which it is printed. Thank you from the bottom of my heart for considering the case I presented in the foregoing pages.

Ross K. Nichols
February 2021

Bibliography

Albright, W. F. "A Biblical Fragment from the Maccabean Age: The Nash Papyrus." *Journal of Biblical Literature* LVI (1937): 145–76.

Allegro, John Marco. *The Shapira Affair.* New York: Doubleday & Company, 1965.

Baedeker, Karl, ed. *Palestine and Syria: Handbook for Travelers.* Leipzig: Karl Baedeker, 1876.

Balint, Benjamin, and Merav Mack. "Jerusalem's Master Forger?" Essay. Pages 152–58 in *Jerusalem: City of the Book.* Yale University Press, 2019.

Berlin, Adele, Marc Zvi Brettler, and Michael Fishbane, eds. *The Jewish Study Bible: Jewish Publication Society Tanakh Translation.* New York: Oxford University Press, 2004.

Berman, Joshua. *Ani Maamin: Biblical Criticism, Historical Truth, and the Thirteen Principles of Faith.* Maggid, 2020.

Besant, Walter. *Palestine Exploration Fund: Twenty-One Years' Work in the Holy Land: (a Record and a Summary), June 22, 1865–June 22, 1886.* London: Bentley, 1886.

———, and Samuel Squire Sprigge. *Autobiography of Sir Walter Besant, with a Prefatory Note.* New York: Dodd, Mead and Company, 1902.

Bleek, Freidrich. *Einleitung in Das Alte Testament.* Berlin: G. Reiner, 1860.

Carter, A.C.R. "Shapira the Bible Forger." Essay. Pages 216–19 in *Let Me Tell You.* London: Hutchinson & Co., 1940.

Cassuto, Umberto. *The Documentary Hypothesis and the Composition of the Pentateuch: Eight Lectures.* Jerusalem: Shalem Press, 2006.

Clermont-Ganneau, Charles. "Genuine and False Inscriptions in Palestine." *Palestine Exploration Quarterly* 16, no. 1 (1884): 89–100.

———. "The Shapira Collection." *Palestine Exploration Quarterly* 6, no. 3 (1874): 201–7.

———. *Les Fraudes Archéologiques En Palestine: Suivies De Quelques Monuments Phéniciens Apocryphes.* Paris: Ernest Leroux, Editeur, 1885.

Conder, Claude R. "Lieut. Claude R. Conder's Reports." *Palestine Exploration Quarterly* 7, no. 3 (1875): 125–68.

———, Charles Tyrwhitt-Drake, and Charles Frederick. "Notes on the Drawings and Copies of Inscriptions from the 'Shapira Collection' Sent Home by Lieut. Conder and Mr. Drake." *Palestine Exploration Fund Quarterly Statement* (1873): 79–80.

————, Herbert H. Kitchener. "Khurbet Kumrân." Essay. Pages 210–11 in *The Survey of Western Palestine*. London: Palestine Exploration Society, 1883.

Crown, A. D. "The Fate of the Shapira Scroll." *Revue de Qumrân* 7, no. 3. 27 (1970): 421–23.

de Goeje, M. J., ed. *Actes Du Sixième Congrès International des Orientalistes, tenu en 1883 à Leide, Part I: Compte-Rendu Des Séances*. Vol. 1, 44, Leide: Brill, 1884–1885.

Delitzsch, Franz. "Schapira's Pseudo-Deuteronomium." *Allgemeine Evangelische-Lutherisch Kirchenzeitung,* no. 36 (Sept 7, 1883); 844–846; no. 37 (Sept 14, 1883): 869–871; no. 38 (Sept 21, 1883): 893–894; no. 39 (Sept 28, 1883): 914–916; no. 6 (Feb 8, 1884): 129–130.

————. "Die Handschriftlichen Funde Shapira's." *Allgemeine Evangelische-Lutherische Kirchenzeitung* no. 15 (Apr 11, 1884): 343–344.

Deuel, Leo. "The Shapira Mystery." Essay. Pages 402–21 in *Testaments of Time, The Search for Lost Manuscripts and Records*. New York, New York: Knopf, 1965.

"Dr. Shapira's Suicide." *The New York Times,* March 30, 1884.

Driver, S. R. *A Treatise on the Use of Tenses in Hebrew and Some Other Syntactical Questions*. London: Oxford University Press, 1874.

Ebers, Georg, correspondence with Eduard Meyer. "Der Briefwechsel zwischen Georg Ebers und Eduard Meyer (1874–1898)." Vorbemerkung von G. Audring. https://www.geschichte.hu-berlin.de/de/bereiche-und-lehrstuehle/alte-geschichte/forschung/briefe-meyer/ebers.

"Facsimile of the Shapira MS." *The Athenæum,* 8 September 1883, no. 2915 edition, 305.

Fenton, Paul B. "Moses Shapira's Journey to the Yemen." Essay. Pages lxviii–lxxxi in *Mittuv Yosef, Yosef Tobi Jubilee Volume, The Jews of Yemen: History and Culture (The Center for the Study of Jewish Culture in Spain and Islamic Countries)*. Edited by Ayelet Oettinger and Danny Bar-Maoz. Vol. Volume Two. Haifa: University of Haifa, 2011.

Fields, Weston W. *Dead Sea Scrolls: a Full History*. Vol. 1. 1947–1960. Leiden: Brill, 2009.

Francis, Patricia. "Philip Brookes Mason (1842–1903): Surgeon, General Practitioner and Naturalist." *Archives of Natural History* 42.1 (2015): 126–39.

Friedman, Richard Elliott. *The Bible with Sources Revealed*. New York, New York: HarperOne, 2003.

————. *Who Wrote the Bible?* New York, New York: HarperCollins, 1987.

Gibson, Shimon. *Jerusalem in Original Photographs, 1850–1920*. London: Stacey International, 2003.

————, Yoni Shapira, and Rupert L. Chapman. *Tourists, Travellers and Hotels in Nineteenth-Century Jerusalem*. Leeds, UK: Maney Publishers, 2013.

Gilbert, Martin. *Jerusalem: Rebirth of a City.* New York, New York: Elisabeth Sifton Books-Viking, 1985.

Ginsburg, Christian David. "The Karaites: Their History and Literature." *Proceedings of the Literary and Philosophical Society of Liverpool* (1861): 155–70.

———, *The Moabite Stone: a Fac-Simile of the Original Inscription, with an English Translation, and a Historical and Critical Commentary.* 2nd ed. London: Reeves and Turner, 1871.

Goshen-Gottstein, M. H. "The Shapira Forgery and the Qumran Scrolls." *Journal of Jewish Studies* 7, no. 3–4 (1956): 187–93.

Guérin Victor. *Description géographique, Historique Et archéologique De La Palestine.* Paris: Imprimé par autorisation de l'empereur à l'Impr. Impériale, 1868.

Guil, Shlomo. "In Search of the Shop of Moses Wilhelm Shapira, the Leading Figure of the 19th Century Archaeological Enigma." *Academia.edu* (2012): 1–20. https://www.academia.edu/2127379/In_Search_of_the_Shop_of_Moses_ Wilhelm_Shapira_the_Leading_Figure_of_the_19TH_Century_Archaeol ogical_Enigma.

———. "The Shapira Scroll Was an Authentic Dead Sea Scroll." *Palestine Exploration Quarterly* 149, no. 1 (2017): 6–27.

———. "The Text of the Shapira Dead Sea Deuteronomy Scroll." *Academia.edu* (2018): 1–13.

Guthe, Hermann. "Die Siloahinschrift." *Zeitschrift Der Deutschen Morgenländischen Gesellschaft* 36 (1882): 725–50.

———. *Fragmente Einer Lederhandschrift Enthaltend Moses's Letzte Rede an Die Kinder Israel.* Leipzig: Druck und Verlag von Breitkopf & Hartel, 1883.

———. *Fragments of a Leather Manuscript Containing Moses' Last Words to the Children of Israel.* Edited by Ross K Nichols. Translated by Mitchell Golde. Unpublished, 2020.

Harding, G. Lankester. "The Dead Sea Scrolls." *Palestine Exploration Quarterly* 81 (1949).

Harry, Myriam. *La petite fille de Jérusalem.* Paris: A. Fayard et Cie, 1914.

———. *The Little Daughter of Jerusalem.* Translated by Phoebe Allen. New York: E. P. Dutton & Company, 1919.

Heath, Dunbar I. "The Moabite Jars." *The Journal of the Anthropological Institute of Great Britain and Ireland* 2 (1873): 331–41.

Heide, Martin. "The Moabitica and Their Aftermath: How to Handle a Forgery Affair with an International Impact." Essay. Pages 193–241 in *New Inscriptions and Seals Relating to the Biblical World.* Edited by Meir and Edith Lubetski. Atlanta: Society of Biblical Literature, 2012.

Jefferson, Helen G. "The Shapira Manuscript and the Qumran Scrolls." *Revue de Qumrân.* 6, no. 3. 23 (1968): 391–99.

Kautzsch, E., and A. Socin. *Die Aechtheit Der Moabitischen Alterthümer geprüft.* Strassburg: Karl J. Trübner, 1876.

Kean, James. *Among the Holy Places: a Pilgrimage through Palestine.* London: T.F. Unwin, 1908.

King, Rev. James. *Moab's Patriarchal Stone: Being an Account of the Moabite Stone, Its Story and Teaching.* London: Bickers and Son, 1878.

Klein., F. A. "The Original Discovery of the Moabite Stone." *Palestine Exploration Quarterly* 2, no. 6 (1869): 281–83.

Mansoor, Menahem. "The Case of Shapira's Dead Sea (Deuteronomy) Scrolls of 1883." *Transactions of the Wisconsin Academy of Sciences, Arts, and Letters* (1958): 183–225.

———. *The Dead Sea Scrolls. A College Textbook and a Study Guide.* Leiden, Netherlands: E. J. Brill, 1964.

Meyer, Eduard, correspondence with Adolf Erman. "Der Briefwechsel zwischen Eduard Meyer und Adolf Erman (1881–1930)." Unter Mitwirkung von Yasser Sabek und Sascha Winkelmann bearbeitet von G. Audring Vorbemerkung. https://www.geschichte.hu-berlin.de/de/bereiche-und-lehrstuehle/alte-geschichte/forschung/briefe-meyer/erman.

Molendijk, Arie L. "Religion at the 1883 Colonial and Export Trade Exhibition in Amsterdam." *Zeitschrift für Neuere Theologiegeshichte / Journal for the History of Modern Theology* 11.2 (2004): 215–45.

Nichols, Ross K. "A Comparison of the Ten Words in English with Explanatory Notes." *Academia.edu* (2020).

"Papers Relative to M. W. Shapira's Forged MS. of Deuteronomy (A.D. 1883–1884)." *Add. MS 41294,* London: British Library.

Petermann, H. "The Moabite Stone." *Palestine Exploration Quarterly* 3, no. 3 (1871): 135–39.

Press, Michael. "'The Lying Pen of the Scribes': A Nineteenth-Century Dead Sea Scroll." *Futures of the Past* 2, no. 3 (2014). https://theappendix.net/issues/2014/7/the-lying-pen-of-the-scribes-a-nineteenth-century-dead-sea-scroll.

Rabinowicz, Oskar K. "The Shapira Scroll: A Nineteenth-Century Forgery." *The Jewish Quarterly Review* 56, no. 1 (1965): 1.

———, and S. Zeitlin. "The Shapira Forgery Mystery—Critical Notes." *The Jewish Quarterly Review* 47, no. 2 (1956): 170–95. https://www.jstor.org/stable/1453227.

Reiner, Fred. "C. D. Ginsburg and the Shapira Affair: A Nineteenth-Century Dead Sea Scroll Controversy." *The British Library Journal* (1995): 109–27.

———. "Tracking the Shapira Case: A Biblical Scandal Revisited." *Biblical Archaeology Review* 23 (3), May/June, 1997, 32–41.

Rosenberg, Rabbi A. J., ed. *The Book of Kings 2, A New Translation of the Text, Rashi and a Commentary Digest.* New York: The Judaica Press Inc., 1989.

Sabo, Yoram. "Between Apostate and Forger: Moses Wilhelm Shapira and the Moabite Pottery." *Academia* (n.d.). https://www.academia.edu/24911481/Between_Apostate_and_Forger_Moses_Wilhelm_Shapira_and_the_Moabite_Pottery_Affair.

———. *Soḥer Ha-Megilot Masa' Be-'iḳvot Ha-Otsar Ha-Yehudi Ha-Avud = The Scroll Merchant: in Search of Moses Wilhelm Shapira's Lost Jewish Treasure.* Bene Beraḳ: ha-Ḳibuts ha-me'uḥad, 2018. (Hebrew)

———. *Shapira & I.* Israel: Ruth Films, 2014.

Schröeder, Paul. *Die Phönizische Sprache Entwurf Einer Grammatik Nebst Sprach-Und Schriftproben.* Halle: Buchhandlung des Waisenhauses, 1869.

"Shapira's MSS." *The Old Testament Student* 3, no. 1 (1883): 23–25.

Silberman, Neil Asher. "Discovery at Qumran." Essay. Pages 36–38 in *The Hidden Scrolls, Christianity, Judaism, & the War for the Dead Sea Scrolls.* New York, New York: G. P. Putnam's Sons, 1994.

———. "One Million Pounds Sterling, The Rise and Fall of Moses Wilhelm Shapira, 1883–1885." Essay. Pages 131–46 in *Digging for God and Country: Exploration, Archeology, and the Secret Struggle for the Holy Land, 1799–1917.* New York, New York: Doubleday, 1982.

———. "Race for a Relic, The Affair of The Moabite Stone 1868–1870." Essay. Pages 100–112 in *Digging for God and Country: Exploration, Archeology, and the Secret Struggle for the Holy Land, 1799–1917.* New York, New York: Doubleday, 1982.

Smith, James. *A Pilgrimage to Palestine: an Account of a Visit to Lower Palestine, 1893–1894.* Aberdeen: Lawrence and Bullen, 1895.

Steen, Eveline Van Der. *Near Eastern Tribal Societies During the Nineteenth Century: Economy, Society and Politics between Tent and Town (Approaches to Anthropological Archaeology).* New York: Routledge, 2019.

"Suicide of Dr. Shapira." *St. James Gazette,* March 12, 1884.

Taylor, Joan E. *The Essenes, the Scrolls, and the Dead Sea.* Oxford: Oxford Univ. Press, 2014.

Teicher, Jacob L. "The Genuineness of the Shapira Manuscripts." *The Times Literary Supplement,* no. 2873, 22 March 1957: 184.

"The Moabite Pottery." *Palestine Exploration Quarterly* 10, no. 2 (1878): 88–102.

"The Shape of the Moabite Stone." *Palestine Exploration Quarterly* 8, no. 2 (1876): 181–82.

"The Shapira Collection." *Palestine Exploration Quarterly* 6, no. 2 (1874): 114–24.

"The Shapira Collection." *Palestine Exploration Quarterly* 6, no. 2 (1874): 202–7.

"The Shapira Manuscript of Deuteronomy." *Scientific American* 16, no. 408supp (1883): 6516–16.

"The Shapira Manuscripts." *Palestine Exploration Quarterly* 15, no. 4 (1883): 195–209.

"The Shapira Ms. of Deuteronomy." *The Athenæum,* August 11, 1883, No. 2911 edition, 178–9.

"The Shapira Ms. of Deuteronomy." *The Athenæum,* August 18, 1883, No. 2912 edition, 206.

"The Shapira Ms. of Deuteronomy." *The Athenæum,* August 25, 1883, No. 2913 edition, 242–4.

Tigay, Chanan. *The Lost Book of Moses: the Hunt for the World's Oldest Bible.* New York, New York: Ecco, an imprint of HarperCollins, 2016.

Tov, Emanuel. *Textual Criticism of the Hebrew Bible.* 3rd ed. Minneapolis (Minn.): Fortress Press, 2012.

Trever, John C. *The Untold Story of Qumran.* Westwood, New Jersey: Revell, 1965.

Vermès, Géza. *The Complete Dead Sea Scrolls in English.* London: Penguin, 1997.

Warren, Charles. "The Moabite Stone." *Palestine Exploration Quarterly* 2, no. 5 (1869): 169–83.

———, Grove, E. Deutsch, and Charles Clermont-Ganneau. "The Moabite Stone." *Palestine Exploration Fund Quarterly Statement* 2:5 (1869): 169–83.

Wilson, Edmund. "The Scrolls from the Dead Sea." *New Yorker,* May 14, 1955.

Yahuda, A. S. "The Story of a Forgery and the Mēša Inscription." *The Jewish Quarterly Review* 35, no. 2 (1944): 139.

Made in the USA
Columbia, SC
09 January 2023

75820283R00120